The Parents' Solution Book

THE PARENTS' SOLUTION BOOK

*by Lea Bramnick
and Anita Simon*

A Perigee Book

Perigee Books
are published by
The Putnam Publishing Group
200 Madison Avenue
New York, NY 10016

Library of Congress Cataloging in Publication Data

Bramnick, Lea S.
The parents' solution book.

Includes index.
1. Parenting.   2. Child rearing.   I. Simon, Anita.
II. Title.
HQ755.8.B72   1984   649′.1   84-7068
ISBN 0-399-51076-1

Illustrations by Kathleen O'Connor
First Perigee edition, 1984
Printed in the United States of America
1 2 3 4 5 6 7 8 9 10

To Michael and Gary who have enriched
my life and taught me so much
LB

To Bert, Boris, Ruth, Sheryl and David, with love
AS

Acknowledgments

Our warm appreciation to those who contributed their expertise and who reviewed the various sections of the book: Gunther Abraham, PhD. Child psychologist, Devereux Foundation, Philadelphia; Yvonne Agazarian, EdD. Psychologist in private practice and president SAVI Communications, Philadelphia; Claudia Byram, PhD. Child psychologist in private practice, Philadelphia; Robison D. Harley, MD, FACS. Senior Consultant, Pediatric Opthamology and Strabismus, Wills Eye Hospital, Philadelphia; Herbert Kean, MD. Clinical Associate Professor, Thomas Jefferson University; Ronald Kehler. Counsellor, Bala Cynwyd Middle School, Bala Cynwyd; Ruth Leventhal, PhD. Dean, School of Health Sciences. Hunter College, CUNY; Bernard Margolis, MD. Pediatrician in private practice, Philadelphia; Arnold Randel, DMD. Periodontist in private practice, Philadelphia; and Jonathan D. Volinsky, DMD. Dentist in private practice, Philadelphia, Associate Dental School University of Pennsylvania. We are also grateful to Lt. Donald Smith of the Fire Prevention Division of the Philadelphia Fire Department, and to Captain Karl Filachek and Officer Bob Shalala of the Police Community Relations

Division of the Philadelphia Police Department for their help.

To Sylvia Shapiro, Felix Rimburg, Hope Byer, Roberta Shaid, and Rae Eisenberg, who offered us personal support, encouragement, and help, we extend our heartfelt thanks.

Special thanks are due to the staffs of Tribeca Communications, Inc. and Franklin Watts for the countless hours required to transform the authors' work of love into a book.

Contents

Introduction

This book is written to assist the parents of the five- to twelve-year-old child, who know full well how the bustle and business of caring for a family gobbles up time and energy like a giant monster.

Help is not easily available to parents who need it. You know whom to call when something doesn't work well around the house—the plumber, the electrician, the repairman—and although they may not come right away, eventually they do solve the problem. Lawyers, accountants, doctors, and dentists help us with other real-world difficulties. But one of the most important tasks of our lives—parenting—requires no advance training or licensing, and, what is worse, there are very few people we can call on precisely when we are faced with a problem. Even being a parent before may not help with a younger child, because raising each child is a unique experience.

This book will help you to step back and look at your alternatives before you are in the middle of a difficult situation. We establish some guidelines for effective parenting and focus on specifically "what to do" and "what to say" in basic, everyday situations that often perplex parents. We suggest ways to make the good times better and offer ideas that may help you get closer to your children.

As educators, we have long been convinced that the principles that allow an excellent teacher to work happily and effectively with twenty-five or more different children in a variety of situations would be valuable tools for parents as well. Modern educational theory tells us a great deal about how adults can interact with children in ways that increase the chances for learning and for building successful relationships.

Our criterion for deciding what would be included in the book was "Will it help parents know what to do or what to say?" We have not provided theoretical or research data on child development, because there are many books on the market containing this information. What we found missing was a pragmatic handbook for parents of elementary-school-aged children.

The book is organized in five chapters, covering areas of major concern to parents:

Chapter 1: Deals with everyday activities: how to organize to get the day off to a good start, through to tucking your kids into bed at night and planning for the next day. It is arranged according to the time of day, morning through evening, and gives guidelines about the activities you and your child do each day.

Chapter 2: Deals with leisure time: vacations, holidays, day trips, and the ten minutes you take just to snuggle with your kids.

Chapter 3: Deals with children's health and safety. Topics range from preparing your child for visiting the dentist to training your child to be safe on the streets.

Chapter 4: Deals with the maturing child. It covers areas of responsibility that developing children are learning to handle, and how to ease them into new roles with a sense of celebration.

Chapter 5: Deals with helping children cope with serious issues, recognizing problems, settling arguments, disciplining, helping your child care for others and show it, and networking.

Our goal has been to provide hints, tips, activities, and sample dialogues to help make some of the universally difficult times, if not easy, at least more predictable and manageable.

No parent can follow all of the suggestions in this or any other childrearing book. That would be impossible and unreasonable, because books are usually about the ideal, and real-life parents sometimes get tired, angry, or forgetful and feel like telling their kids to buzz off.

Still, we're hoping that this book will promote sharing and caring, will help family members listen to one another so their messages can be heard and all their needs can be met. We hope that the times adults and kids spend together will be joyous, helpful, and nurturing, and that they will create wonderful memories.

The Parents'
Solution Book

Planning Prevents Problems
Mornings—Getting it Together for the Day
Breakfast
Getting There—Carpools
Lunch
After School
When Parents Are Not Home After School
Caring for Kids
Dinner
Alone Time
Bedtime

1
Everyday Activities

Planning Prevents Problems

Every day a family faces a multitude of things that need doing: housework and homework, social events and school activities, meals and chores, family together time and each person's alone time. To avoid hassles and make sure each family member is taken care of, all of these needs should be planned for.

Parents should think of planning, not as a task done totally by adults, but as something done in partnership with the child—until the child can begin to plan for himself. Remember that the ability to plan must be learned, developed, and your child will not make plans perfectly at the beginning. First times will be hard for you, too! However, your family's planning and follow-through abilities will improve with practice and experience.

Most parents do the planning for their children: parents plan what's for dinner, where to go on weekends, when their children can have friends over or go to other children's homes, when to go shopping and what to buy, what chores are to be done, by whom, and when. But if parents involve their children in planning what, how, and when, the children are more apt to have a sense of pleasure and responsibility about those activities. If children have taken part in organizing a spring-cleaning day or a shopping trip, they are more likely to be motivated to make the day or the excursion a success—because they have helped to establish the goals.

Getting into the habit of using calendars and schedules takes some extra time at the beginning of the school year. However, it will save parents countless hours of agony later on—perhaps preventing a last-minute choice between an important office function and a school activity that is important to their child. (Often seemingly little things matter most to children.) A neighbor of ours, now in her fifties, still remembers with regret that her mother didn't attend her fifth grade play when she had the lead. Through good planning a family can avoid neglecting any event that is meaningful to one of its members.

In September, gather all the dates that are available for meetings, social events, concerts, sports events, and after-school activities. Most schools plan for these events a year in advance. Collect similar schedules at work and from your church or synagogue, scouts, sports teams, theater group— all organizations in which a family member is involved.

Hang a calendar where it will be convenient and accessible for everyone. Choose one with daily blocks big enough to enter all of these events. When filling in the calendar, be sure to include:

- days you drive carpool
- class trips
- special after-school lessons
- school and religious holidays
- late school openings and early dismissals
- parents' activities
- work-related trips and meetings
- visits from out-of-town friends and relatives
- team games in which your child participates
- medical appointments
- parties

Once you have the family calendar, help your family get into the habit of using it. At the beginning of every month or on each allowance day, ask if there are any changes or new information to add to the family calendar. Keep a pencil on a string taped near the calendar. Remind family members to put things on the calendar and to tell other members about changes. Keep reinforcing the idea that only by planning ahead and marking the calendar can family members be sure that parents and children will be free to attend important events. As activities are posted on the calendar, look for potential conflicts. Often schedule problems can be solved easily if they are spotted early.

RESOLVING SCHEDULE CONFLICTS

Establish priorities. Each family member should understand, for example, that school is the first priority for the children and the kids are of primary importance to the parents. Then if a conflict arises between completing a homework assignment on time and going to a ball game, there really is no choice—school comes first.

Almost everything can be negotiated, however, so keep your mind open to all options. Try to "stretch" time. Sometimes parts of two events can fit into one time slot—for instance, you might go to the first part of a meeting at one child's school and the last act of a play at your other child's school.

Look for alternative times. If you can't get to an important event, try to arrange for a substitute visit. Sometimes school (and other) events are held twice. An orchestra concert may be given during the day for the students and in the evening for adults. A parent may be able to arrange with the school to attend the concert during the day if going at night presents a scheduling problem.

If you find yourself locked into an either-or choice, make the decision in favor of a one-time-only event. Sometimes activities are repeated at different times of the year—a gym-

nastic program may be given in the fall and again in the spring. In case of a conflict in the fall, parents can tell the child, *after checking the date* so it can be a firm promise, that they will attend the event in the spring.

It is usually important to the child that someone from home attend her* special events, but it doesn't always have to be Mom or Dad. Maybe an older brother or sister can get an early dismissal for an afternoon program, or plan to ride with a neighbor to attend an evening program. This arrangement may satisfy the need of a younger child to have someone "watch me." Grandparents, aunts, and uncles are other good substitutes and should be invited even when the parents will be there. Taking a picture of the child during the program can help the child show and tell her parents later.

When there's nothing you can do about it and there's no one else who can go, that's the time to say, *Even though I care so much about what you are doing and want to be with you to share that special day, there's nothing I can do about it this time.* Then plan for a time, even if it has to be a very short period of time, when you and your child can be together, uninterrupted, so she can tell you about everything you missed.

*A NOTE FROM THE EDITORS:

The information and advice provided in this book is intended for parents of both girls and boys. Personal pronouns have been used interchangeably without regard to gender because the issues addressed are not sex specific.

Mornings—Getting It Together for the Day

Scenes such as the following are played out between parents and children in millions of homes and offices every day: you are at work and the phone rings. Your child says, *I forgot my gym shorts and I really need them.* Or, you are at home with a sick child when your older child calls from school to say, *I left my homework in my room and I'll get a bad mark if I don't hand it in this afternoon.*

There is no way for you to be helpful in such cases. This creates several problems: you and your child feel upset and probably angry, and your child does not get what he forgot. More importantly, the child may not be receiving the training he needs in order to be able to meet his own responsibilities. If you want your children to be responsible for their own things, give them the opportunity to develop organizing skills: encourage them to collect what they need for the day *before* they leave home.

The school day requires not only your child's presence, but also his possessions: books, sports equipment, gymsuit, lunch or lunch money, materials for class projects, homework, permission slips—the list can seem endless.

THE WEEKLY CHECKLIST

During a quiet time at the beginning of the school year sit down with each child and make a list of needs for every day of the week. Leave room for last-minute additions. Tape the list on the refrigerator at the children's eye level and help your

	Mon.	Tues.	Wed.	Thurs.	Fri.
Jessica	gym shorts	music	show and tell	soccer stuff	dance class
Daniel	show and tell	art class	gym shorts	music	tennis racquet

child form the habit of checking it before he leaves the house each morning. This works with young children, too. If they don't read yet, draw pictures of the items that are needed for each day. When you first begin this weekly checklist, you will probably forget some things. Keep adding to the list, making it more complete each week.

NIGHT BEFORE PLANS

Encourage your child to talk out his schedule for the next day with you as he gets ready for bed. Help him to think about the things he'll need for each subject in school, any after-school activities, lunch plans (bringing or buying), music lessons, scouts, special events, and so forth. Teach your child to gather as many of these articles as possible the night before, and to leave a note to himself on his underwear or schoolbooks to remind him to get the remaining items in the morning. It is best to plan the night before, because it is easier to think about what you need when you are calm and relaxed than when you are rushing in the morning.

IN FRONT OF THE DOOR SYSTEM

Teach your child to put all the things he needs for the day's activities near the door he will leave by. If there is something that must stay in a special place until your child can take it, such as a carton of milk or a bicycle, teach him to tape a note to the doorknob so he can remember to go back and get it before he leaves.

THE REFRIGERATOR SYSTEM

If you put something that you never leave the house without next to the item you want to remember, chances are you will take both with you. Some good "never leave home without them" items are eyeglasses and coats. Placing your car keys in the refrigerator next to the food you promised to send for the class party may help you remember to take it. The more you plan ahead, the less aggravation you'll face.

Breakfast

Breakfast is an opportunity to get the day off to a wonderful start. It is also a necessity for young children, who have probably not eaten anything in the twelve hours before the morning meal. Trying to get through till recess or lunch on an empty stomach and a low blood-sugar level is detrimental to a child's productivity. Young children need to replenish their food energy, and their requirements in proportion to their body weight are greater than adults. While their parents are maintaining a more or less constant body weight, children are growing—so they require calories more often. Parents should try not to sacrifice the fifteen minutes it takes to prepare a morning meal for an extra fifteen minutes of sleep. Kids are more likely to eat a good breakfast if their parents set a good example by planning and eating a well-balanced breakfast in an unhurried manner.

A ten-year study by the University of Iowa Medical College showed that, among both children and adults, eating a nutritious breakfast was associated with better physical and mental performance. In particular, the study revealed that those who ate breakfast were more productive during the late morning. They also had a faster reaction time (which may mean they are less prone to accidents) and less muscular fatigue than those who skipped breakfast. Children who had no breakfast were more likely to be listless and have trouble concentrating. Furthermore, skipping or skimping on breakfast did not help weight control. Meal-skippers in general are more likely to be obese than people who eat three meals a day. A study of college women showed that those who skipped breakfast consumed more snacks—high in calories and deficient in nutrients—than those who ate breakfast.

Unbelievable as it sounds to those who hate mornings, there are things that parents can do to make breakfast time pleasant for everyone. Concentrate on finding and making simple recipes that are good for you and fun to eat—these become an incentive for eating a good breakfast.

Look for recipes that can be made quickly, require little clean-up, taste delicious, and are good for you. Plan what you'll have for breakfast in the same way you plan dinner. Look for new and unexpected dishes—the breakfast menu need not be traditional. Try a grilled cheese sandwich set up in the refrigerator the night before and grilled in the morning. Leftover pizza, with its balanced protein, vitamins, minerals, and fibers, is a nourishing food, as is a toasted peanut butter and banana sandwich.

If you are rushed in the morning, it may make sense for your family to make some of the breakfast preparations the night before—set the table, for example, or write a good-day or good-luck note for your child to find when she gets to the breakfast table.

Whatever you do, you'll need a plan for morning chores which everyone agrees with: decide who clears the breakfast dishes, who wipes the table, who sweeps, who takes out the trash, who sets up for lunch or dinner.

Getting There—Carpools

For a carpool you need responsible drivers in convenient locations. There are several ways to find suitable people: word of mouth, notes tacked up in neighborhood stores or on the school bulletin board, or requesting a list of people who live in the vicinity from the office of your child's school. Remember, your carpool will be limited in size by the number of people that the smallest car in your carpool can carry safely. Nothing is sadder to the carpool planner than to find that a potential carpool driver who lives two houses away has only a two-seater!

Before beginning a carpool it is vital to check with your insurance agent concerning your coverage. Be prepared to provide *all* the facts about your proposed carpool, and request written confirmation that you and your passengers are adequately protected.

It is a fact of life that as our children's world is enlarged—we take them on public transportation, leave them at the day-care centers, hire sitters, and have other people drive them—the risks increase. So, it is important to be careful about whom you select as carpool drivers.

The next step is deciding when each person will drive. There can be an advantage in doing the scheduling yourself. This allows you to pick the week you want to drive, not the one when you will be out of town or chairing the PTA dinner. Nevertheless, it is most equitable to rotate alphabetically. If you have been in the same carpool for years, perhaps reversing alphabetical order is good for a change. Volunteering to organize the carpool enables you to suggest the carpool system that best suits your own needs. Carpools can be arranged by trips (everybody drives an equal number of trips each week), by weeks (each person takes a turn driving every trip for a week), or by the days of the week (someone drives Monday, someone else on Tuesday, etc.).

Make copies of the carpool schedule and give one to each family in the carpool. Be sure to include each child's name, parents' names, addresses, and phone numbers at home and at work. Enter the carpool schedule on your calendar, put one copy on your bulletin board, store another one in the glove compartment of your car, and keep a third copy at work.

There is one essential carpool rule: the car does not move if anyone is misbehaving. Misbehaving can be anything from the kids not fastening their seat belts, to their being too noisy or too physical, to their doing something that might distract the driver. In setting up your carpool, see that all the drivers agree to pull over and stop whenever any child is doing anything inappropriate. This will drastically cut down on arguments and misbehavior. Kids catch on fast and start to discipline one another when they see the car pulling over to the side of the road.

A few other suggestions:

- Have your child ready (with all his possessions) and waiting at the time the driver is supposed to pick him up.

- Ask that each child know her own full name, address, and phone number. This is helpful if another family member substitutes for you when it's your turn to drive.

- Believe children when they say that they don't feel well. Pull over to the side of the road as soon as it is safe and determine what's the matter.

- Choose whichever plan about eating in the car that pleases you. Either no eating in the car is the rule or kids can eat in your carpool. If you decide eating is okay, bring a snack every once in a while for the youngsters in your carpool. It will make the day nicer!

- If your child is not going, call the carpool driver as early as possible to let him know.

- Don't stop the driver for conversation when he drops your child off. Take care of changing driving days and make social or school plans by phone, so that the driver can stay on schedule.

- Change carpool days only when absolutely necessary and then give as much notice as possible. If someone asks you to change carpool days try to be accommodating if at all possible. Don't count days and expect to be paid back instantaneously. Gracious, considerate behavior is the key to successful carpool relationships.

Lunch

It is important to send your younger children to school with enough money to meet their needs, but it is not prudent to let them carry around extra, unnecessary money. Make giving exact-change lunch money easy by getting rolls of coins at the bank every week. For young children, develop a technique for remembering to give them the money if they are buying their lunch, and as they get older help them to be responsible for this themselves. They might want to use one of the reminder systems mentioned earlier, like putting the lunch money in an envelope by the front door with other things they have to take with them in the morning.

Decide with your kids whether they want to buy lunch or take lunch to school. It should be okay for one child in the family to decide to bring lunch and for the other children to want to buy it at school. Devise a plan for how and when the lunch will be made, and who will make it. Create a back-up system for when there is "nothing to eat" in the house. A shelf that always holds some canned tuna, peanut butter and jelly, or whatever your family likes that can be stored, is a good idea for emergencies. Try to check it before each shopping trip. Sometimes lunch may not be the traditional sandwich. In a pinch, try fruit and cheese, crackers and peanut butter, or a leftover chicken leg.

Letting children make lunch for themselves is one of the simplest ways to help them learn some measure of independence. When you and your child feel that he is ready to take on this responsibility, first try some dry runs (once a week is a good way to begin), with you as a back-up. This way, you can finish packing the lunch quickly if time is short. Even the youngest child can contribute to his own lunch by spreading the egg salad or picking out the fresh fruit. The more you use your child's own ideas, the more certain you can be that he will eat and enjoy what he takes. Be sure to include a napkin and, when you feel like it, a note that says, *Have a good day, Good luck at scouts, Hope you enjoyed lunch,* or *I love you.*

Children may find pleasure in decorating lunch bags for themselves or their friends. It's a good rainy-day activity. Sports bags, initial bags, and bags that look like animals can be easily made. A dozen tied with a ribbon make a super gift.

Sometimes in the hustle and bustle we miss excellent opportunities for family fun times. Lunchtime with the family on weekends, holidays, and vacations can be a treat. It's a wonderful time to picnic, eat on the back stoop, or share an unusual meal around the table that the whole family will enjoy. The simplest lunch can be fun when you get a chance to eat in an unhurried manner at home. Sometimes, everyone who is at home can participate in preparing the meal.

After School

It is important for you and your child to understand that when you leave for your jobs in the morning or prepare to do the household tasks, you are going to work and that when your child leaves for school in the morning, he is going to his work, too. Think about how you feel when you come home after a full day at work and what you like to do: relax a little, have something to eat, plan for your evening activities, or even sound off about what happened during the day. Your child has many similar feelings at the end of the school day.

Whether parents are home after school or not, it is their responsibility to help their children fill their afterschool time appropriately. To do this, parents must be clear in their own minds about what they expect from kids after school.

There are many activities that children can participate in after school. You may have more options than you think, even if you are a working mother. When you compare the price of an afterschool sitter with some of the programs available in your area, you may have some pleasant surprises. For information about programs at schools, community centers, and churches or synagogues, ask other parents and look in local newspapers.

The problem arises in planning it all so that a combination of playtime and worktime is accomplished with a minimum of strain. Divide after-school time into sections, making sure both your own needs and your children's needs will be met.

It's a good idea to give children a chance to relax right after school. Give them their choice of activities before they start chores or homework. Such time can be easily separated into "must do's" and "playtime." Must do's include a list agreed upon by parents and children.

When Parents Are Not Home After School

If parents will regularly not be home after school, they must be certain beforehand that their children will be comfortable with returning to an empty house day after day. We have learned that this is sometimes very frightening to children. In some extreme cases, children get so scared that they hide in closets, under the bed, or in the bathroom until someone returns home.

Here are a few suggestions to help the child stay at home alone:

- Talk with your child about where you will be when she comes home after school. Tell her about your work or your meetings, whom you will be with—anything that can make what you are doing real to her.

- Talk with your child about what she will be doing when she comes home. Plan a schedule with her: include where and with whom she will play, when she will do homework and chores, where she'll spend her alone time, where to look for snacks.

- Finally, let your child find out what the house feels and sounds like when it is empty. While you stay outside, have her go into the empty house alone and explore it. Then, talk about how it is different "empty" from how it is when people are there. Reinforce how nice the differences are—no one to interrupt reading, TV-watching, etc.—so that being in the empty house becomes a "different," not a bad, experience.

Guidelines are necessary when children return to an empty house each day. Once you have sat down and discussed the rules you believe are necessary for your child's safety and well-being, write them down and post them in a permanent place in your home. A sample follows:

After-school Rules

1. Call Mom or Dad when you come home at _____.
                                    (phone numbers)
2. Do your chores.
3. Clean up after your snack.
4. If you go out, leave a note telling us where you will be.

5. NO
• inviting kids in when no adults are home.
• using the stove.
• using knives.

If you always come home later than your children, there are many things that you can do to show your kids that you care and are thinking about them when you are not there. Leave a snack that they especially like or a note that reads *Hope it was a good day* with a comment on something the child was involved in that day, such as: *Hope the math test went well*, or *Thought about you at 2:00 while you were at the play audition*. This shows a child your thoughts are with her. Notes left for no reason other than to show you care can brighten a bad day or make a good one even better.

It is a good idea to have, in a central location, a list of "Things to Do When There is Nothing to Do" for children who are home alone. This list can be your clear answer to *I'm bored, No one's home to play with,* and *I don't have any toys I like.* Here are some suggestions:

- Have a special list of words and ask your child to make as many smaller words from each word as possible. Be sure to update the list regularly.

- Choose a word (or a letter, for a young child) and ask your child to count how many times he can find it in a paragraph or on a page. Or, as an alternative, ask the child to count how many times he hears the word in a certain time period in a conversation, on radio or on TV.

- Ask your child to make up a new ending for a familiar story, nursery rhyme, or TV program.

- Draw a family tree and suggest that your child help fill it in.

- Ask your child to do some work around the house equal to his ability—raking leaves or scrubbing patio furniture are two good ideas.

Every once in a while you can show you care by leaving a trinket, a new book or magazine, or a note telling about something nice you've planned; or by calling unexpectedly just to find out how things are going.

A common after-school problem often has a scenario like this: after Jennifer leaves for school, her mother finds out that she needs Jen to run an errand after school. She leaves instructions for Jennifer, then leaves for work. When Jennifer comes home and finds the note she becomes upset, because a school assignment requires her to do a lot of extra homework that night. In addition, she must complete her chores and other homework before her play practice. What should she do?

Jennifer needs to be taught that she should call her parent to explain her problem, provided the parent's work situation allows for personal calls. And Jennifer's parents ought to know that school is their child's first priority. If there is an unresolvable time conflict, then her parents must make some adjustments.

In a situation where the parent is not reachable by phone, both parent and child should agree in advance on priorities in the event of such conflicts. Such conflicts will inevitably come up now and then, and parents and children should take the time to talk about the decision that was made, discuss the outcome, and set some guidelines to make things go more smoothly the next time. Use these conflicts as building blocks to improve your child's decision-making process. Such situations actually help build the child's understanding of priorities.

There are procedures that you should design in advance to take care of "unexpected" events and emergencies that crop up in all of our lives. A clearly written list of whom to call for what emergencies should be posted in an agreed-upon place (inside a certain kitchen-cabinet door, perhaps, or on a section of the bulletin board that you reserve for this use).

Your list should include:

- emergency numbers—police, fire, poison control center, doctor, dentist, ambulance

- a day-by-day schedule of where parents can be reached, including phone numbers

- names and numbers of friends, family members, and neighbors whom a child can contact in case parents cannot be reached

• people who can fix emergency situations in the home (child should consult an adult for permission to call)— plumber, electrician, gas company, electric company, water company, repairmen for major appliances. Be certain there are working flashlights throughout your home in locations your child is familiar with.

Take the time to explain this list to the children. Have them act out common emergencies: what to do if a fuse blows, if the ceiling starts leaking, if they smell gas escaping, if all the lights go out, if they find water in the cellar, or if the refrigerator or freezer stops running. Have the children say aloud which situation they are facing, and show you what they would do, whom they would call, and what they would say.

Also, teach them how to call the police and fire emergency numbers for immediate action, demonstrating how to give the necessary information fully, accurately, and clearly.

Build older children's ability to stay at home alone by giving them a series of short "at home alone" situations where a parent is easily reached. For example, you might go to a nearby neighbor's for coffee, go to borrow something from a friend in the neighborhood, or go on a one-item shopping trip—anyplace that allows you to return home quickly. If feasible, call once to see how things are going when you leave the child alone.

Building on your children's ability to stay alone for short periods of time in the afternoon allows you to move on to leaving them home alone at night when they are old enough. All the same rules apply. When to begin allowing children to stay alone should be a mutual decision, not one that you impose on your child or that your child demands before you're both ready.

When more than one child is left at home, they often fight or get wild. It is important to set guidelines: no cooking, no use of the stove, no use of sharp scissors or knives. Clearly defining what foods and snacks they are allowed to eat, what TV shows they are allowed to watch, and what to do if arguments occur, is vital. Teach them to go to different rooms if they are very angry with each other, before they start really battling.

Whenever children are home alone, leave the name and phone number of a neighbor who will be home that day or night. This is important in case the children need someone immediately. For obvious reasons, teach your children that if they ever leave the house when they are expected to be there, they should leave a note saying where they can be reached and when they will return. Finally, be sure to tell the children, *If you get scared or worried while we're away, this is what to do.* Then review the list of back-up people, and the place where you keep the names of neighbors to call. Explain that it is fine to call; that there is no reason for them to stay at home alone if they are frightened.

Get into the habit of phoning when you can't be home on time. If *you* phone each time you are going to be late, you create an example your children will follow.

Be certain your children always have "call cash" (a special sum of money in the right denomination that they should carry whenever they are out). It is difficult for children to call if only public phones are available and they do not have the correct change. Instruct your children that call cash is never spent for anything other than an emergency call home.

If you are in a situation that prevents *you* from calling (stuck on the expressway, or on a late train), explain this to your child when you get home, and tell her that any other time you would have called. This time you couldn't. Help her understand that the concern and worry she felt about where you were and what happened is what *you* feel when *she* is late and doesn't call to let you know what's going on.

Before parents leave children alone, certain subjects should be explained and discussed. Few families take time to discuss with their children the use of good judgment. Judgment cannot be found in a book the way rules can. It is developed through conversations and experiences that take place in the family setting. One effective way to give your children practice in using good judgment is to have them pretend. For example, *Pretend your parents are out and you are home with your friends, after school. You are having an exciting basketball game, you're not finished and really want to stay outside, but it's the time you set with us to be inside to talk to us when we call. What can you do?* Through this discussion, you can help your child learn to be where she's supposed to be (to get the call) but then to negotiate about going back outside for another twenty minutes to finish the game.

The concept that you want to get across is thinking through what should be done, and then finding a way for both parties to meet their responsibilities and also their needs. Through these discussions, cover the other important topics of good judgment: how to keep each other informed when apart, changes in plans, giving new information, meeting special needs, and so forth. Act out likely situations.

Teach an older child who will be home alone telephone safety. If someone the child doesn't know calls and asks for one of her parents, the child should respond by saying something like, *My mother cannot come to the phone at the moment, I'll ask her to call you back in a little while.* Then the child should ask for the caller's name and number. This does not convey to the caller that the child is home alone.

Discuss with your child why he should never give information to callers he does not know. Train your child not to answer questions like, *Are you going to be home this afternoon? What's your address? Is your mother home?* The best reply is always, *May I have your number? My mother can't come to the phone right now.* Role-play with your child so he learns not to be "encouraged" into conversation with strangers.

Instruct children not to open the door for someone they do not know. If it's a package or a telegram, no matter how urgent it seems to be, they should instruct the delivery person to leave it outside the front door.

Although many of the things that parents and children talk about are negotiable, it's vital to impress upon your child that certain things are not negotiable and that the rules for being safe are among them. Children should never open the door to strangers when they are alone. Here again, impress on your child the point that there is a small minority of people in this world who are really mean or mentally disturbed, and might harm her or take what doesn't belong to them. Learning these facts of life is part of the child's education.

AUTHORIZING MEDICAL HELP WHEN PARENTS ARE NOT AVAILABLE

Physicians frequently cannot or will not render non-emergency medical treatment to minors without a parent's permission. Even in emergency rooms, if your child needs treatment for a broken bone or a deep cut or some other ailment that is not life-threatening, she may have to wait until you can be contacted to give your personal okay. (This is in part because many doctors have been sued by parents who have objected to the "unauthorized" treatment that the doctors gave in the parents' absence.) Your child may have to wait for hours to receive treatment if you are out of touch, unless you take steps to give your approval by proxy to whomever has been left in charge of your children in your absence.

Dr. Lewis Goldfrank, Director of Emergency Services at Bellevue Hospital in New York City, suggests that entrusting the responsibility for making decisions about medical assistance for your child should be done with the greatest care. Dr.

Goldfrank advises parents to leave word about which doctor to call and what hospital to go to. Also leave the names of whomever you want to be contacted (relative, neighbor). In addition, spell out exactly what you want to have done; for example, if you want your family doctor to be called, leave the number; if you prefer the emergency room at a major teaching hospital, leave the address; if you want a second opinion, say so. It would be a good idea to have your family doctor develop this written plan with you.

Written authorization will enable an emergency room staff or an unfamiliar doctor to treat your child in your absence. Authorization could be in the form of a letter that says, "To whom it may concern: (Name of person) is authorized by us to exercise his or her discretion in authorizing any medical or surgical treatment for our child (name of child) which he or she may deem necessary."[1] The letter should be signed by you and notarized, and left with whomever is taking care of your child in your absence, or where the child can get at it himself if he is alone. Be sure to get such authorization from the parents of a child you are taking care of, or taking away on a trip with you.

Caring for Kids

You can resolve the conflict between needing to be at work and needing to have children cared for by arranging with another family to have children come home together to one house one week and the other house another week, or find a

[1] *The New York Times*, Thursday, January 22, 1981 article "Insuring Medical Aid When Parents Are Absent," by Suzanne Ramos, quoting Anthony Zumbana, Assistant Vice-President of March & McLennan, New York insurance broker in the health care field.

family who is willing to have your child stay with them after school while you watch their children on weekends.

If these arrangements can't be made and your child is still apprehensive, or you don't want him home alone, consider getting a sitter or placing him in a child care center. The following are some guidelines for finding baby-sitters and child-care centers.

GETTING A BABY-SITTER

The best way we know to get a sitter is to choose someone who immediately springs to mind—someone whom your child already knows and who is familiar with your house: a neighbor's teenager, a family member of the right age, or a senior citizen who lives near your home. Proximity is very important; it's inconvenient to have to arrange for a sitter to be picked up after school and delivered home before dinner. If no one you know is available, the next best thing is word of mouth. Ask around for someone who has successfully cared for a friend's child. If you cannot find someone you know, it is vital that you get at least three references, including one from the school that the sitter attends. Look for such traits as punctuality, a sense of responsibility, concern for your children, consistency. It is a good idea to question the sitter about anything that you think is important, asking him such questions as:

- If Larry fell and cut himself, what would you do? If Susan got a bump or bruise, what would you do?

- What would you do if you found you were going to be late getting to our house to sit?

- What would you do if the children said they were hungry?

It is important for you to decide and make clear to the sitter and the children what is expected. Is the sitter expected just to "be there," that is, is it okay for the sitter to do homework or watch TV, or are you paying the sitter to be a companion to the children? Is the sitter someone with whom your chldren will enjoy spending time?

Prepare your child for staying with the sitter by having the sitter come over a few times while you are home. This allows you to observe how the sitter interacts with your child. Explain to your child that the sitter is taking your place, and the child is to follow the sitter's instructions when you are not there. Tell the child that if he feels very strongly that something is going wrong, the child is to call you to check out what he has been told. Fill the sitter in on your child's likes and dislikes, special needs, nicknames, allergies, medications, favorite toys, favorite games, favorite foods; tell the sitter what things the child must not do, and what the child must do.

After the sitter has begun work, take time to review with your child how things are going. Don't ask your child about the sitter specifically—children will often complain about sitters just because they are strangers and their ways are unfamiliar. But do ask how things went and what they did, to get the child talking. Also take time to give the sitter a call, to keep on a personal, friendly basis, and to hear any needs he may have. Remember to invest time and energy in the care and feeding of your sitter because you want him to do the best possible job in caring for your child.

Increasingly, since more often both parents work, older children are taking care of their younger brothers and sisters after school or on Saturdays. They need the same kind of instruction that you would want an outside baby-sitter to have. Some areas of the country have baby-sitting courses for youngsters. They learn to feed babies, what to do if an intruder comes to the door, how to handle common emergencies, and so forth. If you can find such a course in your community, taught by a competent instructor, consider enrolling your older children. If no such course is available, you will have to give the instruction yourself. You and the child can talk about how to handle situations that might come up that he would be concerned about.

CHILD CARE

Another alternative to having your child stay home alone after school is placing your child in a child-care setting. There are many and varied types of child-care situations, ranging from private homes to large child-care centers.

It is necessary to search for the proper child-care center as carefully as you will search for the right college for your child, and many visits as an observer are required to get a clear picture of what goes on while your child is attending the center.

A primary initial consideration should be convenience— the proximity to your work, the route going and coming, and the location of the center in relation to your child's school. (Can your child walk there as if he were walking home? Can the school bus drop him there?)

During your visits, ask questions. If you see four teachers, ask how often those four teachers are there, ask how many teachers at a minimum are always with the children. If you see the children doing a creative activity, ask what percentage of the day they spend in that kind of activity. Do they do it every day? What else do they do? Another vital question is what happens if there is an accident. Ask to see the guidelines, which should include directions for exactly what happens if there is an accident: Who is called? What are their qualifications? What doctor is called if it is serious? With what hospital is the doctor affiliated, and where would the child be taken if he needed to go to a hospital? How far away is the affiliated nurse or doctor from the center?

You will also want to know what the philosophy of the center is. Is it basically a baby-sitting facility that has equipment and supplies for the children to make use of as they wish, or is it a program of activities in which children are expected to participate? Can older children choose to do their homework rather than participate in activities?

Other items which should be part of your concern when you go to observe are the following, which come from a government booklet.[1]

☐ Does the facility have an active license, if appropriate? Is the staff licensed, if appropriate?

☐ Does the place look good to you?
  • Clean
  • Comfortable throughout
  • Safe equipment in good repair
  • Bathrooms clean and sufficient for all-aged children
  • Outdoor areas safe and fenced in

☐ Does the place look safe to you?
  • Fire extinguishers and smoke detectors, fire exits
  • Strong screens or bars on windows above the first floor
  • First-aid kits where readily available
  • Caps on electrical outlets and heaters covered
  • Medicines and household cleaners, poisons, matches, and sharp instruments stored in safe places.

[1]You can get a free copy of this helpful booklet, *A Parent's Guide to Day Care*, by writing to Department 76, Washington, D.C. 20401. Ask for Publication No. (ODHS) 80-30254, LSDS.

Dinner

Before dinner, parents have the problem of switching from the framework of the work day into that of family life. Children have a similar problem. Naturally, they want to play as long as possible, and tend to race in just before dinner is served. For most, their minds stay where they'd like their bodies to be—outside playing with their friends.

One way to overcome this problem is having the children come in a little earlier in order to change their mood. Helping with dinner can get them in the mood for food. Inviting the children to set the table or help in the preparation of a dish can change the atmosphere from active playing time to a relaxed environment for dinner.

This transitional time also affords the opportunity to think about organizing tasks for the evening. Does the child have to write a report, do special homework, or practice the piano or trumpet? Help your child get into the habit of scheduling evening plans just as he would schedule playtime, schoolwork, and other activities.

AVOIDING HASSLES AT
THE DINNER TABLE

To avoid hassles at dinner, make sure that the sizes of the portions are really what children are able to eat. Often parents put food on children's plates without knowing how hungry the children are. It's silly to get into arguments about eating all the food on the plate when it is just too much food. The "clean plate club" and forcing children to eat all of their food are things of the past. Allow your children to eat as much as they want of a balanced diet—don't fuss about special foods. There are always substitutes, if you are concerned that your child should have a particular nutrient. For example, if your child doesn't like spinach, there are many other green vegetables you can serve, prepared raw, cooked in soups or in stews, or mixed with noodles. The object is to encourage your children to taste everything. What you want to avoid are the tenseness and arguments that can arise over eating.

Do not bribe your children to eat. Don't use the "If you don't eat your vegetables, you can't have dessert" technique. Try the positive approach, saying, *This tastes so good to me, please try it.* Most importantly, don't try to convince your kids with intimidating slogans: *You eat like a bird,* or *Why don't you eat like your sister?* When told children are starving in India, most kids suggest that their liver and spinach be packed up and sent overseas. It is terrible to be singled out as the child who is a poor eater. Make food and mealtime an adventure, not a chore to be gotten through quickly.

TABLE MANNERS

Dinner will be much more pleasant if you use good table manners consistently and teach your children to do the same. Adults should try to serve as models for the children, because that's really how kids learn. If you want your children to have good manners and be interesting conversationalists, you must expose them to the right environment daily.

You can start with easy rules for your children: teach them to place their napkins on their laps; to tip soup bowls away from themselves and fill the spoon by pushing it away as well; to sip soup from the side of the spoon or from the end without making noise; to say please when they want something rather than just grab for it; not to speak with their mouths full of food, or make too much noise when they chew. Teach older children to make sure that there is enough food for all before taking a lot of their favorite food from the serving plate.

Many families have a rule that no one begins to eat before all family members are seated at the table. This is to encourage children to focus on other people and to develop a sense of appreciation for the person who prepared and served the meal. In addition, it also allows that person to be part of the whole meal. This is where serving hot food onto prewarmed plates is helpful—it assures that everyone gets to eat while the food is hot. Train your children to help serve and clear, to notice if someone needs something (more ice, another napkin, etc.). This early training will make your children more comfortable and socially competent as teenagers and adults.

DINNER TABLE CONVERSATION

Conversing at the dinner table is a wonderful way for children to think about what happened to them during the day. It creates a sharing climate for the whole family. Some families ask children to talk about something they've done at school and also something they've read about or learned that interested them. This makes the children more attentive to school, and also more aware of the newspapers, television, and the library, so that they have something interesting to contribute to the conversation at the evening meal. Listening to others' questions and information is a valuable lesson best learned at home. During dinner turn off the television; this leaves time for conversation.

THE DINNER TABLE
ATMOSPHERE

Try to set the table as if you were having company. If the people who live with you are the ones you care about the most, why shouldn't you try to make meals prettiest and most delicious for them?

Often it means reaching for some plates that are in the back of the closet—but after all, wouldn't the green beans look better on the yellow plates? Or it may mean remembering to chill the plates for salad (you still have to wash the same number of dishes) or zig-zagging a lemon for the fish instead of just cutting it in half.

Centerpieces can be anything from garden greens, fruit, a plant, something a family member created, part of a child's rock collection, or a bunch of flowers, to a newspaper article someone thinks is important.

If you have "take out" fried chicken, you can serve the chicken and french fries from baskets lined with pretty paper napkins or bandana print napkins (fewer dishes to wash). Why not place celery and carrot sticks in a juice glass next to each person's plate? It becomes a personal salad bouquet.

There can be lots of different kinds of meals. Try a reading meal, where you all bring a book, newspaper, or magazine to the table.

On a nice day, take plates and eat all or part of dinner outside on the steps, around a table, or on a blanket on the grass. If you're lucky enough to have a fireplace, in winter you can have tray dinners in front of the fire. Sometimes talk and eat, sometimes just eat and read near the fireplace. Roasted marshmallows are always fun at dessert time. Sometimes you all might watch an important TV program while you eat:

what better way to explain, discuss, and share a vital news event or a long-awaited special?

Enjoy celebration dinners. Be sure to celebrate going back to school—dinner on the first day of school should be an event.

On birthdays, the birthday person can choose the menu, from appetizer to dessert. Half-birthdays, unbirthdays, or "for no special reason" days are fun times, too. Holidays can always become occasions. They can be stretched out as you celebrate the Day Before or the Day After, the Week Before, and so on.

Dinnertime is often the one time of the day when the family is together. Usually family members are happy to see one another, to tell about what happened at school, at work, at play. It is often the place to share a problem and get help in finding a solution, talk about a place to go on vacation, plan how to paint part of the house, or decide what the family will do on the weekend.

A mealtime discussion about how hard it is to remember that everyone's message is important because your message is the most important to you, can make dining more pleasant. *Even though it's tough, you've got to wait to tell about your special information. It's like a busy intersection— someone has to get the red light, even though everyone is in a hurry. Sometimes you need a green light for talking so you don't have a conversation crash.*

It's important that both parents and kids contribute during dinner—what are your plans as well as your kids' plans? What went well? What do you want to change? Is there a problem that can be solved? Encourage older children to help younger children solve school problems. Since the big brother probably attended the same school as his younger sibling, he will have some knowledge of the teachers, the layout of the building, and how the school functions.

The mealtime feeling seems to set the tone for a house. Of course, members of families love each other, but whether they like each other often shows up most at the dinner table. Sometimes we're silent, most times we talk. We share our thoughts and our hopes, our plans and our fantasies, the day's events and the future, what pleases and what disappoints us.

Alone Time

The most important thing you can give to your child is yourself—your time, attention, understanding, and help.

When two people try to find time to be alone together they are showing their commitment to one another. Decide how much time you can give your child and when you can best give it. And then make sure you do! Remove yourself from distractions—turn off the TV, do not take phone calls. When you talk, choose topics that are of interest to your child. Do not use this time to discuss keeping his room neat or your hard day. Alone Time can be anything from cuddling for a few minutes to a big outing.

The first time you leave the other kids behind or go to another room to spend time with one child, they may feel disappointed, angry, or sad. Though you explain that each child will have opportunities, it often takes time for children to adjust to unhappiness about being left out. This is an important lesson for children, however, because learning to handle frustrations and disappointments is part of growing up. Acknowledge the left-out child's feelings by saying something like, *I know it makes you unhappy when I spend time alone with your sister.* Then follow the child's lead, listen and offer help. You might suggest things for that child to do alone or arrange his Alone Time with you. Be sure to arrange Alone Time with each of your children.

It is important that you create some free time for yourself and also for you and your mate as a couple. DO NOT DISTURB signs like those that hang on hotel room doors can be home-made and used on your own door. Children learn to watch for signals from an early age—the smile or tone of voice that indicates approval, or the red light at the street corner that means STOP, or a sign on a bedroom door that signals *I need some time alone.*

Decide how much time you'll need and set a clock to show the child when you'll be available. Being able to match his own clock with a family clock becomes an activity in itself. Plan an activity for the child—a game, a chore (moving books, folding towels), or a visit to a friend's house—to insure your Alone Time. An appealing snack, including something to drink, prepared and left in an accessible place often removes the need for interruption. There is one impor-tant rule concerning Alone Time: it is vital that you match the amount of Alone Time realistically to the period of time a child can be expected to stay by himself.

Once there are kids in the house, it sometimes seems impossible to find the time just to be together with your mate in an unhurried, leisurely, loving way. While romance fre-quently results in kids, kids do not correspondingly promote romance. However, if you seek out opportunities, you can find the important time you need—to be alone as a couple, and to be alone as individuals—for your own personal growth and pleasure.

- Encourage sleepovers, not only to your children's friends' houses, but also to grandparents', cousins', or other rela-tives' houses.

- Have a baby-sitter to gain some time alone at home. Let the sitter take the children to the movies, the zoo, the park, the museum. These arrangements can work equally well on a weekend afternoon or after school.

- Arrange for grandparents or a sitter to be at your home when the child comes home from school. If they then stay through dinner and the evening, this can give you a whole day on your own. You might take a holiday away from the house by booking a room at a hotel after arranging for grandparents to be at home after school. This gives the grandparents a day with the children and parents a day without the children. A reminder: anytime your children are going to come home and find someone other than you there, they need to be told about it in advance and to know when they can expect you home.

- You can also pre-arrange with the school that the grandparents will pick up the children after school and take them to the grandparents' place. Then you can pick the children up at the grandparents', so the children won't show up before you're ready for them.

Bedtime

Try to create a quiet time for your children before they go to sleep. One way to make this happen is to have a reading time, either as a group or alone. Young children can be read to by a parent or by an older brother or sister. Read as a family, with those who can read doing the reading, and the younger children listening and knowing that when they get old enough they will take their places as readers. Even ten minutes of this activity will help get children in the mood for bed. Quiet discussions and listening to music can also be relaxing ways to end the day.

Introduce your children to one of the great pleasures of the civilized world—reading in bed. When your child is young, make it your responsibility to see that there is always an interesting book by his bedside. Encourage older children to go to the library to pick out books that they would like to read. This can create good life-long reading habits. Reach a mutually satisfactory decision concerning how long to read each night.

An important part of each day is thinking about the day that just passed and taking time to review what went well and what could have gone better. When your child is getting ready for bed, encourage him to think about what happened that day and talk about it—the parts he liked, those he didn't like, what he would like to change, and how he could accomplish that. When your child is evaluating his own day, that is definitely *not* the time for you to lecture him about what he did wrong. If you encourage your child to talk to you about things he thinks he should have done better, and then scold him for things that went wrong, you will only discourage your child from talking and sharing with you.

What you can do is paraphrase by reflecting or repeating to the child what you heard him say in a supportive way, so that the child is sure you heard him. Put what the child said into your own words without changing the meaning. For example, if your child says, *I should have studied my spelling better*, you should *not* say, *Well, I told you you'd better study if you want good grades.* Think how you would feel if your spouse said that to you after you had just flunked your driver's test! Instead, *paraphrase*; say something like, *You feel next time you'd like to study more before a hard test.* This reaffirms what the child has decided, and shows you are listening.

Before bedtime is also the time for each person to gather together what he needs for the next day. Ask your child to check the calendar and his daily checklist to see what's needed for tomorrow: gymsuit, musical instrument, papers for a special project. You want to get your child into the habit of planning and then preparing for the next day. This is also a good time to talk about how you want the next day to go. You can share things you both want—his getting to school early enough to get a library book before school (that means breakfast ten minutes earlier), talking to the gym teacher about making the team, or your own plans for a meeting, or for shopping.

When children are young, parents take the time to tuck them in and say good night. Don't lose that as children get older. It's worth the extra trip to keep this ritual going. Often, before children go to sleep, you can learn incredible things about what they feel and hope. And very often you can be helpful in making some of those things happen. Sometimes you can learn what's worrying them or what is bewildering them. These quiet moments together can be the most important part of the day for parents as well as children.

We can enjoy our days more if our expectations are realistic and we teach our kids to be realistic—to know that some things will go as well as we planned, but some won't. You can add to your kids' sense of success and competence by reminding them of the things they did well that day: *I noticed that you remembered to say thank you when Aunt Bert picked you up,* or *You really seemed to be trying to do your work more neatly.* In this way, you convey to your child that you are aware of his progress and are glad that you shared the day.

Introducing New Activities
Sports
Food Shopping
Cooking
Games, Computers, and Collections
Birthdays
Celebrations
Home from School—A Forced Vacation
Reading
TV
Movie, Theater, Dance, Music
Conversation
Grandparents
Travel

2
Quality Time

Quality Time gathers family members together for a short, warm hug or for a long, leisurely vacation. It means giving a few minutes of quiet, uninterrupted time when you can't give an hour. It implies, *If I can't be there or listen, I say when I can and keep my word.* It means connecting by telephone when you can't be there in person. It means reaching out, listening, touching, trying to share and care. The message in your heart can be conveyed to your child in seconds with a loving pat on the back or a kiss on the cheek. Quality Time means changing gears, clearing your head, and focusing on your child. It also means showing your children, by your example, that time you spend together is important, precious, and enjoyable. Try to create Quality Time—grab it when the opportunity arises, savor it, cherish it! Quality Time is measured in memories that will last a lifetime.

For the most part, weekdays are very crowded with work, school, and keeping the house going, while weekends are crowded with sports, social, and religious life, "catching up," and shopping. Holidays are crowded with family gatherings, travel, and all the necessary preparations. Vacations are crowded with getting there and seeing everything. So, if you want Quality Time with your family, you have to work to make it happen by planning.

Why bother? Because you'll have children who enjoy being together and contributing to your family's experiences, who have the skills to relate meaningfully to others, and who have good memories of childhood. Our kids are with us such a short time. The atmosphere and environment that parents create in these few years become a child's foundation for the future. Children who are raised in a family setting where they are treated like packages, to be used and transported in good working order, or taken out when convenient, are likely to treat their own children that way. It takes extra time, planning, listening, and caring to build Quality Time. When you're hassled, harried, and hurried it is often difficult to place a value on creating "together" times. But we believe the rewards are worth it.

This chapter provides some ideas for improving the quality of life between generations—between you and your kids. It's based on the concept that the more unfamiliar something is, the worse it's likely to seem. Unfamiliar foods (like grasshoppers and eels) are much less palatable to most of us than a juicy steak, but that same juicy steak may be totally inedible to a vegetarian. The very quality of being "less familiar" makes a thing seem less good. Sometimes we have to overcome tremendous prejudices to feel that something alien is as good as something we've grown up liking.

Having advance information and experience helps make people feel good—your kids as well as you. This concept is important to remember when dealing with between-generation issues. What is familiar, and therefore good, to your kids (the latest in music, hairstyles, dress) may be perceived by you as "strange," "weird," or "immature." Likewise, when we ask our children to watch a ballet, go to a symphony concert, listen to blues or jazz, eat a new food, sit home and read plays out loud, go on a totally different kind of vacation, we are thought to be "out of it," not "with it," dull, or old. So to build the best together times, request everyone's input, encourage everyone to listen and try to use as many offered suggestions as possible.

Introducing New Activities

What's the best way to introduce new ideas to kids—to get them to go to a new place or eat a new food? The answer to this question is to start training your children very early.

Only by orienting them toward experimentation while they are growing up can you make new things exciting rather than frightening for them.

Research is confirming what most parents already know: children are born with different temperaments. Some are easygoing and take to new things cheerfully, others are fussier and have to be coaxed to try new foods, toys, or activities. But you can expand any child's capacity to enjoy a new experience by experimenting and talking about it: *Let's walk home a different way today. Let's try that funny new vegetable we read about, spaghetti squash. Let's go someplace new this weekend.*

Talk about your own experiences with new things—people you've just met, new foods you've tried, going places for the first time, new things you've done, and how you felt before and after you did them. Encourage your children to tell you how they feel about trying new things, and accept those feelings—say something that will make the child glad he told you instead of sorry he bothered: *I'm glad you told me that. I understand how you feel. I didn't know you felt that way. I remember feeling like that when I tried something new. Lots of kids feel that way.*

Talk to your older children about how unfamiliar things often seem unpleasant or bad, and that one of the ways to increase our options for enjoyment is to become familiar with a wider variety of things—foods, people, places, books, sports, activities, and so forth. This means trying more and more things until they become familiar to us, so we can make informed judgments about what we like and what we don't.

Sports

Sports are a popular family pastime. Learning to play a new game can provide many happy hours of shared time. It doesn't matter if different members of your family root or play for different teams. Even watching a game together makes for a good time. Sometimes parents feel that they should know the answers to every question their children ask. Often, instead of saying, *I don't know, let's find out together*, or *I always wondered that but never took time to look it up*, or *I'll go to the library with you*, parents discourage the conversation or put down the topic or the questioner because they feel threatened. If that happens, much is lost. It's important to create opportunities for your child to learn about sports. You can do this by reading books together. You might try the following:

Rules of the Game, by the Diagram Group (Paddington Press Ltd., 1977)

The Answer Book of Sports, by Bill Mazer (Grosset and Dunlap, 1973)

There are hundreds of sports books for children. A trip to the public library with your child may result in your discovering just what your family wants.

Attending local school, semi-pro, or major league team games together, as well as watching them on television, can create get-togethers, memories, and draw the family closer throughout the year. Reading parts of the sports section to a younger child or discussing articles or editorials in the sports section with older children can be a very satisfying shared activity.

Sports stories and sports events offer many conversation starters: how and why people acted as they did, the consequences of their behavior, what led up to their actions, and personal opinions about all of it can catalyze some fascinating discussions. Learning to ponder an issue, figuring out how you feel, and being able to express your views are lifetime skills that can be developed through an interest in sports. Preparing to go to the game as well as talking about it afterward stimulate good times and easy conversation. Often one or both parents don't get involved in a particular sport that their child likes because they feel they don't know enough about it. It's really okay for a parent to know as little (or less) about the topic as the child. Learning from your child or with your child can be as valuable an experience as teaching a child. We know two children who developed a treasured friendship while watching sports on television and discussing the games with a person who became very special to them. The memories of those times remain a joy to them as they mature.

It's also okay for one parent or child not to like a sport that others in the family like, and to use the time alone for a different social activity. It can be enriching for children to have time with one parent or for both parents to spend time alone with one of their children.

Perhaps the most important way to encourage your child to become skillful at a sport is to be there. When she's playing, or managing the team, or simply on the bench, your supportive presence is required from time to time. It's not much fun to attend your child's soccer game when you have dinner guests coming or a speech to write for a 9 A.M. presentation, but kids care about their parents' being there, and your presence can help them stick to a sport long enough to develop understanding, good skills, and a camaraderie with team members.

Sometimes your child may not even get to play during the game, or during the season. It's at times like these that the parents' support of the team helps the child develop a sense of sportsmanship and team spirit.

If your child expresses interest in learning to play a sport, help her make that goal realistic by:

- arranging for equipment. It often makes sense to try to borrow equipment for a while, to give your child a chance to see if she will really enjoy getting involved in a particular sport.

- helping her learn the game. Take her to the library to get books so she can learn the rules, signals, history, famous teams and players.

- helping her enjoy the sport. Practice with her by pitching balls (soft balls for younger children) or throwing tennis balls for her to hit, etc.

- helping her build a plan for getting proficient in a sport. She can set up practice sessions, lessons, or an exercise routine.

Show support for different skills, talents, and interests among your children. Even if some of your children do not love sports, encourage them to attend games and matches in which their siblings participate. Similarly, the sports-oriented children should be encouraged to attend their siblings' plays, debates, concerts, and so forth. This is the stuff that bonds family members and creates good times.

HOW TO HELP YOUR CHILD
AFTER A SPORTS LOSS

Sports also help your child learn that she won't always be a winner. Everyone has to learn to cope with the disappointment and frustration of losing. The only rule we know of to help at these times is, don't let the subject go underground. Talking about the hard times should be as much a part of your family life as celebrating the good times. If the child brings up the subject first, try to follow her lead. For example, if she's angry and says things like, *The other team wasn't fair*, or *The ref was blind*, accept the angry feelings as a start. If she's sad, accept those feelings, too. This will encourage the child to continue talking. When she's gotten better control of her feelings (by talking them out with you), then you can either let the topic go, or do whatever teaching seems appropriate (either immediately or at a later time). Try to help your child to understand that if she doesn't lose some of the time, then she is not challenging herself enough—the game's too easy to be a real sporting event. What matters is how much fun, how much learning, and how much good teamwork (or individual skill) the child exhibited; not who won or lost. Accepting these ideas takes a long time and more maturity than the child has now, but it's appropriate to introduce them at this age. If the child does not bring up the topic, you do it. *I'm sorry your team lost today, you had a wonderful save in the fourth inning*, or *I really liked the way your team kept right in there till the end.*

Kids sometimes feel like now is forever, this is the only championship, and there will never be another time to win. To them it somehow feels like this competition is the last chance. Once you can get your child to talk to you about this feeling, you can help her by exploring what future sporting events there are, and what plans she's making to play in them. Sometimes a child feels badly because she knows that she played as hard as she could, and still she lost. Something that may help here is reinforcing the idea that it would be a bad thing if she never lost. Make it clear that you know she played as well as she could, but that if the two teams are really evenly matched, hers will lose half of the time; and if they are playing a better team they will lose more than that. Only if they are playing a team that is worse than their team will they win all or most of the time. Help the child to see how bad that would be for her skill development. The bottom line is still that losing feels bad, however. Don't discourage your child from voicing disappointment. She (and you) should be able to say after an upsetting loss, *Boy am I mad!* or *I'm really disappointed*—without being put down for it.

When there are losers, there are winners. Your child may need help handling her disappointment about losses, but she also needs training in how to congratulate the winners. The older the child, the easier it will be to accept a loss, to say *The other team really outplayed us today*, or *We just couldn't get it together*. The younger child is more likely to blame a loss on unfairness. Teaching the child to recognize the good play of others is important. You can help by pointing out sportsmanlike behavior you see on television or read about in the papers—for example, when a coach says, *We were outplayed*, or a star football player congratulates his counterpart on the other team.

Food Shopping

Some errands that are necessary to keep the family going can be turned into family outings. Food shopping is a good example. Encourage family members to add favorite items to an ongoing marketing list posted in the kitchen. Help them understand that everybody may not get their preference each time, but that they'll all be kept in mind. Taking one child to the store can be a way of creating alone time. Make a separate list of items that the child can pick up while you get other things. This saves time and allows the child to be really helpful. Even a young child can look for coupons in the paper at home with you, and then match them with the real articles at the store. It is a good beginning reading exercise and another way of utilizing children's efforts and energy while spending time together. You can drop off an older and younger child at the store to do certain types of shopping for you, thereby creating time well spent together by siblings.

It is certainly worth the time to teach your children to be discriminating and informed shoppers. Explain consumer information as the need arises. Knowing how to be a wise buyer is a vital skill. Teach your children these shopping guidelines:

When buying milk or other dairy products, check the container to be certain there are no dents, leaks, or bad odors. Look at the date printed or stamped on the top of the container. This date is the last day that the product may be sold. It can be kept for a week after that date in your home refrigerator.

When buying food packed in bags or boxes, check the corners to be sure there are no openings—corners usually tear first. Shake the bag or box gently to be certain there are no holes. Look at the closing to be sure it is tightly sealed. The package should look clean and fresh, not dirty or old. Check the freshness date on the package if there is one. Choose a package with the latest date.

When buying canned goods, avoid cans that leak,

bulge, are dented, rusted, or discolored, or that smell bad-ly. Never use or even taste food in a questionable can; it could give you food poisoning. Take the can back to the store unopened. Usually the store will refund your money.

Courteous behavior makes shopping more pleasant. Dis-cussions can help children understand why good manners are helpful everywhere, including the supermarket. Choose examples that relate to your child's experience—getting in line in front of someone else, grabbing for the last item, nib-bling on merchandise that isn't yours—to help him under-stand why certain behavior is not acceptable.

In everything we do we are models for our children, and this includes shopping at the supermarket. If Mom or Dad bor-rows a supermarket cart to wheel groceries home or to move something from the house to the garage, it is unreasonable to be angry when their children use one to deliver papers or as a toy.

Let family members know that everyone is expected to help put groceries away. It makes a dull job fun, gets it done with a minimum of effort, and enhances family community spirit.

Cooking

Everyone knows that visits to the zoo and camping trips are fun and also are good learning experiences for children. But few people realize that some of the best fun and best learning can be shared with their children at home—in the usually forbidden territory called "The Kitchen."

Pots, pans, lids, spatulas, whisks, and measuring cups can capture a baby's attention for hours. Children can find that same fascination in this special room as they grow older. Use children's known abilities as a springboard to success in cooking. If children can finger paint, they can also spread soft mixtures. If they can roll clay, they can use a rolling pin. If they can tear paper, they can tear salad greens. Cooking is a real-life skill. Children can only pretend to drive a car or to be a teacher or superhero. But they do not have to pretend to make good foods. They can actually cook; in fact, they can become accomplished cooks.

Before you get your child excited about cooking with you, ask yourself some important questions:

- Are you willing to take time from your busy schedule to cook with your child?

- Will you let your child be satisfied with the results, even if your expectations are not met completely?

- Are you willing to risk having the recipe fail, to have peanut butter sandwiches instead of a glorious new dish?

- Are you willing to begin over, spill a little, drop a lot, give it another chance, and still keep your good humor?

Here are some hints that we believe can smooth away potential problems and pave the way for successful cooking. Prepare comfortable work spaces. You may choose to arrange some cabinets so that the ingredients and equipment are in easy reach for the recipes your child is learning to prepare. If some things are off limits, store them away from the things your child can use. Your toddler is safest out of the kitchen when you cook with an older child.

Before you start each cooking session, you and your child should read the whole recipe. Check to be sure you have all of the ingredients and equipment needed. Do not substitute ingredients, or change the recipe in any way the first time the two of you make it. Change, alter, and adapt only after you both have an understanding of the basic recipe and have made it successfully a few times. The younger the child, the more he will need the security that comes from repetition.

Pre-measure any ingredients that you can. This saves valuable time and reduces tension when you are following step-by-step directions. Use one tray to hold all ingredients, and another tray to hold all tools. Remember that larger bowls and pans reduce the risk of spills when children mix and stir.

Put each ingredient away after you've used it. In that way, you'll have an automatic check on what must still be added. The less cluttered the kitchen is, the easier it is to work. When you have finished using tools (except knives), put them in a bowl of sudsy water. In this way, you can prevent food sticking. Knives should be washed and stored away immediately after use, or rinsed and placed where they can't be grabbed accidentally.

If your child loses interest in part of the process, ask if he wants to watch or do another task such as setting the table or washing utensils in fluffy suds (no knives or other sharp objects), while you continue cooking. When more than one child is working with you, they'll invariably want equal time. You can help them to alternate tasks (one can mix and one sauté this time and switch jobs next time) or you can divide each task into equal time with the use of a timer. You and the kids can decide in advance which way you'll do it. Note, however, that the child who didn't get the chance to perform a process today is well motivated to do it the next time. It's much easier to be working with a child who says, *It's my turn*, instead of the familiar, *Do I have to do that again?*

If your child has difficulty with a particular task, help him over the specific rough spot and then *let him continue alone.*

It's easy to get carried away and start doing all the cooking by yourself. In general, the less you must explain and show, the more your child will learn and enjoy. If you find yourself telling too much, *stop!* Ask a question instead, to get your child talking about the next step, or about what was fun already. Only through actual work successes can the child learn to think of himself as one who can accomplish.

Games, Computers, and Collections

One of the most important rules about agreeing to play a game with your kids is to be sure you set aside enough time to complete the activity. Nothing is more frustrating than having a player leave in the middle. It is a good idea to ask someone else to grab the phone when it rings, stir the stew, or listen for the doorbell. If that isn't possible, then say that at the beginning, so your children understand that they have you except for unavoidable interruptions.

There are many kinds of games that foster family togetherness. It is often a good investment to purchase a ping-pong table, pool table, or a badminton set for the family (garage sales are good places to find bargains). These are games that require several people to play and create ongoing relationships. Having a jigsaw puzzle out where everybody can fit a piece or two and then gather around as the puzzle fills in is a simple activity that brings people together. Card games and board games provide easy and inexpensive means for sharing family time. Creating a series—the best two out of three games—builds a feeling of continuity and ongoing conversation. A series of games can be played intermittently and give the children something to look forward to each day for several days. Funny games like charades create opportunities to be silly and laugh a lot. Games sitting on the shelf are useless. Give some thought to how you can use them in your own family setting to foster Quality Time together.

One of the ways that parents can get out of the middle, when several kids are engaged in a game and start the "he's not playing fair," "that's not right, he shouldn't have done that" routine is to refer the children back to the rules. They'll probably need your help, but you should help them find out what is the appropriate or right thing, according to the rules of the game they are playing. If there is no set of printed rules, then help them decide what is "closest" in the rules. Or, you can introduce the idea of a third party arbitrator, by asking the kids to pick someone whose opinion they agree to stand by without argument.

When we were young, reading science fiction was a popular pastime, and one of the pervading themes was the fear that computers and robots would take over the world. Today many adults have a distrust of the computer and its powers. However, this is not true of our children, who see the computer as one more tool for people to use, like the airplane and the television.

Technology is growing explosively and during the next decade there will be a revolution in information processing. Homes of the not-so-distant future may have computer rooms, just like today's homes have kitchens. Technologists predict the computer room will be the entertainment center (with a wide variety of games and video devices), the information center (where you pay bills, handle financial matters, maybe even do your shopping), the energy conservation center (regulating your home's energy flow throughout the day and night), the learning center (where programs will be available to teach anything from multiplication tables and Chinese to effective management), the security center (burglar prevention system), and the communication center (phone, teletype, and other links with the outside).

Chances are, your child already knows more about the world of the computer than you do, and, if not, it makes sense for you to develop a positive, supportive attitude toward her acquiring such knowledge, because it is the language of the future. No child who is currently in elementary school will be considered well educated when she graduates from high school unless she knows a computer language and has some comprehension of the world of technology.

As technology improves, the price of computers will come down. Home computers are now within the price range of some families. Home computers are wonderful for exposing your children to the mechanics of programming and the joys of a stimulating self-teaching environment. Computers are doing what educators have always wanted to do—making learning fun. Programs are available for home use in traditional school subjects, as well as a wide range of entertaining topics. For example, an airplane program lets your child be a pilot and calculate the effects of wind direction and velocity, throttle thrust, and other real-life variables in trying to plan a flight that goes the longest distance. This kind of fun learning helps pack a lot of extra education into a day. Home computers can provide fun and are an excellent substitute for television.

When a child has a particular interest in a sport, in science, or in almost anything, that interest can become the foundation for a collection: bugs, rocks, baseball cards, comic books, shells, stamps, coins. Stamps and coins from different countries can lead to an interest in history and geography.

Collections can be something for a child and parent to share. This shared interest can often be a catalyst for conversation, especially when all else fails.

A collection can be your child's entree into a new world of greater independence. He can become an expert in his chosen area of interest, knowing more about the subject than his friends or anyone in the family. Collections can be vehicles for making new friends—both adults and children—with a common interest in the hobby. Also, the times you take your child to another child's house to look at his collection or to trade, or the times you go with your child to a convention or exhibit are all good opportunities for being together.

Birthdays

With a little effort, birthday celebrations can be inexpensive yet very special. What fun to wake up and find a congratulations message in your bedroom: HAPPY BIRTHDAY written in bright colors on a long length of paper towels or several sheets of newspapers published on the child's birthday can be wound around the bedroom to start the day in a festive manner. A birthday card and some balloons blown up and left in the child's bedroom can also create a special mood.

Let your child plan the menu for breakfast, lunch, and dinner on his birthday. He will probably pick something that you are accustomed to making, but, because he chooses it, it sets the day apart and can become a family birthday tradition.

Birthday parties require planning and cooperation. In thinking about how many children to invite you'll want to consider the kind of party—inside or outside; the size of your house or apartment (can everybody sit down to eat their ice cream and cake); how much it will cost; how many people you feel will be comfortable for the type of party planned.

Party invitations should not be given out at school unless the whole class is invited. Even though it saves stamps, think how your child would feel if invitations were given out to a group of classmates and he was not invited. If your child is not inviting everyone, he should be taught not to flaunt the fact that he is having a party.

It may sometimes happen that your kids are not invited to a party. Encourage them to talk about it with you; *You sound really disappointed about not being invited to the party. Would you like to talk about it?* Remind them of their last birthday party and how many people were there, and help them to remember that there were people whom they didn't invite. Explain that at different times you want to share things with different people. After the child has had the chance to talk about what is disappointing to him about not being invited, help him to focus on something positive, by asking what would be a fun thing to do instead. If it is a big disappointment, he may need your company and support at this time to plan something special.

It's fun to choose a theme for a party—outer space, cowboys, cars, horses, the circus, and baseball are all fun themes for kids. Carry the theme out even in the invitations. Your children can cut suitable pictures from magazines to make the invitations, writing the pertinent information on or under the picture. You can have each invitation photocopied and let your child cut it into five or six pieces like a puzzle. Place each puzzle in an envelope. Then the guests can put it together to find out whose party it is; when and where to come, etc. Be sure to include the time the party ends as well as when it begins. Addressing and stamping the invitations and sending thank-you notes should be the child's responsibility once he is capable of assuming it.

Special activities carefully planned in advance can make your child's party unique. For example, provide the guests with materials for making their own costumes—old bathrobes, old hats, outdated clothing, absorbent cotton (for making beards and such), boxes, tape, etc. Let the guests make themselves into characters. Tell them to use any of the materials they see to make the costume they want. Depending on their age level, give them ten minutes (for five-year-olds who will put on only a few articles of clothing) to half an hour (for twelve-year-olds who will be cutting boxes, pasting things together, and constructing things). Once they've made the costumes, suggest putting on a play. You can get them started with just a few words about a plot.

- "All of these people are on a boat to . . ."

- "This group lives on the Planet Atina. Something remarkable is about to happen. It is . . ."

- "Everyone here has seen something strange happen. They have gathered together to . . ."

Another idea for a child's party is a carnival. Boxes can turn into bean-bag or penny tosses; trash cans can be used for ball-toss games; plastic milk containers can be hung on a line as targets. Take a deck of cards and a child with an imagination and you can have a fortuneteller. A few signs and balloons create a wonderful carnival atmosphere.

Another idea is a treasure hunt. The treasure can be inexpensive—fun gifts or food can be used.

First decide how close the locations for leaving clues have to be. (Age level of the children will determine this decision—whether children can cross streets for example.) Place one clue in an envelope for each person or each team at every location. Be sure the clue is clearly labeled with a team name (red, green, blue, or whatever) or each person's name. Avoid sending players to the locations in the same order. Decide if certain locations should have an adult monitor. Gather prizes for all participants; use things from the attic,

books that are new to young readers, ice cream sundaes, and so on. Here are some sample treasure-hunt clues:

Next door but I won't help you.
Is it right or left to the next clue?
On the ground flowers you will see
And in the middle the next clue from me.

Walk back to our house
Where there is a tree
Look at the bottom
The next clue you will see.

Candy bars and comic books
Are what they sell there.
Go to the drug store—
The next clue will be there.
*[Use any store that is convenient
and substitute a new first line.]*

To mail a letter you have to go far—
To the corner near the red car.
Look carefully: there is an envelope for you.
The message inside will tell you what next to do.

The playground is fun,
Baseball is too.
If you get to the swing fast,
You'll find the next clue.

Come down Main Street.
Turn in at our place.
Look at the front door.
The clue is staring you in the face.

Go to Karen's house, don't be too quick.
The porch is the place to pick.
Search carefully—the envelope will be found
Very, very close to the ground.

Round and round and round you go.
First go fast, then go slow.

The park is great, the merry-go-round so much fun.
Hurry, hurry, you're almost done!

Back to the party it's time to go—
To Elm Street, don't be slow.
Go to the place where we bar-b-q.
Hope you had fun following the clues.

A mural party can be fun for elementary-school-aged children. Open a roll of shelf paper and provide crayons and magic markers. Mark off the paper in segments, and have each child draw one section of a mural. Tell them to draw anything they want—a scene, a person, a group, an animal—an inside scene or outside scene. Have each child sign his section. What fun it is to fold it up, then unroll it, and have the group make up a story as the scenes unfold.

Other ideas for birthday entertainment that require more expenditure are: hiring or recruiting talent, such as a juggler, a magician, a fortuneteller, a cartoonist who does caricatures, the use of ponies or horses, puppeteers or story-tellers. The extreme would be hiring someone to arrange and cater the whole party.

A "go fly a kite" party makes for exciting outdoor fun, as does building and flying model airplanes (gliders). Giving each child a puzzle and having a prize for whomever puts his together fastest is great for a rainy-day party.

Give a special event party: take children to the circus, a special movie, or children's theater; go to the zoo, science museum, aquarium, or art museum; visit a farm where you can pick apples or gather strawberries; go bowling. Some of these places require making arrangements for transportation and getting other adults to help you monitor. You can offer the child who is interested in sports a choice of taking three or four of her friends to a sporting event or having fifteen friends to a house party. College sporting events are often outstanding, and fun for kids to see. They are usually less expensive than professional events.

For a young child's birthday party, an older child dressed in the costume of a superhero or *Peanuts* character could be hired to help at the event. He can assist with the opening of presents and serving of food, be a wonderful surprise guest for the children, and a helper for the adults. (Older children who enjoy spending time with younger kids might consider investing in a costume and hiring themselves out as helper/ entertainers for neighborhood parties.)

Food for a party should be whatever you find enjoyable preparing. There's no point in giving a child a fabulous birthday party which leaves his parents frazzled the week before the event and exhausted the week after.

The food can complement the theme of the party. Tuna and egg salad can be shaped into whatever form you want. You can put a couple of sandwich fillings such as cream cheese, egg salad, tuna salad, sliced chicken, lettuce, tomato, grated or sliced cheese out and have kids "build their own" sandwich into pita bread. Children can build their own sundaes as well, with a few ice cream flavors and topping choices. This means less for the adults to do and gives the kids more involvement and enjoyment. If they are going to build their own, have all the ingredients out and arranged attractively and logically. Call a few children at a time to the table to prevent pushing, squabbles, and accidents.

We've often found that when the party is over, there sits Joey, whose parents have not come to pick him up after everyone else is gone. Expect this to happen, even though you've told parents when to pick the children up, because in any crowd there are likely to be emergencies that cause delays. Have a toy or book ready to give to the child, so that he can remain happily occupied without your constant attention while he waits. Teach your child to be a good host and keep him company if possible.

As the day ends, in some way mark the event with an inexpensive extra present or a note tucked near your child's pillow. A book, a puzzle, something that says, *It was a wonderful day, and I celebrate with you the fact that you were born.*

Celebrations

Why not use any reason you can for a family celebration? Make holidays inexpensive, easy-to-do celebrations. Give them your own flavor by developing and maintaining family traditions. You can imbue ornaments, recipes, and things around your house with unique meaning by making them a part of holiday celebrations.

A wonderful shared activity is looking up a holiday in an encyclopedia or cookbook. Finding the history, customs, and food associated with each celebration is a fun learning experience for adults and children. Talking to other people about their holiday traditions enhances your own celebrations.

A NEIGHBORHOOD PARTY

A very special kind of party is one that you invite your neighbors to. It can be held for no reason or it can help you celebrate something that is meaningful to your family: a Christmas or Chanukah party is a good example. You want your children to be able to share and explain their holidays with the broader community. Let the kids help build the guest list and include the parents of their friends (even if you don't know them) as well as your own friends and their children.

Sunday afternoons are a good time for this kind of party. You can serve the foods of the holiday as a snack or for dinner. Encourage your kids to tell the story of the holiday. Records or tapes of the holiday music create a festive atmosphere. Have music sheets or write the words of some of the songs on a big piece of paper or poster board; this lets everyone participate in the festivities with a sing-along.

Let the kids prepare games appropriate to that holiday and explain any rules. Encouraging the kids to do as much as possible gives them pride in their heritage.

Whether it is for a holiday or just for a family get-together, try to make something happen that you can build into a tradition or ceremony. This is the stuff that good memories are made of. If your extended family doesn't meet as a rule, why not start a family get-together? It is important to teach your children that they are part of an extended group. They have a family with a history, a present, and a future.

NEW YEAR'S EVE

Families with young children may want to consider turning the clock ahead so that everyone can celebrate the welcoming of the New Year together. At 6 P.M. the clock can be turned to 10 P.M. to get ready, and have guests start arriving at "10:30" for New Year's dinner. At "midnight" the New Year is toasted in with punch and ginger ale and by "1 A.M." everyone is tired and ready to go home.

NEW YEAR'S DAY

Celebrate this day by inviting friends over to watch the football games, see the parades, and share meals. Having the same people over for a number of years builds expectations of good times, and traditions of special fun and memories with family and friends. When your family has an especially good time with another family, that's the time to say, *Let's do it again next year.*

VALENTINE'S DAY

Get the family to plan a red, heart-shaped dinner. Tomato juice first, beets and red cabbage as the vegetables, and a heart-shaped meatloaf for the main course. Have something red for dessert—let your family be as creative as they can. Encourage the family to send each other cards, homemade or purchased.

ST. PATRICK'S DAY

Have a green dinner. Use your imagination!

EASTER

An Easter midnight breakfast is a special treat for the older child, with guests and a table decorated with jelly beans, fresh flowers, and buffet foods. Sunrise service and an Easter egg hunt are nice family traditions. Remember to keep a list of places the eggs have been hidden; there are always some that no one finds. On holidays with religious significance you might have a party for children of different faiths. The origins and customs of the holiday can be explained, along with the sharing of appropriate food and gifts.

PASSOVER

Create meaningful jobs for children: they can help to bring out the Passover dishes, unpack them, prepare the Seder

Plate, learn to cook special food for the Passover meal, and set the table. Children will carry these traditions into adulthood.

MEMORIAL DAY

Go on a picnic. Even if it's just on your block—but *you* start the idea.

INDEPENDENCE DAY

Make a wonderful red, white, and blue dessert using cream cheese with strawberries and blueberries.

BACK TO SCHOOL

Celebrate the opening of school by making the kids' favorite dinner on Back-To-School Eve and spending the evening doing something the children enjoy. Let them know you're very excited about school starting and think it's an important enough event to celebrate.

ROSH HASHANA

Celebrate Rosh Hashana, the Jewish New Year, by enjoying honey cake, round challahs, and apple slices dipped in honey to symbolize the wish for a sweet year. Encourage family get-togethers where good wishes and good times are abundant.

YOM KIPPUR

Even young children can appreciate the values of Yom Kippur, the Jewish Day of Atonement. But parents are often faced with a dilemma about what to do when their young children want to fast to "keep" this holiday. A good system seems to be to allow the very young child to skip part of breakfast. In following years he may skip all of breakfast, then skip all of lunch, and so forth. In that way, the child will learn to fast by degrees.

HALLOWEEN

Halloween is the two-thousand-year-old holiday that's the biggest costume party of the year. Young children can create a pumpkin face by using vegetables to decorate it, so they don't have to cut with sharp knives. Serve a stew in a pumpkin or pumpkin soup!

Safety tips for Halloween:
- When children go trick or treating, dressing up is one of the fun things to do. In their zeal to be "in costume," children often reach for materials with which to decorate themselves that are inappropriate and truly not safe. Marking crayons and glue are the two most offensive items. If a child uses commerical glue on his face to attach mustache, beard, sideburns, etc., the glue either has to wear off or be rubbed off. Use eyebrow pencil, lipstick, etc., for face decoration. Theatrical make-up is a wonderful alternative, if available. It is simple to apply and easy to get off.

- Masks should not impede visibility or breathing. The costume should not restrict movement and should be made of fireproof material. Costumes should be suitable for the weather.

- Children should carry some light—a small flashlight, a strip of reflecting tape on their bags, or a light-colored shopping bag to hold the treats. Children should be taught to observe all safety rules: looking both ways before crossing streets, crossing at corners, not talking to strangers on the street. Young children should always have an adult to accompany them. Older chidren should trick or treat in a group.

- Unfortunately, there has been an increase in the amount of dangerous objects such as razor blades embedded in apples, oranges, cookies, and other common Halloween treats. Your child needs protection from this danger. A hard and fast rule should be that the child eats nothing until he brings it home. Make it an annual event that the child comes home and dumps all his goodies out so the family can "ooh" and "ah" together. But the parent should check each item to see that it is in its original factory wrap. If it is not, it should be cut in half or quarters before it is given to the child to eat.

- Since children generally get more goodies than they can healthfully consume in one evening, a nice idea is to get a Halloween container of some sort for each child (like a pumpkin basket from the variety store), and each child can "bank" his goodies there for future consumption. Then you can allot an amount that he can have each day thereafter. This lets the child feel that he's not losing his possessions, and still keeps the number of stomach aches to the bare minimum.

THANKSGIVING

Let the children make special holiday place cards, place mats, table decorations, and part of the Thanksgiving dinner. Allow the children to become "famous" for some food preparation. A fun recipe for children to make is an uncooked cranberry-orange relish.

CHRISTMAS AND CHANUKAH

Increasingly, these holidays are turning into commercial nightmares, with gift buying looming as a source of anxiety instead of joy. Try to give your child the meaning of these holidays as much as possible by de-emphasizing expensive presents and emphasizing things of family value. For Christmas, encourage children to make their own tree decorations and their own presents to give to people who are important to them. Jelly that you've made together in the summer or fruit that you've put up together are good gift ideas. Save pictures that were drawn throughout the year and put them in frames as wonderful family gifts for your child to give to grandparents, favorite aunts, and so forth. Watch for things your children make during the year as potential gifts. For Chanukah try to have everyone light his own menorah. Encourage children to make their own decorations and gifts. Children should also be involved in making the foods of the holidays as much as is appropriate for their age level.

There are some tips to make your house safer during the holidays:

- Don't hide presents in places that will encourage children to climb and fall if they spot them.

- Be sure the tree is firmly placed, so that it cannot easily tip over as children help with the decorations.

- Tell your children never to turn on the lights without an adult at home.

- Be sure there are no Christmas tree light cords across walkways and doorways.

- Give children safe materials for making presents. They should not work with sharp or electrical tools.

- Holiday plants are pretty but often poisonous; berries and mistletoe are two examples.

- Make sure that appealing half-finished alcoholic drinks are not left around for a child to sample.

- Be especially careful of plastic wrappings and plastic bags. Throw them away immediately.

- When a child is old enough, teach him how to safely strike a match to light the Chanukah candles.

- Tell your children never to light Chanukah candles without an adult present. Don't leave menorah candles lighted when no adult is home.

Parents often wonder how to handle their child's belief in Santa Claus. Your child will probably let you know when he is ready to give up the Santa Claus fantasy. For example, if your young child says *My friend told me there's no Santa Claus, that's not true, is it?* he probably wants to retain his belief. However, when an older child says *I saw three Santa Clauses in town today. There isn't a real Santa Claus, is there?* he is ready to relinquish his belief. He can move toward the concept of Santa Claus as a representation of the ideals of the holiday—caring, giving, sharing.

Unquestionably, preparing for a major holiday involves a lot of extra work. It is easy to let a few things go each year. However, if the holiday is watered down a little bit each year, eventually the spirit of the holiday may erode. Since traditions are what give children a feeling of roots, of belonging, and a sense of identity, it is important not only to keep them alive, but to have your children contribute to them with innovations that may become their own traditions.

A PARTY FOR NO REASON AT ALL

It is a treat to have a party for no reason at all. This can be announced simply by blowing up three or four balloons and putting them on the dinner table, or by making a sign that says, THIS HAS BEEN A GOOD DAY! Parties for no reason at all create strong, good family feelings and can happen just by making a special menu at home or going out unexpectedly for a treat. Any surprises that you've prepared can fill this function.

Home from School— A Forced Vacation

A school day spent at home because of a minor illness can create warm memories: with loads of pillows, the bed becomes a throne. Some library books, paper, crayons, favorite games, paper dolls, telephone calls, all the same things we have downstairs, take on a new look from the perspective of a kingdom in bed. Best of all are the special sick-foods: soup, pudding, ice-cream—they certainly taste different and much better from a tray, and the extra attention doesn't hurt any, either.

Even though children don't stay in bed much anymore when they are sick, some of the same ideas are helpful. The major criteria for an activity should be its appropriateness to the child's stage of development and to the type of illness. Remember, some medicines make a child drowsy or ornery, so question the doctor about side effects when medication is prescribed for your child.

Certain activities lend themselves to the passive behavior of the sick child: playing cards; hobbies; games; being read to; telephone calls from friends and relatives; arts and crafts that provide free play when the child is restricted in other ways; quickly sprouting plants; collections such as stamps; drying flowers; organizing football or baseball cards; talking into a tape recorder. Even chores, like sorting and folding laundry, can help break the monotony. Parents can do their own chores in the child's room to keep him company.

It is impossible to measure the positive results of some extra hugs and cuddling, a warm, quiet conversation, and the feeling of closeness when parent and child are home alone during the day. Being sick can contribute a great deal to being well.

Reading

Reading together is a pre-television family activity that is great fun and worthy of a comeback. The whole family can enjoy reading plays together (you'll need enough copies for all the readers to be able to see their parts). Children are much more spontaneously effective actors than adults, and they really enjoy getting into plays and role-play, once they understand how to do it and that no one will laugh at them if they make a mistake. Something else your family might enjoy is ad libbing a play they've seen or a story they've read.

Children also like to listen to and read stories aloud. You and your family can read poetry, or read and discuss items of importance, humor, or interest from non-fiction books, newspapers, and magazines.

When children live in a family in which books are important—when newspapers and magazines are left "invitingly" available; when parents consider a night reading a well-spent evening—children have a better chance of learning to read and appreciating the world of reading. The introduction to reading is through language, and the more you talk to and listen to your child, and ask and answer questions, the better equipped he will be for learning about the written word. Explaining new words by relating them to his real environment—tastes, sounds, smells, touch—allows the child to anchor the new words in his vocabulary. Praise your child when he has said something particularly well, or used a new word.

The most significant contribution parents can make to their children's becoming good readers is to read to them. Read poetry, nonsense rhymes, short stories, the instructions on game boards, how to work the new toy or put the bicycle together, the directions that Aunt Lil sent for getting to her new home.

Make reading time a pleasurable time—an arm around the shoulder, cuddling on the sofa—close, comfortable, and warm feelings as you turn the pages of the book. Let your children see that this is time that you value, and they will tend to value it, too. Encourage children who are beginning to read to pick out words that they know on signs, on boxes, on television, or in newspapers. Correct them gently, if at all, when they are wrong. Concentrate on what they are doing right. Beginning reading should be fun, like a game, and not work.

Teach your children that they can find out valuable information from reading and by looking things up together in reference books. For example, when they hear on the news that there is a tornado in Kansas or a hot-air balloon is making a trans-Atlantic crossing, get out the atlas or the encyclopedia and find Kansas or trace the route of the balloon. It seems that reading runs in families—children who read are often children who were read to. And, if it hasn't started yet in your family, it's a tradition well worth beginning.

TV

Statistics show that the average child between the ages of two and eleven watches TV for 3½ to 4 hours a day. *You* can control the amount of TV your child watches. If you are concerned that your child is watching too much television, be sure that you are not sending him there in the same way you would send him to a baby-sitter; in essence saying leave me alone. We believe controlling television is important. Here are some suggestions for managing TV watching:

Check the TV schedule at the beginning of each week to see if there is any program pertaining to your child's schoolwork—for example, a historical movie about a period of time he is studying, or a travel movie about a place he is studying. Next check the schedule for programs that match your child's special interests—such as sports, science, cooking, or whatever. Then look to see if there are any quality programs that your child alone or the whole family might enjoy.

You and your child should reach a mutual decision about how much free-choice time a child his age should have each day. This is time when your child may choose any program he wants within whatever limits you've spelled out in advance. Be certain he understands the limits.

If you feel strongly that there should be no TV after school, or after dinner, or after 10 P.M.; or that your child should not watch violent or sexually explicit material on television, then *you* must set the limits. Each family should determine its own set of rules.

Settle on a system in advance to decide what to do if two family members want to watch different shows that are broadcast at the same time. Taking turns or flipping a coin with the loser going first next time there is a conflict might work for your family. If you don't develop a decision-making system in advance, either you will be put in the middle (leaving you open to charges of favoritism from the loser), or you will have to listen to the kids fight over it so long that they will miss both programs.

Remember, kids will do as you *do*, not necessarily as you say. If *you* watch television for hours each night while telling your kids not to, they will want to do it all the more, and they will find ways to get around your cleverest strategies to wean them away from the tube.

If you feel television-watching has gotten out of hand in your family, you might consider getting a TV lock that can be installed on the TV plug and opened only by a special key. Major manufacturers of television sets are planning to introduce various electronic devices that you might find useful in limiting your children's use of the TV. Before purchasing a new set you may want to inquire about the availability of a set with a built-in mechanism or an adapter for blocking out channels (network or cable), video games, or videocassettes. Or, the television could be removed from the room where the children work or study, and put out of sight. Of course, the advantage of a lock-box, adapter, or built-in device, is that the set is readily available for shows you want the family to see.

If you and your kids have agreed about restricting their TV viewing, a simple sign taped to the set instructing NO TV TO-NIGHT, or NO TV BETWEEEN 4:00 AND 6:00 can serve as a reminder and eliminate the need to nag.

TV can be a source of tremendous family alienation as people sit side-by-side with no real human contact for hours on end. But it can also be a source of stimulation for family interaction, if adults and kids actively watch together. Discuss shows you've all seen. This can be as simple as asking, *Did you like it?* and *Why?*, or *How did you feel about that scary [violent, sad, etc.] program?* Let your child know how you feel about it as well. Explain that you too were worried (angry, upset, relieved, or scared). It will help him to express his worries as well as his pleasures if he realizes that you've had those feelings yourself and that you understand and are interested in his feelings, too.

Help children to develop aesthetic values by asking, *Is the story good?*, or *What did you think of the photography?* Ask thought-provoking questions; *What did you think would happen next? Would you like to live in that climate? How do you think they got into that situation?* An observant parent can use a TV program as a way of discussing values; *What did you agree with? Did you see any other ways to solve that problem? How do you think angry feelings are handled in our family? How are they handled in that family?* Plan TV together time by scheduling the viewing of a program in the same way you plan a trip to the movies. Make a special treat to eat while you watch. Buy or make funny or decorated note paper on which to jot down questions or ideas to talk about later. Even taking time to laugh about a comedy creates an environment of sharing.

Movie, Theater, Dance, Music

There are several ways of presenting new movie, theater, dance, and music experiences to children. Once the adult has invested his energy and resources in purchasing tickets, he clearly has more than just a financial investment in this experience. In essence he is saying to his child, *I like this, I think it is good, I want to share it with you, I want you to like it, too.*

Complete preparation in advance: Some parents find their children take to the theater, ballet, and even opera very well by hearing the music frequently at home before attending the event. In that way, the songs and themes are familiar to them, and the only new experience they have to assimilate is the visual. For children who take to change slowly, this may be a good method.

Partial preparation in advance: Some orientation is given about the story line, or some of the main characters, and perhaps one of the songs is played.

Surprise: Some parents prefer to have the entire experience be a surprise to the child.

The first thing to recognize is that if your child doesn't like something you wanted him to, then you are likely to feel angry or disappointed. It's helpful to recognize that there can be lots of reasons for a child's not liking something. It may be that he's too young for this experience at this time, or that you need to try a different preparation technique for him (perhaps preparing him so he's more familiar with the event next time). Don't make a scene if he didn't like it. Encourage him to talk about what he did and didn't like.

Conversation

We all want to have meaningful, fun, exciting, interesting conversations within our families. Sometimes that's hard to do. And more often than not we get the "How are you? Fine. What's new? Nothing." routine. Once these questions are answered, there seems to be little else to say. Parents of young children have opportunities to change that pattern by beginning early to talk to and listen to their children. We are often surprised by the perception and depth of understanding and feeling expressed by children when they are interviewed on TV by an astute reporter. Clearly the children have varied and interesting opinions about local issues as well as world problems. A skilled interviewer gives children the opportunity and encouragement to voice their ideas without regard to "right or wrong"; the focus is just on what they are thinking. The process of learning to be a good conversationalist is very difficult to begin at age fifteen but easy to make a way of life at age five. Again, making time for this to happen is the key issue. You cannot teach your child to be a good conversationalist if you talk with him only about critical matters. Light subjects must be as much a part of conversation as somber, weighty, terribly important issues.

If your family has fallen into the almost-no-conversation rut, we suggest a few things to talk about:

- his favorite sport (how's he doing, is he in a competition, when is the next game, match, etc.)

- favorite entertainment (TV show, movie, singer, would he like to attend a "live" event, what does he like about his favorites)

- highs and lows (favorite people—what does he like about them; what do they do or not do that he likes; what have they accomplished that he thinks is super; biggest recent disappointment or set-back; is there anything you can do to help now, help next time; what makes him maddest, saddest)

- school (best: teacher, subject, after-school activity, friends; worst: subject, teacher, happenings at school)

- at home (best: foods, good times, household jobs, after-school lessons, family celebration or events, pets, trips or vacations; worst: chores, foods, after-school lessons, family events, trips or vacations)

- image (does he feel popular at school, feel liked, feel "in," feel lonely; does he feel competent about schoolwork or sometimes overwhelmed; does he feel competent in sports, in competition, in hobbies)

- You can also discuss a current local issue that will affect one or all members of the family (such as the closing of the recreational facilities, the opening of a new tennis program, changes in school bus schedules). Be sure you listen to your kids' ideas and opinions.

- Talk about current events on a global scale: an article about Japan if a favorite uncle is going there; information about an ethnic, religious, or political issue meaningful to all of you.

Other good topics are things *you* are doing or learning: projects you are working on at your job or on your own; activities you're interested in; your hobbies and why you like them and what you are doing; civic or political events you are involved in; your feelings, hopes, concerns, and pleasures. Why? Because conversation is a learned art, and you are your child's best teacher.

WALK WITH YOUR KIDS!

Short walks, long walks, going for an ice-cream cone, going out for no reason at all. If kids don't learn to take walks when they're young, the chances are pretty good they'll never learn to like it. Taking a walk with your child is a wonderful chance to chat about his life and yours, to share a good time, to try to solve a problem, or just to be together. Remember, there are no telephones, TV, or doorbells when you are out walking.

Grandparents

Grandparents are a gift to children. They accept, encourage, praise, and give unending amounts of love.

When people of different generations get together, what do they talk about? There's usually more interest on the part of the older generation to be together than there is on the part of the younger generation. Grandchildren need more from these meetings to make them appealing than does Grandma or Grandpa. You can bridge the gap between the older and younger generations by creating activities, events, and conversations that will help grandparents and grandchildren meet happily together.

One interesting idea is a house inventory. Many items in the grandparents' house have special stories: old photographs, tablecloths, knickknacks. Children can help make an inventory by listing, photographing, and then writing about these possessions. They learn a little about the things that may some day be theirs and a lot about their grandparents' lives: *Who gave Aunt Tanya that lamp? Where did Aunt Bea's blue willow dishes come from? How does this old-fashioned kitchen equipment work?* Things that children take for granted because they have "always" been in their grandparents' house generate new meaning and interest in grandparents' lives when the children learn about them. They can help children understand some of the family's history.

Many older people have loads and loads of old pictures waiting to be labeled and pasted in albums. Young children can help grandparents by sorting out the pictures: *This was the summer at the beach. This was right before the war. This was just before your father was born.* If they sort the pictures chronologically and put them into groups, it becomes easy to tell the story from the album. Sorting the pictures together is one activity, and then perhaps the child can take them away, paste them in an album, and give the grandparents a present of the album at a later date.

Life reviews done with a tape recorder are interesting as well. Prepared questions are useful for the taping sessions: *What happened when you came to this country? What was America like when you came here? What was it like when you were my age? When did you see your first airplane? How much did things cost when you were young? What did you do on Sundays? When did you first meet Grandmother?* These questions usually have fascinating answers and give children an intimate slice of history.

Creating the family tree together can be a heartwarming and informative experience for the family as a whole. A project such as planting a garden and tending it, with the grandparents doing as much as they can and the child doing the weeding, stretching, and bending, is a good way to share time. Learning to cook some of the things the way the grandparents do is a long-lasting, fun experience. It is also one in which you don't have to be together all the time. A weekly visit can help tend a garden and a monthly trip to visit a grandparent can produce twelve cooking lessons a year.

Knitting, crocheting, weaving, refinishing furniture, carpentry, and whittling are all skills that many older people may have and could teach to their grandchildren. In this way the arts and skills of past generations can be passed on. Music is another way of sharing time. Old-World songs, ethnic music, and translations of some of the songs will make children laugh and give grandparents wonderful reminiscences.

What you are trying to build, when generations get together, are happy times and good memories. In order to do that, you have to create a bridge, and it is the *parents* that make the bridge between their parents and their children.

Travel

Few things in the world are all they are cracked up to be, and vacations are no exception. Often we believe that removing ourselves and our families to a wonderful new location will also remove us from our problems and our problem behavior.

Leaving the pressures of school, work, and social obligations makes us hope that we also leave behind conflicts. We seem to expect that a halo effect will follow us, creating marvelous times, good conversations, and feelings of camaraderie and togetherness. The result is that many adults get overly concerned about spending a lot of money and not having a good enough time. Performance anxiety—the feeling that each day must be a grand and glorious experience—can ruin a perfectly fine vacation. The solution? Try not to have false expectations, and try to take the good times and the less-than-good times as they come, with the expectation that, even though you are on vacation, you will have both.

Plan to go places that both adults and children will enjoy—not somewhere just because your child likes it or because it's your favorite place. Often, something brand-new to all of you can create a wonderful experience, and the investment of time and effort in planning brings great rewards.

Choosing the right place to go is very important. When taking your children to a museum or historical site, be sure they are interested in seeing it. It is not a good use of your time or your children's time to take them to national monuments or shrines they haven't studied about in school.

It is perfectly okay, however, for you to explain to your children that visiting such a place of interest is something that *you* want to do, and that they have the choice of accompanying you, reading in the car, or going to another place you've arranged. What's important is to avoid making children feel they "ought" to enjoy something they clearly are not enjoying. This can negatively color their feelings about such places for the future.

Before you leave on a long trip, put kids in the mood by asking them to draw some pictures of the places you plan to visit. Tell them it doesn't matter if they have never been there before; encourage them to use their imaginations, and then they can see how close to the real thing their impressions were. That kind of preparation helps everyone to record vivid impressions of the new place.

Chart your route on a map. Even if your trip is a short one, it's fun to mark off places of interest, from point A to point B. Even younger children can get a grasp of directions by seeing how things are located in relation to each other.

Read or tell about the places or areas you are going to visit. Highlight interesting buildings, rivers, bridges, and historical sites that you will pass on your way, to make the trip more meaningful and fun. Local American Automobile Association (AAA) offices have good regional travel books and maps. Try the local Chamber of Commerce and travel agencies for additional free information and maps.

Give your children and yourself the chance to be informed by reading about what you're going to see and do before you arrive. AAA information books provide just enough information to highlight historical points and important geographical features of the area you are driving through. This reading does not have to be done as "homework." Reading in the car helps pass the time and builds anticipation about what's coming next. Some people are more comfortable reading in the car than others. Use the person who is most comfortable to read to the others about sights you are going to see and the places you are riding through.

If your child has a tape recorder, surprise him by packing it and some of his favorite tapes. For younger children it's a nice treat to pack some books and your tape-recorded reading of some of their favorite stories. This can keep a young child occupied during a long, uninteresting stretch of turnpike. Unless the tape recorder has earphones, be sure that what you give your children to listen to is something you too want to hear.

Stock your car with moist towelettes, tissues, a first-aid kit, and a camera and film. Allow each child to pack a small bag with some things that are familiar and important to him. Let him take it in the car with him. For example, he might pack a favorite stuffed animal, a game, a small toy car, a night light (if it's an overnight trip), and some favorite books.

Arrive early at places that will be crowded so you don't have to stand in long lines. Before you arrive, give children an appropriate amount of money to spend. Then, allow them to make their own decisions about how to spend it. Plan what to see and do before arriving. Allow time to talk, explore, and rest. Set time goals out loud with the children. For example: *We must leave by eight o'clock, what do you want to be sure you do before then?* Don't arrive hungry. If the car trip is long, pack crunchy, crumbless snacks.

Try to buy all tickets at one time so you don't have to stand in many lines. Name-tag young children and arrange where to meet if the child gets lost. Teach your children to answer when they hear you call their names. Tell them to say, *Here I am, next to the lion's cage,* or *near the flower garden,* so you can find them easily.

Listen to your children's comments as you investigate and observe. Answer any questions they may have even if the answer seems obvious to you. What you do will have a greater influence on your child than what you say. So, how you handle the flat tire (panic versus action), or the emergency (futile complaining or getting the problem solved), shows your child how to handle difficult situations in the future.

When taking your child to a museum, it is best to decide with him which one section you and he would like to see first. If you do not have this information before you go to the museum, stop once you are inside, look over the floor plan or calendar of events, and together select the place that seems the most interesting.

It's best to see the thing of the highest interest before the child gets too tired to enjoy it. Take into consideration the amount of walking, the child's attention span, and the amount and quality of the information on which the child can focus. When you've seen this section of the museum, you can ask which of the other sections the child would like to see. Keep following this process of seeing a section and then making another choice until the child's interest or energy begins to wane.

GAMES FOR CAR TRIPS

Children often get bored and start squabbling when they are confined in a car for a long ride. Travel games can degenerate into fisticuffs because the oldest child "always wins" or the youngest "doesn't play fair" or any of the thousand and one reasons that kids have for expressing their strong needs for active stimulation.

That's why we suggest planning some activities and games that do not have to have a winner. There are many categories of catchy games to keep kids amused, alert, and thinking as they ride along. None of the games need pencils, scissors, or tools that could be dangerous if the car stops unexpectedly.

Little Words From Big Words.

One person chooses a word, for example, *elephant*. Everyone tries to discover the little words that can be found in the big word: an, pat, leap, tea, plant.

Funny Sentences.

One person chooses a word. Each person tries to make a funny sentence using the letters of the word as the first letter of each word in the sentence. For example, *finger*: Frank is never giving Emily ribbons.

Double Words.

One person chooses a word which is "two" words, for example, *doubleplay*. The next person chooses a double word whose first part is the end of the previous double word. For example, *doubleplay, playground, groundhog*. Play until you run out of words to build.

I Choose The Letter.

One person chooses a letter. Everyone names as many things beginning with that letter as possible. Variations are things in the car, out of the window, in your kitchen at home.

Number Words.

One person chooses a number. Everyone else tries to think of a word with as many letters as the number. Example: number *6*, word *fishes* (6 letters); number *12*, word *Pennsylvania*.

Conversation.

Have a conversation without using a certain letter. People drop out when they say a word with the forbidden letter.

Buzz.

Choose a number to be the buzz number—for example, *four*. Then start counting off in a circle. Each time the number, or a multiple of the number, is said, substitute the word "buzz": *1, 2, 3, buzz, 5, 6, 7, buzz,* etc. Buzz is also said for numbers with 4 in them, like 14, 40, 41, etc. For 44, say "buzz buzz."

Variation on Buzz—Fizz Buzz.

To make the game even more exciting for older children, use buzz for one number and fizz for another number, example buzz for 3 and fizz for 5. Counting would go *1, 2, buzz, 4, fizz, buzz, 7,* and so on.

What Do I Do?

One person describes a job or profession. All other players try to guess what it is.

Where Am I?

One person describes a place. All the other players ask questions about this place and try to guess where it is.

What Am I?

One person pretends he or she is an object (typewriter, boiling water, bubble gum, etc.). All the other players try to guess what the mystery object is.

Who Am I?

One person gives the initials of a secret person. All the other players ask questions about this person and try to guess who he or she is. The person who correctly guesses begins the next round.

Surprise Bag: What's In the Bag?

Bring a small cloth bag full of familiar objects. (Be sure to make a list of things as you put them in the bag, so you will remember what's there as the game is being played.) Ask players to guess what is in the bag by feeling the objects through the cloth. Some ideas are: old toothbrush, marble, comb, pencil sharpener, emery board, small stuffed animals.

I'm Going To . . .

The leader begins by saying, "I'm going to _____" and names the place where the group is going. He continues by saying "and I'm taking _____" naming an object. Next person repeats "I'm going to _____ and I'm taking _____" naming the object the first person named, then adding her own. The next person remembers the past two objects in order, and adds a third, etc. For older children, limit the objects to a category: movie stars, furry animals, fruit, etc.

For variety have the leader start with an object beginning with the letter A. The next person repeats that item and adds one beginning with B, etc.

Remembering Pictures.

Bring some small interesting pictures. Show a picture to each person in the car, then put it out of sight. Ask each to remember what was in the picture.

HEALTH AND SAFETY ON VACATIONS

Take a few minutes before the start of a vacation to line up a source for emergency medical care: the name of a doctor or the address and phone number of the emergency room at the local hospital. In an emergency, seconds will be important.

If, despite precautions, you need medical help, you can contact the following services for assistance:[1]

- Intermedic
  777 Third Avenue
  New York, New York 10017
  This agency offers a yearly family membership that provides access to doctors in 200 cities and 90 countries.

[1]*Ladies' Home Journal*, April 1982.

- IAMET (International Association for Medical Assistance to Travelers)
  350 Fifth Avenue, Suite 5620
  New York, New York 10001
  IAMET can put you in touch with English-speaking physicians in 450 cities and 20 countries. This organization offers information on the climate, sanitation, and immunization laws of countries throughout the world.

- United States State Department's Citizen's Emergency Center
  Washington, D.C. 20520

- When traveling in a foreign country, you can call the nearest American embassy or consulate. Ask someone to get in touch with the Emergency Center to find you a doctor. The Emergency Center can also keep you informed about epidemics, illnesses, and political conditions for a given area prior to your visit.

The best medical advice seems to be to enjoy everything in moderation, particularly sports, sun, and food. Your children have less experience than you in the controls needed to stay healthy on vacation. Your guidance can prevent hours of needless discomfort from sunburn and stomachaches.

Unless you and the children are tan, avoid the direct rays of the sun when they are strongest—between 10 A.M. and 2 P.M.—or at most be exposed for twenty minutes. For longer exposures, apply a protective sunscreen lotion or wear clothing that can get sandy or wet without creating a problem. Numbers on sunscreen containers now indicate the effectiveness of the protection: the higher the number, the greater the protection. Remember, children burn more easily than adults, so while you are just beginning to tan, your child may be developing a serious burn.

If you are vacationing near water, teach your children to play close to where you are sitting; if they have to move their play area, you should move your sitting area. Never should they be allowed to go into the water without a "buddy" or a parent. The calmest sea can hide a strong undertow. Also, train your child to swim near the lifeguard if there is one. You must be a model for this: if you disobey the lifeguard's instructions, your child will, too.

If your child gets lost at the beach, alert the lifeguards and ask everyone around you to search in different directions. Be loud and repetitive; call the child's name constantly and walk somewhere near the water's edge, so the child, if she is in the water, can hear you.

Teach your child to ask for help from a lifeguard or police officer if she gets lost. Be sure that your child knows the address and phone number where the family is vacationing. The best way to cut down on lost-child panics is to teach your child to stay still once she discovers that she doesn't know where you are. Assure her that you will come to find her. If you are both moving around, finding one another will probably be more difficult.

Vacationing in cold climates requires the packing of special clothes to keep your child warm and comfortable. Layers of clothes are more effective in keeping people warm than one heavy piece of clothing. Layers of air get trapped between the articles of clothing and the warm air acts as insulation. Loose-fitting clothes are warmer than tight-fitting ones. The first layer should be thermal underwear; top that with a layer or two of wool clothing. The outer layer covering should be a windbreaker or an insulated suit.

Frostbite is a danger, so the extremities (fingers, toes, and ears) have to be carefully protected against the cold. Gloves under mittens give the best protection for fingers and allow flexibility if mittens have to be removed to put on skis or adjust sled ropes. Layering works well for feet, too: wear cotton socks under wool socks under waterproof boots. Ears need to be protected either with earmuffs or a hat that has ear flaps. A large percentage of the body's heat will be lost through the head if it is uncovered. A hat or headmask will provide warmth, as will a scarf loosely wrapped around the head and protecting the mouth. If you notice signs of frostbite (a feeling of extreme cold and pain, a burning sensation, numbness, or a bluish or whitish tinge to the skin), it is important to get the area warmed. Do *not* use hot water; use warm water and movement. Don't rub frostbite with snow—the skin is delicate.

If you are traveling in areas in which conditions can be dangerous (forests, mountains, extreme heat or cold), be sure that your child is trained in safety precautions and knows what to do if she gets separated or lost.

If your child has a serious health problem, it's a good idea to carry a medical information sheet prepared by your doctor. Keep it with your drivers' licenses, passports, and other papers. Be sure it includes your name and address as well as the child's, medical insurance information, blood type, an explanation by your doctor of the medical problem, medicines currently being taken and what doses, and any drug allergies. A medical information bracelet or necklace might also be useful, in case your child gets separated from you and needs emergency help.

Carry medicines in their original containers showing the name of the medicine, the dosage, the date you obtained it, and the doctor's name. The generic name of the medicine should be included, because brand names may vary from place to place. In addition to prescribed medications you might also take along extra eyeglasses and medications for fever, constipation, diarrhea, and allergies. On certain trips you may want to take a first-aid kit containing antiseptic sprays or cream, bandages, a thermometer, a needle, tweezers, insect repellent, and sunscreen and, if necessary, spoons for administering liquid medicines.

TRAVEL BY PLANE

Children have grown up familiar with airplanes and are probably less afraid of flying than many adults. However, most first-time flyers, including kids, experience some discomfort from the unfamiliar sensation.

Before you go to the airport, talk to your kids about the trip. Get a map and let them trace the route the plane will fly. You might even talk about how long it would take to drive and compare it with how long it will take the plane to get there.

Describe what will happen at the airport: tell your children that your luggage will be labeled and taken away to ride in the baggage compartment, and you'll pick it up at the other end of the trip. Buying the tickets, checking in, or getting the seat assignments will be the next step. You may have to go through a metal-detection system, so explain to your kids that they will walk through a metal gate, one at a time, and all bags and carry-on luggage will go through an X-ray machine. Tell them this procedure takes only a few seconds and that they will feel nothing. They will simply walk through an area similar to the check-out aisle in the supermarket. Explain that airports are very concerned that no one with a gun gets on the plane, and this is how they stop guns or sharp dangerous instruments from getting onto the plane. Try to give them a sense of security. Tell them that everything is done to insure their safety. Emphasize the exciting aspects of air travel.

Explain that there may be a long walk to the plane and (in many cities) they will go directly from the terminal into the plane without ever going outside or seeing the whole airplane.

Briefly describe the interior of the plane. Describe wearing a seat belt, and tell the child how to get into and out of one. Tell your child that it is safest to wear the seat belt all the time he is in his seat.

Describe what will happen when the plane takes off. There will be different sounds as the pilot maneuvers parts of the plane—puts up the flaps, raises the wheels—and the child may feel some pressure in his ears as the cabin pressure is adjusted for the climb. Ask the child what he thinks the land will look like from up in the air, and then when you're flying get him to talk about how it compares to what he thought it would be like.

It is possible for religious or health reasons to request special meals on a plane trip. Kosher, vegetarian, low-salt, and low-cholesterol meals are available, but you must give the airline advance notice. It is best to do this when you make reservations, but it must be done at least twenty-four hours before your flight. A child may prefer the fresh fruit on a vegetarian platter to the hot dish. Also, some airlines may provide a hot dog or a peanut butter and jelly sandwich if a child's plate is requested in advance. If you have ordered a child's meal, inform the flight attendant when you board so that this special meal is not given to another by mistake.

Although you don't want your children running up and down the aisles, you should take them for a walk at least once an hour. This is good for you as well as them. Jet lag and travel fatigue are combatted by getting your circulation going at least once an hour. Take the children for water, or for a visit to the bathroom, or, if there are empty seats in a different section, change seats for a while.

CHILDREN FLYING ALONE

In these days of split families, more children are flying alone than ever before. Many airlines arrange special treatment for children who fly unattended. For the most part, those under five must be accompanied by a parent or other adult, and those twelve or older are treated as adults and must be able to take care of themselves, although most airline personnel will help a youngster if they possibly can.

You will be expected to bring the child to the airport and stay with her until she has gotten on the plane. You'll also be asked to give information about who is meeting the child at the other end, along with an address and phone number in case of problems.

Of course, you'll be expected to brief the child on what will happen (boarding procedure, what the plane will look like, how long the trip will be, how she is expected to behave), and to provide things for her to do during the flight. Airlines report that card playing is a favorite activity for children, and they can frequently find someone to play with if you provide cards for them to take along. Also, the child will probably enjoy taking a familiar toy or game, as well as a new book or a magazine with activities in it. Don't pack away medicines or other things that will be needed in flight. Give the child a carry-on bag which includes these as well as toys and games.

Check with the airline about the procedure they want you to use to board the child. Arriving early at the airport is a help, both for the airline and for you and your child, so that you will have a relaxed time getting ready to get on the plane. Be sure to take a few moments with your child at the airport to ask if she has any questions, and just to let her talk about what she is thinking and feeling. Even if you are not feeling cheerful, try not to "rain on your child's parade" with any prejudices, fears, or anxieties you may have about flying. Chances are your child feels excited and happy about the trip although she may be sad about leaving you. You can share her sadness about the separation, but you need to support her excitement about the new adventure of flying alone. This will help your child to feel confident about her growing independence.

If your child expresses apprehension about the flight, accept those feelings by saying something like, *Everyone feels nervous when she does something new—that's a perfectly natural feeling.* Or, *You will get to see some very beautiful and exciting things in the air, and maybe the pilot will let you see the inside of the cockpit when you get on the plane.* Focus on something to help your child feel happy and excited instead of fearful.

AFTER THE TRIP

Family travel experiences create opportunities for many happy discussions. Take some time after your trip to talk about who enjoyed what, and how the next trip could be better. An interesting question for adults and kids is to ask themselves, *How was the trip different from how I thought it would be?* It is important to respect everyone's ideas in these discussions, otherwise the kid you put down won't talk freely to you the next time.

Follow-ups are fun, too! Drawing pictures, writing letters about the trip to grandparents, and filling albums with photos, pictures, and souvenirs, can involve the whole family.

3
Health and Safety

Choosing a Doctor for Your Children

Most parents do not start from scratch when looking for a pediatrician. They have neighbors, friends, relatives, or other physicians who recommend a doctor for their children. No matter how you come to consider a particular pediatrician, check out all his qualifications before you select him as your children's doctor.

Consider age: you will want a doctor who is young enough to know modern medicine, old enough to have some experience, and not so old as to be ready for retirement before your child outgrows him. You will probably want a doctor who is board-certified in pediatrics. If possible, choose someone who is on the staff of a good teaching hospital affiliated with a medical school. This will be helpful in case your child needs special testing or hospitalization.

You should interview the pediatrician before taking your child for a visit. Ask about fees, office hours, house calls, telephone accessibility, and what medical insurance plans the doctor accepts.

No doctor works twenty-four hours a day, seven days a week. It is important that you know, and feel you can work with, the other doctor or doctors who are on call for your doctor when he is off duty. This is particularly true in a clinic or group practice. Choose a doctor who is conveniently located for you and who does not make you and your child sit a long time in a waiting room before he sees you.

If possible, your child should visit the doctor for the first time when he is well, for a check-up. It is hard for the child to determine how he feels about a physician if the initial visit is for an illness or injury, when the child is not at his best.

A good pediatrician is aware of children's developmental patterns and will probe areas that are relevant to the child's social and physical growth. An alert physician will ask children about smoking, and drug use, and will discuss their sexual development. A competent pediatrician will help your child learn good health habits and will practice preventive medicine.

It's important to find a pediatrician with whom both you and your children can feel comfortable, and who believes in continuous education to prevent medical problems. Routine health care for your child should include a discussion about home health care with the doctor or someone on the doctor's staff during each office visit. That person—whether a physician, a nurse, or a physician's assistant—should talk to your child about normal, healthy bodily functions and what the child should be doing to keep his body healthy. If the child is aware of how his body functions when it is healthy, he can let you know when something is wrong.

Health education is very important for elementary-school-aged children. They may be self-conscious about their genital areas and feel shy about telling you if they have a pain in the testicles, burning during urination, constipation, or diarrhea. You and the doctor should talk to your children about their bodies in a matter-of-fact manner to ease any embarrassment they may feel.

If a child is continuously upset by visits to the doctor, talk to the child and try to find out why. If he seems to like the doctor and merely objects to injections, then with maturity this problem will probably disappear. But if the child says that he doesn't like the doctor, or that the doctor doesn't listen to him, or that he can't talk with the doctor because the doctor is too busy, you should talk with the doctor about it. If

after subsequent visits the child continues to be overly concerned, consider changing doctors, because your child's attitudes toward health care are set at this early age. It is important that your child learn to have confidence and trust in the
doctor so that he doesn't hesitate to seek medical help when
needed and feels free to raise questions with health professionals about his concerns. Many needless deaths occur
because people are afraid to ask a doctor about symptoms
that concern them and so don't seek medical advice while
treatment is still possible. Don't be intimidated by physicians: it is your responsibility to get all the answers to questions you have about your family's health, and it is the
physician's responsibility to provide those answers.

When You Should Call the Doctor

You should call the doctor *immediately* if your child:

- appears very ill
- has difficulty breathing
- has a high fever
- loses consciousness
- is disoriented or exhibits peculiar behavior
- is experiencing great pain
- is bleeding badly
- has an earache
- has convulsions
- has pain in the testicle (pain in the testicle of a boy may
  indicate that the cord leading to the testicles is twisted,
  cutting off the blood supply; this condition requires
  immediate surgery)

- has a visual disturbance
- has persistent vomiting
- has a headache following a head injury

You should call the doctor later if:

- a low-grade fever goes into its second day
- an unusual rash that you can't identify persists
- the child has persistent headaches, if a mild headache goes into its second day, or if a severe headache lasts more than eight hours
- a cough lasts a few days without improving
- diarrhea or constipation persists

When you call the doctor, provide all the necessary information as quickly as possible. Be ready with your name, your child's name (to avoid any confusion with his siblings or a child with a similar name) and age, symptoms, and the duration of the symptoms.

Immunization— It's the Law

Immunization protects your child from preventable diseases. It is vital to find out what the local, state, and federal laws are in your area about immunization before your child starts school. It is probable that your child's school will not admit him if he doesn't have the proper documentation about his immunization. There are only two exemptions to immunization requirements, medical and religious, and even for these, written explanation must almost always be submitted to the school.

Ask your pediatrician for a list of immunizations and boosters that your child will be expected to get and the ages at which they should be administered. Some pediatricians have booklets or listings available for their patients with this information, and a place for you to note when your child gets immunizations and boosters. Ask about this when you visit the doctor.

Whether you make up a check list yourself, or your doctor gives you a booklet in which to record immunizations for your child, it is vital that you keep a permanent, updated record of your child's immunization history. Your child will need this all through school and into college. Take the check list to the doctor's office each time your child goes, so the doctor can update your medical record for you.

Preparing a Child to Visit the Doctor

Making the appointment for a child's medical check-up is the parent's responsibility. You will build your child's trust in you by telling her the truth about these visits. It makes sense, even to the young child, to visit the doctor when she is sick because the doctor has the skills and training to help her feel better. It makes less sense to the child to go when she is feeling well and then to come away in pain (as happens when she gets an injection). You can help your child feel more comfortable and in control by giving her as much information as she can handle to understand what is going to happen and why.

For young children you can say something as simple as, *Visiting the doctor helps protect you from getting sick. You know that you wouldn't cross the street if you saw a*

car coming. Well, the doctor watches the things that hap-
pen in your body to see if anything is coming that she can
protect you from.

If you know from your immunization chart that your child
is due for a shot or a booster, make sure you mention it to the
child before you visit the doctor, so the child can be prepared.
For some reason, many adults hate and fear getting injections. Actually, sticking your finger with a sewing needle or
banging your finger with a hammer hurts as much or more
than a shot. What seems to make the pain feel worse is the
anticipation that it *will* hurt. So, it is important that you do
not convey your own anxiety about experiencing pain to your
child. Be honest, and say that it will hurt for one minute (and
then time one minute so she can understand how long that
is), but do not make a big deal of it. Don't say, *I can't look* or *I
can't stand shots*—you'll only teach your child to fear and
worry about shots more than is necessary.

Be sure that you and your child use your time with the doctor to the best advantage. Your child might understand the
analogy of talking to a traffic officer, whose time can't be
wasted because she is busy directing traffic. Likewise, your
child can't waste the time of the doctor, who has lots of boys
and girls to help. When your child talks to a traffic officer,
she should have her questions ready: *Where is Fifth and
Elm?* In the same way, she has to have her questions ready
for the doctor: *Why does my chest hurt when I run to
school?* This kind of training can be applied to other areas of
the child's life, where she has to have her thoughts organized
in order to collect information quickly.

Here is a tip that costs you nothing and can be extremely
helpful to both you and your doctor: construct a family tree
which shows important medical facts about each close blood
relative—cause of death, major diseases, genetic disorders,
medical problems that appear in your immediate family and

in other relatives, any physical or mental handicaps. This kind of record can be invaluable. More and more, doctors are finding that information like this helps them understand what our complaints and ailments really mean. Often a potential medical problem can be avoided by knowing what happened in the past. For example, a history of heart problems among your relatives may lead your doctor to carefully check you and your children for signs of a similar disorder. You should bring the family medical tree to the doctor's office when the child goes for an examination, especially when seeing a physician for the first time. Keep the tree updated by adding new information regularly—once a year, or before scheduled doctor appointments.

Children five to twelve years old should have a check-up every six months, if they have not been seen for a sickness since the last check-up. If they have been to a doctor in the meantime, their next check-up should be six months from the date of the last visit.

When Your Child Should Stay Home from School

When your child is very sick, there is no question: he stays home from school. And when he's feeling well, he goes to school. It's when he says, *I don't feel well*, but nothing is noticeably wrong that parents have a hard time deciding if he should go to school or rest at home.

Keep your child home if he has a fever. Since different children have different "normal" temperatures, take your child's temperature at a variety of different times on different days when he is well, to find out what his normal temperature really is. Be sure to tell your child why you are taking his temperature so much. Tell him that "temperature" is an individual measurement, although 98.6° is the average human temperature.

Keep your child home if he is vomiting, or if he has diarrhea or an undiagnosed rash.

Keep your child home if he looks sick. Sometimes when the child tells you he has a earache, stomachache, or headache, your only real clue is how he looks.

Preparing a Child for an Eye Examination

Experts say that all children should have their eyes examined by a specialist who is trained to spot medical problems in the eye, as well as vision problems. Often young children don't know that they aren't seeing properly, and it's important to catch a child's real or potential vision problems before he starts school.

Prior to the visit to the eye doctor, make a list of questions you have concerning your child's eyes such as: Does he squint? Does he hold things unusually close to look at them? Is he particularly sensitive to light? Does he tilt his head to one side to look at things? Tell the doctor about any family members who have special eye problems so that this information can be made part of the child's record.

To prepare your child for the eye examination, explain that the room will be darkened and the doctor will get very close to the child while he is examining his eyes. (You might even demonstrate how the doctor will look in the child's eyes with the lighted examining instrument.) Tell your child that the doctor will cover one eye to test the other one separately, and that he might give him strange glasses to wear with different lenses to find out if they help him see better.

Explain that the child's eyes will be checked for "far" and

"near" vision. Depth perception will be measured by asking the child to wear a special pair of glasses while he looks at a special book. The eye is one of the few parts of the body that can be examined internally without an X-ray. Eye examinations rarely hurt, but they sometimes feel funny.

After the examination, the doctor will summarize his feelings and make recommendations. He might say that the child needs glasses; or that he need not come back for three years; or he might suggest that the child sit closer to the board at school (in which case the parent should request a note from the doctor to send to the school).

Preparing a Child for an Ear Examination

If your child doesn't pay attention, daydreams, has a discipline problem or does not answer when spoken to, he may have a hearing problem. Take him to a doctor who specializes in ear, nose, and throat ailments, or an ear specialty clinic at a major teaching hospital, for a thorough ear examination.

When you take your child for the examination, be prepared with a medical history of your child: his prenatal history; any childhood diseases (especially mumps); a record of his colds, ear infections, and sore throats; any history of hearing problems in your family (especially in your other children); and any specific problems you feel are relevant.

To prepare the child for the examination, tell him that the doctor will look in his ears and that the doctor will stand or sit very close to him. Both of his ears will be examined, as well as his nose, his throat, and the glands in his neck.

After the doctor has looked in his ears, the child will be

taken to the audiologist, a person who tests and measures hearing, sometimes in another section of the office. The child will be seated in a booth and given earphones, and the audiologist will give him certain directions. The child may be asked to repeat words he hears, or he may be asked to raise his hand when he hears a sound.

The audiologist will analyze all of the tests and give a report to the doctor, who will in turn summarize the report and make recommendations to you. Ask if any directions should be given to the child's classroom teacher. If so, request them in writing.

Discuss with the doctor any specific concerns you may have come in with. Ask the doctor if there are changes that should be made at home to help with a child's hearing problem—if you should change his place at the dinner table, call him with a bell instead of by voice, etc.

The First Visit to the Dentist

The best way to introduce the child to the dentist is for the parents to bring the child along when they go to the dentist's office for their own visits. Let the child become familiar with the office as early as possible. When this method is used, children sometimes develop such a positive attitude that they resent being left home when their parents go to the dentist.

When the child has a mouthful of teeth (somewhere around two to three years of age), you can help prepare him for his first visit by making it part of the developing process. Tell him that he is now old enough to be examined by the dentist, too, to make sure that his teeth are okay.

When the child is going to have his teeth cleaned, be sure to explain that the dentist has special mirrors to help look at all of his teeth, and instruments to clean places that his own toothbrush cannot reach.

Tell the child that the dentist is an expert in taking care of teeth and can help keep his teeth healthy. The dentist can prevent minor problems from becoming big ones by taking care of both teeth and gums. Tell the child that the dentist is there to help him, and that semi-annual visits increase his chances of having healthy teeth and gums throughout his life.

During the first appointment, the dentist can invite the child in for his own special time in the chair, or to sit on the parent's lap while the dentist looks at the child's teeth. If the child wishes it, it is better to have him sit in the chair with the parent for the first time than to force him to sit alone.

The dentist will probably only look in the child's mouth and talk to him. Dentists who specialize in working with young children can do a lot toward helping the child feel comfortable about the visits. The more information the child has, the less frightened he'll be. The dentist should provide information about what's going to happen. She may show pictures of a tooth with an unfilled cavity and talk about what a cavity is and why a filling is helpful. If the child needs a filling, the dentist can ask the parent and then the child, after explanation, whether he wants a local anesthetic to have the tooth numbed and whether he'd like to see the tooth after it's filled by looking through the dentist's mirror.

Explain all the dentist's equipment: the electric brush (different from the one at home), the drill (the noise and the funny feeling). Discuss the possibility of pain honestly and develop a signal to alert the child for pain before it happens. Encourage the dentist to discuss and demonstrate at-home care, how-tos, and schedules with your child.

Try to find a dentist whose office is geared to dental education, where each visit re-educates the child about proper dental care. This is usually done by a nurse, dental hygienist or the dentist himself and is called Dental Health Education. Sometimes children see films or slide shows, or they are given demonstrations and booklets about tooth and gum care.

BRUSHING TEETH

Brushing their own teeth is one of the first responsibilities that children have for their well-being. It also seems to be one of the hardest health habits for children to develop.

Some parents give teething infants a toothbrush to play with by pushing it against their gums to soothe them. This makes children and toothbrushes good friends from the beginning. When children have their first teeth, it is the parents' duty to brush them morning and night.

Once the children start learning to brush their own teeth, it is good for parents to do it with them, right from the start, so that the children can imitate the proper motion—down from the top, up from the bottom, and reaching all the way in the back.

We'd like to use this as a place to separate out the use of gimmicks from the use of understanding as motivation for your children. Maintaining a healthy body is a responsibility each of us has, and giving your child the understanding of her responsibility to keep her teeth healthy is part of your job of parenting. So although there are special kinds of toothbrushes and fancy kinds of toothpastes which you can use to induce your children to brush, we recommend teaching your child the relationship between her brushing habits and her ability to have good-looking, healthy teeth throughout adulthood, instead of sore gums and loose, perhaps artificial, teeth.

This is one of the first opportunities you will have to teach your child that what she does reflects only on herself—it does not help or hurt other family members if she doesn't brush properly. When she takes care of her own teeth, it helps her.

BABY TEETH FALL OUT

Baby teeth get loose and eventually fall out! And it's a fairly big happening in the life of the child, not to mention the parents. Mark this event as something special—as a sign of growth, in physical strength, in size, and in being able to handle increased responsibility and privileges. If you are with the child, make sure you save the tooth. If you decide your family is to be visited by the tooth fairy, see that the visit happens each time a tooth comes out. Don't disappoint! Some families we know leave a shiny dime under the pillow each time a tooth falls out, some have a system of starting with a dime, then increasing a dime for each tooth (this will take you up to two dollars for the last tooth). Whatever system you invent for your family—use it as a fun time as you share the joys of your growing child. Ask your dentist the procedure to follow in case of an injury that results in the loss of a second tooth.

X Rays and Children

Once you're certain that an X ray is necessary, prepare the child for this experience so that it is, if not fun for him, at least something that feels like an "event" rather than a trauma.

Explain that the X ray will allow the doctor to study the inside parts of his body and since his leg hurts or his cough isn't better, an X ray will allow the doctor to find the way to make him feel better.

Younger children can understand about an X-ray machine in relation to a camera. Since they are familiar with cameras and know that they are used to take pictures, you can help the young child understand that an X-ray machine functions similarly. A camera takes a picture of the outside of his body, while an X-ray machine takes pictures of the inside. Discuss the similarities and differences: cameras are usually small, X-ray machines are usually larger; cameras usually take pictures from far away, X-ray machines take pictures by having the person be close to and touching part of the machine; cameras usually take pictures of the whole person, X-ray machines generally show only a specific part of the body— the elbow, ankle, etc.

Discuss what will happen if the child is going to have an X ray. As an example, for an X ray of his shoulder, the machine that will take his picture will feel big and cold. The child may have to hold his breath. He will have to be very still. This can be frightening the first time a child has an X ray. Explain the various sensations your child might experience when having an X ray. Assure him that the procedure is quick and painless.

Going to the Hospital

A trip to the hospital is one of the most frightening and threatening situations an adult can face, and it is certainly no less frightening for children. Still, there are lots of things parents can do to make a hospital stay less unpleasant for the child, and to help him come through it positively. Planning makes the difference. As parents, you need to do some very specific research before you are ready to even begin talking to your child about his hospital stay.

You won't be able to help your child understand what is going to happen and why, unless you thoroughly understand it yourself. You need to find out:

- exactly what is wrong
- why it can't be cured out of the hospital
- what other options there are
- what exactly will be done in the hospital
- what the likely results are
- what the less likely but possible results are

After you have all the information that is available, you have to make the final decision about whether and when and where (except in cases of emergency) the hospitalization will occur.

If you have decided with your child's doctor that hospitalization is in the child's best interest, learn exactly what hospital procedures will be done, from the time the child enters the hospital until he leaves.

Ask about any of the following that are appropriate for your child's hospital stay:

- admissions procedures

- first examinations (by whom, where, when, for what)

- other examinations, special procedures, operations

- what tests will be done before the operation (by whom, where, for what, when results will be available)

- how the child will be taken for tests, X rays, etc.

- whether you are allowed to accompany the child for all of the above

- what interviews will be given to the child

- what medicines, needles, etc., will be given to the child

- what pre-operative preparation the child will undergo

- what visiting policies are for parents, siblings, others

- what the room will look like
- whether the child will have a telephone; when it can be used
- whether arrangements can be made for special foods that the child likes
- whether parents can sleep over and be with the child all the time (hospitals vary a lot about this)
- how the child will be taken to the operating room
- what anesthetic will be used and how it will be administered
- where the parents will be during the operation
- where the child will wake up after the operation
- where it will hurt, and for how long
- what things the child will be unable to do during the first day(s) after the operation
- what medicines or shots the child will be given after the operation
- how long the child will be in the hospital
- how long full recovery will take
- whether the child will need an at-home tutor
- what he will be restricted from doing
- what kinds of permanent changes there are likely to be in what the child can do

Your child's doctor may be an excellent source of information about how to talk to your child about his hospital stay. In addition, check to see if your hospital has children's counselors who might help you prepare the child and/or invite him to a pre-hospitalization program or tour.

There are many reactions your child may have to your telling him about being hospitalized, including guilt (*I have to go to the hospital because I was bad*), curiosity, anger, and fear. He has probably learned things about hospitals from friends, TV, books, and conversation in his own home. It is vital that you have obtained clear information so that you can give him the support and knowledge that he will certainly crave, and also correct any confusing or erroneous hospital stories he has heard. Be honest about when it will hurt and to the best of your ability tell him how long he will be in pain.

Before you start getting your child ready to go to the hospital, it's best to get yourself completely prepared. This includes getting together all the medical forms, insurance cards, and other papers you will need. It also includes packing the things you will want to take to the hospital for yourself, even if you are not staying overnight. Pack a toothbrush, magazines, books, a change of clothes—whatever will make you comfortable.

Make an appointment with your child's teacher and then discuss the child's future hospitalization. Ask for any appropriate schoolwork so that your child can continue his studies whenever he feels well enough.

Plan, with other adults in the family, when and how long each of you will be able to stay in the hospital with the child. Other things family members should plan together are:

- work schedules

- other children's schedules (carpools, etc.)

- when other visitors will be there (grandparents, aunts, older children)

- domestic concerns

TELLING THE CHILD

Tell your child about going to the hopsital and what will happen during his hospital stay in a series of short conversations. Many short discussions are easier than one marathon session and will enable you to give each part of the information clearly. Also, this way the child has a chance to ask questions and to digest all the information.

When to tell your child, and how much, depends on the age of the child and on the advice of your doctor. The younger child should be told close to admittance day; the older child will need more time to plan and absorb. For the five-year-old, a few days' notice is probably enough. But any child capable of understanding should be told about the things that he's going to find out about anyway—needles, pain, your not being with him some of the time, some unpleasant tests—so he isn't left alone to face these possibly frightening events without information and your support.

Sometimes parents don't tell the child the things he needs to know because they think someone else will do it. But that is not true concerning a child's impending hospitalization. And although it's very hard to tell bad news to someone you love, and most of us would go to great lengths to avoid doing it, it is the parents' responsibility. Parents' fear of upsetting the child is one reason that children are often pushed into hospitalization without adequate preparation. Out of love, many parents refrain from telling the child what he needs to know, with the result that the child suffers from having to depend on imagination to figure out what is going to happen to him, instead of having the reassurance and information that his parents could have given him. The things we imagine are usually worse than the reality, and kids' imaginations are particularly vivid.

A child was told that he was going to have an incision, described to him as a "small hole." It took a while to find out that the child imagined that it would be like a hole in a bag, and he was terrified about what was going to "fall out" of him. Another youngster had visited his grandfather in the hospital and had seen him receiving I.V. The grandfather subsequently died. When the child learned that he himself would be getting liquid intraveneously after his operation, he was terrified that he too would die.

As careful as you may be, there's no way to anticipate all of your child's fears. Some things you say will be misunderstood. Sometimes the child will hear only part of what you say and blow it out of proportion. Talk with and listen to your child as much as possible, so you can clear up most of his misapprehensions and unrealistic fears. Don't tell the child more than he can handle, and do listen for his questions.

It's helpful to point out to kids what's going to be the same as at home, because what's familiar is comforting and gives a feeling of mastery and control. It's also important to point out the differences, so there aren't too many surprises. (*Your bed will be very high, as if it were on very tall legs. This is so the doctors and nurses don't have to bend over so far when they examine you.*)

The younger the child, the more important it is that his parents be with him as much as possible during his hospitalization. Increasingly, hospitals are making arrangements for parents to stay with their children, even overnight, because they realize the importance of the emotional support that a parent can give the child in an unfamiliar environment. For the young child, the separation itself may be the most frightening aspect of the hospital stay.

Be alert to the fact that a hospital confinement is often a dehumanizing experience for children. The doctors may talk to you or to each other about the child as if he weren't sitting there listening to them. The child will be put into a strange-looking hospital gown and often be undressed or made to feel naked while strangers examine him. An antidote is for you to keep as much personal contact with him as possible. Try to include him in the conversations with the doctors, and, above all, talk together about what is happening and what he wants to know, and let him know that what he is feeling and experiencing is important to you.

Often it is hard for kids to understand why they have to go to the hospital. The kinds of things that you'll want to communicate with your child about this are:

- *Something* (say what the problem is) *is wrong.*

- *We've done all we can do for now at home.*

- *The hospital has certain kinds of treatment which are not available at home.* Or, *The hospital can perform tests to find out what can be done to make you better.*

- *To make you better, the doctor feels a stay in the hospital is necessary. Sometimes, what needs to be done takes longer than one day, so you will be staying overnight* (or for _____ nights). *Then you'll come home.*

In talking with your child, be honest. If you lie to children they may not believe you next time—why should they? Hospitals are *not* wonderful places where children are always smiling. If your doctor tells you that your child's throat will be sore for three days, tell him! You may say something like, *When you wake up after the operation, your throat will be sore. You will feel uncomfortable, especially when you swallow, for a few days while it is healing. But after that, you will have less severe sore throats.* (Emphasize whatever benefits there will be from the operation.)

If possible, it is advisable to take your child to see the hospital where he will be. It's good for him to see his room or a similar room and as much as possible of the equipment that will be in it. Children who undergo cardiac surgery do much better in the critical post-operative period if they have been shown an oxygen tent beforehand (and allowed to get into it); if they have been taken into the recovery room (sometimes called the "wake-up room" for kids), and the room where they will receive treatments; *and* if they are introduced to a child who has been through it all and is recovering. Letting your child talk to another child who has been through the same operation or treatment, and is recovering, is recommended as an important step in overcoming your child's anxiety and pain. This lets him identify with someone who's been there, mastered it, and who can share his "war stories" proudly.

A fringe benefit of talking to your child about this experience is the trust he will feel in you to take care of him if he sees that you are not overwhelmed by what is frightening to him. Your calmness and assurance in talking with him can help reassure him that you are there to protect him. This increases his confidence in you, and his own self-confidence about being able to handle the situation.

Be prepared for your child's irrational feelings. Your child may take out his anger or fear on you for telling him he has to go to the hospital. Assure him that you know how angry it makes him to have to go. Your acceptance of his feelings is important. It means you're allowing him the right to be angry or scared. Don't put down his angry feelings by saying *Be reasonable* or *It's not my fault you have to go* or *Come on now, act grown up.* Instead, try saying *I know this must make you pretty angry* (or *worried*)—*no one likes to go to the hospital* or *I'm glad you're telling me how you feel. Going to the hospital would upset anyone.*

Some children may get depressed and withdrawn instead of angry. Get your child to talk to you by asking questions about how he's feeling and what he imagines will happen. He may be frightened about something unrealistic, or about something realistic, and not know how to put that fear into words. Getting your child to talk about his feelings can help him master his fear.

Often a child facing a traumatic experience has a sense of guilt. He may feel that he is being punished for something he did by having to go to the hospital. Listen to your child: it's the first essential step toward helping him cope.

A child needs to feel as much in control of the situation as possible by being active and making decisions. Allow him to play a big role in packing for the hospital. Give him the opportunity to choose pajamas, toothbrush, soap dish, a familiar toy, as well as several books that can make the hospital room more comfortable.

Explain that the child's own doctor may look different in hospital whites. Even a doctor whom he knows very well may look strange (and potentially frightening) in a hospital mask, if the child isn't prepared for this.

Check-in at the hospital may take some time, so you might plan a surprise activity, game, or book that the child can use alone, because you will have to anwer a lot of questions, and there may be a long wait.

Share information about the admission procedure with your child. Many hospitals do a chest X-ray and blood test and give the child an identification bracelet before he goes to his room. Tell him how vital his cooperation is. It's important that he help the doctors and nurses by doing what they tell him to do.

Let your child unpack and decide where his pajamas should go, where to hang up his robe, and where to put his books and toys so he can reach them. Next, prepare him for the parade of people who will come into the room, most in uniform, to talk with or do things to him. The child needs to know who these people are, what they're going to do, and why. Discuss the possibility that you may have to leave for a short time while the doctor examines him. Be prepared for the fact that you may be asked to leave. You know your child best of all, however, and if you feel it might be reassuring to the child for you to stay, ask the doctor if that is possible. In the event that it is necessary for you to leave, do not go until the child understands what will happen, where you will be, and that you will be back as soon as the procedure is completed. Leave a clock in the child's room to show him when you are coming to visit him. It is important for you to be punctual when you visit a hospitalized child.

Follow the rules of the hospital:

- Don't bring in outside foods if policy forbids this.

- Don't bring in younger sisters and brothers if it's against hospital rules.

- Be as friendly to the staff as possible.

- Do as much for your child yourself as possible. (Nurses are not maids.)

- Ask questions about anything puzzling.

A child's hospitalization is difficult for parents to cope with. The child will be separated from everything that is familiar and put in a strange, new place in which unique and sometimes painful things are being done. And the child may not perceive this as helpful to him. This is why parents may have to say things more than once, be very patient, and reach for hidden resources.

With so much happening, it's hard to remember the kind of

attention that the child(ren) at home will need, but they too may be traumatized by the hospital stay of a sibling. Although it seems almost impossible to find extra tme, it is necessary to save a few special moments for the children at home. Answer questions, plan the making of a get-well card or a big sign that says WELCOME HOME. Take care of school activities and responsibilities by alerting teachers, carpool drivers, and so on, and plan to do your share at a more convenient time. Volunteering to help at the Spring Fair instead of the Christmas Bazaar declares your continuing interest and shows the well child that things will get back to normal.

Preparing a Child for a Parent's Hospital Stay

In the same way that you have to prepare a child for his own stay in a hospital, it's important to prepare him for the hospital stay of another family member, particularly a parent's.

The child may have many worrisome fantasies about where you're going and why you're going, unless you talk to him about it. He may feel angry with you for deserting him. He may feel guilty because he thinks some "bad" thoughts he had about wanting you to disappear or even die caused you to have to go to the hospital. He may feel scared because he thinks you're not coming back. Make it clear that your hospitalization has nothing to do with anything he thought or did or said or wished. Tell him everything you know about your schedule: when you are going, how long you'll be away, what will be happening when you come home.

Children feel comfortable with the familiar, so tell them everything about your stay that they can relate to—what you're going to eat, what your room will be like, what you will watch on television, and who will visit you.

Give a general idea of your treatment, stressing the kindness and the experience of the doctors and nurses. Buy a few small items for your child and tuck them into your hospital bag. Then you can give (or send) them to the child as a surprise that says, *I'm thinking of you even if I'm not home with you.*

As soon as possible after your treatment or operation, call the child on the phone or write him a short letter. Talk to him about his world—homework, friends, what he had for dinner, his pets.

Most hospitals will not let children younger than twelve visit. If your hospital does let your child in, use your judgment about timing. An unconscious patient hooked up to a battery of machines can give even an adult nightmares. But when the parent is in a cheerful frame of mind, and strong enough to entertain and reassure the child, it's time for a visit. An older child may be able to cope with and understand a variety of machines and treatment steps, if the gadgets are explained clearly and simply when he visits his hospitalized parent.

Doing something for the hospitalized parent makes the child feel more in control and occupies his thoughts about his parent in a productive way. Be sure that there are arts-and-crafts materials at home available for him to create cards, posters, and so forth.

Overweight Kids

If your child has a weight problem, you can be most helpful by clearly letting him know that you are concerned about it too, and that you are willing to lend him your total support in solving it.

Being overweight not only has serious health side effects, but also causes agonies (particularly for an overweight adolescent) from either feeling unpopular or feeling he must over-compensate because he is heavy. If you too are overweight, one of the best things you can do for yourself and your child is diet together. We've known several parent-child pairs who have created their own diets with medical supervision or who go to weight-loss programs together, with much success.

Some things you can do:

- Don't give a child more on his plate than he should eat; make sure that the portions you give him are appropriate.

- If the child doesn't finish everything on his plate, don't encourage him to do so.

- Instead of serving family-style, where everyone helps himself, make platters in the kitchen, giving the overweight child less of the things that are fattening, and more of the things that aren't (salads, fruits, green vegetables).

- Make low-calorie food attractive.

- Help the child set manageable goals. Don't talk about losing ten pounds, talk about losing half a pound this week.

- Celebrate each success with a reward—swimming at the "Y", or something that will encourage weight loss. When a child has lost several pounds, a T-shirt or piece of clothing in a smaller size will be appreciated. It can serve as a tangible symbol of his accomplishment.

- Encourage your child to eat only in one room in the house, not in the den or living room or watching TV.

- Build the diet on what the child likes. For example, if the child likes potatoes, they are fine, but help him learn to like them with seasoning instead of butter.

- Encourage the older child to keep a diary of everything he eats during the day. Then you and the child can look at his pattern. If he gets hungry late in the evening, save something from his daily food that is appropriate for munching before bed—a piece of fruit or some carrot sticks rather than a piece of cake or candy.

- Don't use desserts as rewards or comforters.

Plan strategies for coping with the big family dinner, birthday parties, the school fair, and so forth, since they are part of every child's life. Your child will need special help in coping with situations where appealing and fattening foods are easily available in large quantities and where all of his friends and relatives will be eating and enjoying them.

Knowing in advance that this is the case will let you help your child plan what to do:

- Teach your child how to mix and match, saving calories at one meal that he will eat later.

- If your school fair or your kid's parties traditionally do not have fruit, raw vegetables, or unbuttered popcorn available for weight-conscious children, either arrange to have these foods there or encourage your child to bring them.

We are treating the subject of weight loss as a change in life style, rather than as a temporary means to losing a few pounds. This is the only way we've heard about to insure that the weight that is so painfully lost will stay lost. A change in life style means learning to enjoy foods that are good for you, instead of foods that are sugar-laden. Parents should help their children find foods that will be good for them, but that they will also really enjoy (at a party, popcorn instead of candy, pretzels instead of cookies, raw vegetables instead of cake, fruit instead of ice cream).

We all know that ice cream is different from fruit and that there's no way to treat one as a substitute for the other. Effective dieting requires your child's commitment to this life-style change. Reward the child for his successes, not with food but with a smile, a pat on the back, a hug, or a few supportive words: *I saw you were eating fruit salad today—it really looked good, and I was proud you stuck to your diet.* Provide your child with tangible rewards that will encourage him to continue with his weight loss program—clothes in a smaller size, swimming lessons, sports equipment.

Your reward for all this is the increased chance that your child will join the growing number of young people who truly like and enjoy fruits, vegetables, and salads as an alternative to fattening diets.

Medical Emergencies

This is a section that is not fun to read, nor was it fun to write. In fact, we were unable to find a way to present this material to you that would excite you enough to make you talk to your kids about it. And so, we decided just to tell you that this is something we find most people don't talk to their kids about, but should.

It is imperative that you know what to do immediately if your child goes into shock from a sting, gets a serious burn, starts to choke, or if some other serious medical emergency arises. You should educate yourself about what to do in each medical emergency before it happens. Ask a health professional for the best resources for coping with medical emergencies with children in your situation. (For example, if you live near the water you will have different potential dangers to cope with from someone who lives in a desert climate or a very cold climate or near rocky mountains and cliffs.) Ask your doctor to recommend first-aid manuals and reference books that should be part of your family library. Ask your doctor what medicines and supplies you ought to keep in your medicine cabinet. Have first aid supplies accessible and separate from cosmetics and non-emergency medications.

Also, we'll remind you that you should have your list of emergency contact phone numbers easily accessible (doctor, poison control center, ambulance, etc.).

	Name	Phone
Doctor		
Hospital emergency room		
Ambulance service		
Taxi service		
Police emergency		
Poison control center		
Family		
Friends/Neighbors		
Veterinarian		

Ask your doctor to demonstrate the best procedure in the case of choking.

Here's what to tell your child to do if someone is bleeding from a cut:

- Put a clean piece of cloth (like a clean towel) or handkerchief over the cut and push on it with your thumb until the bleeding stops.

- If the cut is bleeding a lot, don't waste time getting a cloth—stop the bleeding right away by putting your thumb over the cut and pushing on it hard.

- Tell your parents or another responsible adult as soon as you can.

- Once the bleeding stops, wash the cut under cold water. Pat dry with a clean cloth or paper towel and cover with an adhesive bandage.

BURNS

Does your child know what to do if she gets a burn? What she should do is immediately get it under cold water. Placing the burned area into ice water or putting ice on the burn is even better, but the important thing is to get the temperature of the burn down immediately. Why? Because even after the affected area has been removed from the heat source the cells are still burning and their temperature is still high enough to be damaging. If you can get the temperature down enough to stop hurting (which cold water will do), you will avoid more damage. How long should you leave the burned area in ice water? Until it no longer hurts when the ice or cold water is removed. Instruct a child *never to put grease or butter on a burn. ALWAYS USE COLD WATER, AND ALWAYS TELL YOUR PARENT WHEN YOU'VE BEEN BURNED.* Of course, serious burns should be seen by a doctor.

Have the police emergency number and your doctor's number posted where your child can find them instantly and be sure that he knows how to make emergency calls.

POISON SAFETY

In cases of poisoning, seconds count! You really must be prepared in advance to know what you are going to do if someone ingests a poison. For many types of poisoning, immediate action can save a life. Have the number of your local poison control center, the emergency room of the nearest hospital, and your family doctor on each phone so that you can call without wasting time looking for the numbers. Be prepared to tell the age of the patient and the exact substance that was swallowed or inhaled. Ask your doctor to acquaint you with the use of syrup of ipecac in some cases of poisoning.

Teach your children to know how to call the poison control center immediately. Teach them to dial the number and give the complete information:

- their name
- age
- address they are calling from
- phone number they are calling from
- name of the person who needs help
- age of that person
- name of the ingested substance

Hello, my name is George Smith. I am eleven years old. I am calling from 555 Fifth Street, the phone number is 555–5555. Sally Stone, age five, swallowed some _____ *cleaning fluid.*
(brand name)

Parents should not keep dangerous substances like corrosive alkalies and acid drain cleaners in the house.

Teach your children that there are things that are dangerous and can cause them physical damage and pain. Do your best to keep these substances out of the child's reach. Give your children a thorough understanding of the problem. Take the time to tell them what they need to know and discuss the consequences of eating or drinking unknown or unprescribed medicines and other substances.

Label all household cleaning materials with a big "X" and teach your children that this means *Poison, don't touch.* Label all medicines with the person's name, date, doctor's name, directions for use, and whether they are for internal or external use. Also, teach your child never to take any medicine that isn't given to him by you or an adult you've authorized to care for him in your absence. Teach your children to take medicine only when it is needed. This is important training for the future, and lays a good foundation for talking to them about drug abuse.

Be aware that, although strictly speaking they are not poisons, instant glues can be dangerous if not handled properly, particularly if the child gets some on his hands and then rubs his eyes. Have your child use these glues only with adult supervision.

Choking

Choking happens so quickly and without warning that it is a terribly frightening experience. If a child chokes, the parents should know what to do by being prepared with information from the pediatrician, from written sources or by having been taught exactly what to do by health professionals.

Bicycle Safety

When the child gets old enough to ride a bike, it's a good idea to introduce bike safety the same way that many states teach automobile safety. Motorists have to pass a test before they get a license to drive, and you might want to give your children the opportunity to learn the most current information about bicycle safety that applies to the area in which you live. Local police stations and the American Automobile Association are excellent sources for these materials.

We believe it is clearly the parents' responsibility to review, explain, and discuss bike safety materials with their child. A child can be only as safe as his understanding of the safety rules allows him to be. He must know that it is important to you that he learn and follow the rules, and that you will follow-up and discipline him if he breaks them. Safety is not your child's primary concern, thus you need to initiate and follow through with safety training, if you want your children to be safe. Police stations and the Automobile Association of America can provide you with bicycle safety materials.

If your child's playground leader, or teacher, gets him primed to talk about safety or sends home materials on safety, it is important to capitalize on your child's motivation to talk about this issue. Don't put off the discussion until "later," which usually becomes "never."

Toy Safety

Toy safety in the home is a parental responsibility.

- Inspect all labels. The word "non–toxic" should appear

on painted toys, "flame retardant/flame resistant" on fabrics, "washable/hygienic materials" on stuffed animals and toys.

- Maintain toys. Check periodically for breakage and potential hazards (for example, edges on wooden toys that might have become sharp or covered with splinters that you should sand smooth). Examine outdoor toys regularly for rust or weak or sharp parts that could become dangerous. Repair or remove broken toys.

- Check the toy box. It should always have a light-weight lid that opens from within, air-holes in case a child gets stuck in it, and no sharp edges that could cut or hinges that could pinch.

- Watch for sharp edges. Toys of brittle plastic or glass can easily be broken, exposing dangerous, sharp edges. Be aware that wooden, metal, or plastic toys sometimes have sharp edges due to poor construction.

- Be wary of loud noises from some caps and noise-making guns which can damage hearing.

- Realize that broken toys can expose dangerous prongs and knife-sharp points. Pins and staples on a doll's clothes, hair, and accessories can easily puncture a child. Even a teddy bear or stuffed toy can have barbed eyes or wired limbs which can cut or stab a child.

- Children should never be permitted to play with darts or other types of equipment that have sharp points. Arrows or darts used by children should have soft cork tips, rubber suction cups, or other protective tips. Also, watch for flying toys, which can injure the eyes.

- Try to get the right toy for the right age. Toys that are safe for older children can be extremely dangerous in the hands of little ones (chemistry sets, toy saws, etc.). Be aware of what toys are played with when older and younger children play together in your home.

- Electric toys that are improperly constructed or wired or that are misused can shock or burn. Electric toys with heating elements are recommended only for children over eight. Children should be taught to use electric toys cautiously and only under adult supervision.

Summer Camp Safety

Parents usually spend a great deal of time and effort inquiring about a dancing school, a music teacher, the teacher their child will have next year, and whose house their child will visit for a one-night sleep-over party. And yet they send their children to summer camp on the basis of a single meeting with a camp director, the viewing of pictures or slides of the facility, and a phone call or two to parents of former campers. We suggest writing to the American Camping Association for its current list of guidelines for choosing camps.

Over half the known summer-camp deaths in the last five years were from drowning. Therefore, parents should be particularly concerned about the camp's swimming facilities and supervisory procedures. The American Camping Association guidelines call for one certified Red Cross lifeguard for every twenty-five campers, with an overall average of one guard for every ten persons in the water. All swimmers should be supervised by a Red Cross Water Safety Instructor, or someone with equivalent certification.

All children should be tested for swimming ability before they are allowed to take out boats or rafts on their own. A master list with the children's names and swimming ability should be posted and consulted before boats are issued to campers.

The swimming area should have a barrier to keep boats out. Also, the camp should have some specific procedures for supervising swimmers—like the buddy system, where each swimmer is watched by (and watches) another.

Be knowledgeable about the qualifications of the camp's medical staff. How many people? In what positions? Where is the local hospital, and how reputable is it? What procedures does the camp medical staff follow in an emergency to guarantee that the child receives immediate care?

You should talk with the camp director about the camp's safety record, the credentials of camp instructors teaching potentially dangerous sports like riflery or boating, and safety procedures.

The American Camping Association suggests that parents not accept pat answers; parents should have the director verify the instructors' and counselors' qualifications for the activities they will be supervising and teaching.

Lightning

Children should be taught the following rules for being safe in a lightning storm:

- Stay away from single trees, flagpoles, and towers.

- Never be the tallest object in an open space, or at the top of a hill. If you find yourself the tallest, crouch or lie flat.

- Each home is built with a lightning rod as protection, so explain to your children that if they are in the house, they are protected. They are also safe in a car. Therefore, if they are indoors or in a car, they should stay there until the lightning storm is over.

Teaching Safety at Home

In order to act safely you must first learn how to be safe. Although this idea may sound silly because safety seems like common sense to the adult, children are not born knowing how to be safe. And so you have to take time to teach safety at home.

In this case, showing is better than telling. Two ways to show children are practicing the safe method yourself, and taking the time to teach safety skills clearly.

The rules that follow apply to every electrical appliance, whether it be the blender in the kitchen, the electric saw in the basement, or the lamp in the living room.

- Before the appliance is plugged in, the cord should be examined to be certain that it is not frayed. Teach your child that "frayed" means the protective rubber coating is worn off and the wires are exposed. Tell him that if wires are exposed, the appliance cannot be used until it has been repaired.

- Arrange your work space so that the appliance is close to the outlet and the cord does not dangle. It is better to move the appliance than to have a cord dangle where people can trip over it.

- Only one appliance should be plugged into an outlet at a time. Don't use adapters that convert a socket into two or more sockets, making it easy to overload the electrical circuits, blow a fuse, or start an electrical fire.

- Everything touching the appliance should be dry, including your hands. It's also important that the floor you are standing on be dry. Water is a good conductor of electricity, and if the child is standing in a wet space when he touches the appliance, he may get shocked.

- Never touch the moving part of the appliance when the appliance is working. Although this seems obvious, children need to be taught to control their impatience when turning off a blender or mixer, and wait for the blades or beaters to stop revolving.

Look around your own kitchen and ask the child to tell you if there are any violations, or where violations might occur that you should both watch for. Teach the rules and ask the child to say them back to you in his own words. Do this together, to help each other remember.

Anytime you notice something irregular in the heating or electrical systems, show and tell your child about it so that if he is going to be home alone, he will have the training that lets him do the same kind of analysis that you do and the follow-through procedures to correct the problem.

Smells— Sometimes you can smell oil or gas, or a wire burning.

Sounds—A crackling sound or "funny noises" in the wires, or a crackling when you plug something in.

Sight— Flashing when you plug something in.

Feel— Wires that feel hot. Walls that feel very hot (particularly around a chimney of a fireplace or the flue of a furnace).

FIRE SAFETY

Research indicates that children truly learn the lessons of fire safety only if they are drilled and practice what to do repeatedly. They do not necessarily learn from being lectured to. Since this is a matter of life or death, and since your child's instincts could lead him into a fatal move in case of a fire, we recommend taking the time to role-play and discuss, on a regular basis, your fire escape plans.

Often children come home from school requesting that their families participate in a fire drill. However, parents do not always follow through—instead they are "too busy" and tend to ignore the child's need to learn fire safety. Practice what has been learned in school by scheduling three or four home fire drills a year, and be sure to follow through.

Install a smoke detector outside of your sleeping areas. The detector ought to be close enough to the bedrooms to be heard by everyone. Prepare a scaled floor plan. Have your child show you on the plan exactly how she would get out of every room of the house in case of a fire. There should be two exits from every room through doors or windows, and your child should know how to leave from both exits. Mark on the plan the place outside the house where the family will go immediately after leaving the house so that it can be quickly determined if anyone is missing. Choose a special landmark (the big tree, the end of the driveway, the pavement in front of the house) and walk out during your practice together to be sure everyone knows where to go. Teach and impress upon each family member the importance of following this rule: *Once out—stay out.*

We suggest that you take a few minutes to remind each family member that people are more important than things. Once everyone understands this, it is easier to follow the rule that everyone gets out of the house first and then the fire department is called from a neighbor's house.

Sit down with the family and talk about the escape routes. Quiz each other: *If you were in the living room and the fire was in the kitchen, what would you do?* And walk through the route, since showing is more effective than telling.

Whatever you do, as soon as smoke or fire is detected, it must be done quickly, safely, and from habit brought about by training. Most fatal home fires occur at night while everyone is sleeping, so fire experts recommend that everyone sleep with their bedroom doors closed, to protect the occupants from heat and smoke. Place fire department numbers on each telephone. Check with your local fire company for complete home-fire-drill instructions.

Choosing a Guardian

The possibility of leaving your elementary-school-aged children parentless is so scary (as well as being highly unlikely), that most parents make no provisions for someone to assume parental responsibilities in the event of the parents' deaths or other circumstances requiring permanent child care. However, choosing a guardian whom you (and your children if they are old enough to discuss it) would want is like a form of insurance—insurance for your child's emotional security in the event that both parents die before the child is grown.

There are two kinds of guardians. One is the person who will actually take care of the children and give them a home. The other is called the "trustee," because he manages the property that you leave in trust to the child. Sometimes they are the same person, but they need not be. Your lawyer should be consulted about this issue.

A will drawn by a reputable lawyer assures that your wishes for your children's care as well as your property can be carried out.

Self-Image
Letting Kids Be Kids
Individual Differences
Teaching Responsibility
Learning to Make Decisions
Sex Role Stereotypes
Promoting High Achievement
Celebrating Milestones
Allowances and Money
Scholastic Development
Meeting New People
Values
Kids in Restaurants
Decorating Your Child's Room
Growing and Giving
Chores
Going on Their Own
Sleepovers
Overnight Camp
Pets
You Can't Do It All

4
Responsibility and the Maturing Child

You recognize that your child has matured physically when you have to let down hems and cuffs or buy new shoes two sizes bigger. But the child is maturing inside as well as outside and this internal development may be harder to comprehend.

The main task of the elementary-school-aged child is to develop the intellectual, social, physical, and emotional skills needed to move from dependence (of the parent-oriented preschooler) to independence (of the middle- or junior-high-school-aged, peer-oriented adolescent).

The task of the parents, therefore, is to be supportive when the child regresses to her "toddler" self and to encourage her independence when she tries out her sophisticated "adult" self—and to stay relatively sane as she fluctuates back and forth. The healthy five-, six-, or seven-year-old is the very essence of the scientist or detective. She wants to know about all things and asks why about everything that interests her—and *everything* interests her! She wants to know about clouds, where little fish come from, why the moon sometimes looks broken, and what holds airplanes up in the sky. It is not accidental that formal schooling starts around this age when the child is most ready to expand her intellectual capabilities. She is motivated by a curiosity which is limitless unless it is killed by her environment.

As you are already well aware, your child is a multi-faceted person. The pre-teenage years are an important period in which to encourage growth in *all* major areas of development. You'll want to support not only the child's mastery of academics but also her social development, her physical development through participation in exercise and athletics, her interest in hobbies and skills, and her artistic development in music, drama, and the visual arts. It is important not only to help the child feel good about taking new steps, but to encour-

age the child to challenge herself to try things she might prefer to ignore (like growing a garden, trying out for the school
play, going out for a school team, making friends with new
children, attending parties).

Since the main task of parents is to give their children
"roots and wings" it is vital for parents to understand that
they are only temporary caretakers of their children. Parenting consists of importing babies and exporting adults. The
main parental tasks are those which will enable the child to
be emotionally, psychologically, and intellectually prepared
to leave home at the appropriate time. If parents are aware of
and prepare for this from elementary-school age on, the
"empty nest" syndrome will not hit so hard. By the time the
child physically leaves home, both she and her parents will
have been on their own for many activities. Thus, besides
encouraging and supporting your child's growing independence, one of your major efforts as your child matures is to
handle your own feelings of loss as your child now wants to
be alone or with friends doing the things she used to do with
you. Consciously build activities into your own lives which
contribute to your own growth as a couple and as individuals.

The elementary-school-aged child learns to outgrow the
feeling that she is the only person in the universe and that
everything she wants is to be done for her immediately. As
she matures she realizes that others have feelings and needs
too, and that life is a process of getting her needs met and
helping others to get their needs met as well. She understands that sometimes when these conflict, she will have to
wait to get her own needs satisfied while others go first, and
only sometimes will she come first. Basically, the child needs
to learn that feelings are different from behavior—a lesson
many adults have never mastered. What this means is that

all people, children included, have feelings and are entitled to those feelings. In fact, not only do we have a *right* to our feelings but we also have little control over whether or not we will feel something. For example, if someone behaves thoughtlessly toward us, we probably feel angry; or if someone we love gets hurt, we probably feel sad or frightened. But although those feelings are not under direct control, our reactions are under our control. That is the lesson the child needs to learn. She is entitled to her feelings but not entitled to "act out" those feelings any way she chooses. So, although an angry infant expresses her feelings in a direct, physical way by striking out at people or objects that frustrate her, we start to train the toddler to put her feelings into words rather than physical action.

We train the school-aged child to "put herself into the other person's shoes" and to try to understand what caused the event that made her angry in the first place. All of these activities require greater social and emotional skills on the part of the child, and greater awareness on the part of the parent about the kinds of skills the child ought to be developing. The basic theme of development here is that the child has a right to her feelings, and should be encouraged to talk about what she feels to people whom she trusts, but that she also needs to develop the skills to decide what verbal behavior is appropriate for use when she feels anger or another of the so-called "hard" emotions: fear, hostility or disappointment.

As your child matures through the elementary-school years, the more opportunities you create for her to expand her horizons, the more competent she will be as an adult to increase her chances for success in the world of work, for loving and being loved by other people, and for self-fulfillment in terms of things that give her pleasure and lead to personal growth.

Self-Image

The development of the child's concept of himself is vital to what he can ultimately become and achieve. We all know people who are severely handicapped only by the image they have of themselves: *I'm ugly, I'm too dumb to try for that job, She'll never want to go out with me, I can't take tests, I can't draw a straight line.* And we all know others who have achieved in spite of severe real-world handicaps because their self-image included the ability to try for what they wanted despite a high chance of failure.

One of the important things you can do to help your child's self-image is to be aware of the dangers of labeling your child. Don't you do it, don't let your child do it, don't let anyone do it! Your child is *not* awkward, shy, non-mechanical, or any of the other things we're likely to feel when a child does something less perfectly than we would like. The truth is that sometimes your child does some particular thing awkwardly, or is reluctant to meet a certain new person, or does not know how to do a specific mechanical task, and so forth. Calling your child uncooperative when he has done one particular uncooperative thing, gives both him and you an instruction which says that he is *supposed* to behave uncooperatively the next time because that is what uncooperative people do.

Instead of labeling in that way, deal with the single event that you are concerned about, and contrast that event to other times when he behaved very cooperatively. Labeling is something that you should prevent your child from doing to himself as well. For example, most children feel ugly, and even feel like freaks at some stage of their development—

because they have to wear braces, or have to wear glasses, or are taller than everyone or shorter, or because their breasts develop too fast or too slowly or too early or too late. The "I don't look as good as everyone else" fear is very common.

When your child says:	You can say:	Do not label:
I'm shorter than everyone else.	Your brother was your height when he was your age. Now he is 5' 10".	Act your age. Don't be stupid.
These braces make me look like a little kid.	Paul is your good friend and he wears braces. Do you think he's a little kid?	Don't be ungrateful. We worked hard for the money to get your braces.
I don't want to go.	I know you aren't anxious to meet our new neighbor, but I believe you'll be more comfortable after you meet her.	Don't be so shy.

Giving a child real-world information about how he is doing—both positive and negative evaluations—is very important for the development of a strong self-image. The parent who tells the child only good things about himself is potentially as harmful to the child's maturation as the parent who can never find anything good to say. If the child hears only positive things about himself, like *He's so wonderful,* or *I can always count on my boy to do the right thing,* or *I knew you'd get an A+ on the exam—I never expected less of you,* the child realizes, consciously or unconsciously, that either the parents are not seeing when he does do things that are wrong or they are thinking that what he does is too bad to talk about and in some way he must be a bad person. This is like giving too many presents, which end up meaning nothing to the child. Too many verbal presents also become meaningless to the child because he knows that they are a formula which is used every time the parents talk about him (or to him), regardless of what he has actually said or done.

Letting Kids Be Kids

Emotionally mature adults maintain a healthy skepticism toward authority figures. They don't take at face value what an expert says, not without at least thinking about whether the authority figure makes sense or has provided a realistic research base for her statements. The elementary-school-aged child cannot deal with abstracts, however. His world is concrete—black and white, right and wrong. Children need, and want, their world to be clearly divided into good and bad.

Although there is a strong tendency in today's culture to look for the foibles and weaknesses in our heroes, if we prematurely try to teach our children to be skeptical about authority figures or heroes, we may deprive them of the needed sense of security they get from believing they live in a world where adults are people who will help and protect them. The younger the child, the more he needs to trust the people he counts on to know the truth and convey it to him. Children need to believe that parents, older family members, teachers, and other authorities have their best interests at heart and are protective of them. When young children have this nurturing experience, it allows them to develop feelings of basic security about themselves and their world. This gives them the base they need so later they'll be able to accept mistakes, imperfections, and weaknesses in other people as well as in themselves.

In addition to needing to believe in their experts, children are also different from adults in needing clear limits set on their behavior. Whereas to adults limits are sometimes felt as confining or restricting, children need limits to make their world feel comfortable and safe. The young child who is told to be home by a certain time, to stay within a certain distance of the house, to stay away from a particular place, or to do homework at a set time, does not have to worry about making decisions that he may not have the skills to make. Limits not only help the young child *stay* safe, they help him *feel* safe by placing him in a predictable environment.

Young children should not be expected to solve your problems. It helps kids mature to let them learn how to deal with their own problems, but they are not equipped to handle adult cares and concerns. Why tell a child about a problem of yours when he cannot be realistically expected to have reasonable input into its solution? Asking a child to be involved with problems that are too big for him to deal with can cause him to feel helpless and incompetent. The ability to solve problems is as much a function of believing that you can solve them as it is of having specific problem-solving information. So the child who is successful at solving problems early in his life has a better chance of being able to handle more difficult problems later. Helping your child participate successfully in the solution of problems that apply to him (budgeting his allowance, budgeting his time, what to do when invited to two parties for the same day) will give him a feeling of effectiveness and competency.

Individual Differences

Promoting individual differences among children is a corner-stone to a healthy self-image. To promote individuation, encourage those things each child does well. Building on each child's strengths will foster differences in hobbies, activities, sports, interests, and skills.

Recognize differences in needs. Buy something now if a child needs it, don't feel you must buy all your children the same thing at the same time so they won't fight. Teach your children the concept that each of them will get what he needs at the appropriate time.

Don't always give treats or new experiences to "the children." Instead, give to the individual child for whom it is particularly relevant. *You are Michael, you are six years old, and you are ready to ride your bike to Jeff's house. You're Gary, you are four and a half, and I've bought you new paints because you're ready to start painting.* This concept is especially important if your children are close in age.

Reinforce differences out loud with your kids when you are giving privileges or going places or buying things. This will encourage the children to think of themselves as different individuals, each valued and each important.

Do not make comparisons between siblings. Comparison encourages rivalry over things which can't be changed. If Joan isn't able to stay alone until age thirteen, while her sister Beverly was able to stay alone when she was twelve, that makes Joan *different* from Beverly, but not better or worse. Also, a comparison on that basis ignores that fact that Joan is able to draw beautifully, while Beverly's picture of a horse looks like a camel.

It is important to impress upon teachers that your children have different interests and aptitudes; to point out the positive differences between them. *You had David in class last year, and he was very good in English and drama. This year you will have his sister Sheryl, who is good in math and particularly interested in science.*

Teaching Responsibility

A child's sense of responsibility develops gradually, through a series of events which slowly transfer responsibility from the adult to the child. For example, you don't suddenly give your young child the responsibility of handling all the money for his weekly expenses. You start by giving him a small weekly allowance that is usually used for treats, and as he grows older you encourage him to use part of that for long-term goals. Children become responsible only over a long period of time.

When children are small, parents don't give them the responsibility for taking care of themselves because the children are not ready, willing, or able to accept that challenge. Parents impose rules for young children in order to keep the children safe and healthy. For example, we tell children, *You may not cross the street* or *You may play only in our yard or in front of our house*, because young children do not have the judgment needed to go farther away safely.

Parents generally impose controls on young children with geographic boundaries (*Stay on our block*) or with a guardian

(*Play where your older brother can watch you*). Then, as children get older, these external boundaries are replaced by internal controls (parents' instructions, which the child remembers and heeds). This is the beginning of the shift from outside controls to what we call a sense of responsibility.

Parents can begin to teach the concept of responsibility by making clear the differences between "then" and "now." You want to get across to your child that when he was very young, you cared for him and made the decisions about his care. *Then* you brushed his teeth for him. *Then* you made his bed and fed him. *Now* he does those things on his own.

Not all children are ready to use sharp knives at nine, or to cross a busy street at seven. Children are ready for particular responsibilities at different ages. Each child should be awarded a responsibility only when he's able to handle it, and he should be made aware that he's being given this responsibility *because* you feel he's now able to fulfill it. You can say, for example, *You were so careful each time you crossed Revere Road, that now I think you are ready to cross Putnam and Prescot Roads, too.* In this way each new responsibility is built on previous success and the child understands how and why it was given. This helps the child realize the meaning and importance of his increasing ability to take care of himself as he moves from childhood into adulthood.

When will your child be ready for different responsibilities? There's no right answer to that question. Human development is so varied and each child is so unique, that the answer has to take into account the things that each parent observes about his own child. You, ultimately, will have to judge when you want your child to start incurring the risks that go with growth—using sharp scissors, knives, electrical appliances; crossing streets; carrying a key; staying home alone—one by one. Heaping many new responsibilities on a child at the same time makes them seem less important and may over-burden your child's decision-making abilities. Allow each new responsibility to become a comfortable habit before you introduce a new one.

When you award a new responsibility, explain to your child why you believe he is ready for it, and describe in detail what is expected of him. You must demonstrate and discuss how to act, what to say, where to go or not to go, or what to do, before you expect a child to take responsibility for something new. Sometimes we call kids irresponsible when in fact they don't know what to do in a new situation because nobody has told them. Taking time to discuss thoroughly what is expected of the child assures the parents that they can rightfully expect the child to do what was rehearsed. If he does not do it, they have a legitimate reason to question why not.

Some of the things that children don't intuitively know, but must be taught are: keeping their rooms neat, keeping in touch with their grandparents, brushing their teeth, being on time, taking care of their bodies, handling money, practicing good manners, developing relationships with other people, doing their homework on time and doing chores. It's impor-tant for you to plan the teaching of these areas of responsi-bility.

Children learn most of what they know by watching what their parents do. So before you lay lots of rules on your kids, look at how you yourselves do things. You can't very well get annoyed with your child for not writing to you from summer camp if you are negligent about keeping in touch with your own parents. Hollering at your child because his room is nev-er neat, when you are the world's greatest collector of clothes on the floor, plus papers and books on all surfaces, simply teaches your child to ignore what you say (except when you physically or psychologically threaten him).

When the child is older, his opportunities to be responsible are increased: *You may go down the street to play at Amy's house, but be sure to stay on this side of the street and come home when I call you.* Then, as the child learns how to tell time, he is expected to be responsible for arriving on time—for dinner, for his piano lesson, for the church choir rehearsal. To help your child develop a sense of responsibility, it's important that you give him real responsibilities.

History indicates that children can probably accept responsibility for their actions at a much earlier age than we think. For example, during World War II some children undertook important roles in resistance movements at age nine and ten. Many cultures consider the fourteen- or fifteen-year-old to be mature enough for marriage.

Often what we mean when we say that we want our children to behave responsibly is that we want them to follow the rules that our culture dictates for people in that situation. We want children to be dependable (to do what they say they will do), to dress appropriately for various events, to greet visitors suitably, and to treat each other considerately.

There are several ways to teach children social responsibility. One of the most common is to scold the child when he does wrong. The reason that hollering at the child is a more common response than teaching him how to do it correctly is that parents are often annoyed by their child's failure.

Tell the child in advance what is expected of him in various situations. Then, reward him when you notice him doing what you asked. This is called positive reinforcement. The climate you establish by talking about the good things the child does is much warmer than the atmosphere you'd create by focusing on the things he does incorrectly.

Children, like the rest of us, love attention. If your child learns that he will get your attention more frequently by being bad, he may figure out more ways to be bad so that you will notice him. If, on the other hand, you pay lots of attention to your child when he is good, you're likely to see more of the good behavior you have rewarded.

Learning to Make Decisions

Parents of young children have the opportunity and the responsibility for making most of the decisions for their children that the children will later make for themselves. For a very young child, the decisions include even where he may and may not go (not out of the front yard; then not around the corner; then not across the street; then only within two blocks of the house).

Having authority to make decisions is one way that we mark the development from childhood to maturity. Young children can't decide to stay up late and watch the late, late show; adults can. Children usually can't decide where to move or where to vacation; adults can.

Look into any elementary-school classroom and, chances are, you'll see different kinds of kids—those who seem alert, always taking the initiative and eager to learn; and those who seem inert and passive, reacting only to what they're told to do. The child who sits back and waits to be told what to do may have been trained to follow pawns' rules: Do what you're told; don't say what you think because you'll be ridiculed; don't try new things because you're likely to fail and be punished. In contrast, children who feel good about taking the initiative have probably been rewarded for following achievers' rules: Speak when you have an idea you'd like to share; try new things (that's how you grow); be prepared to fail (if you don't fail sometimes, you may be aiming too low).

One of the major differences between pawns and achievers is that the latter set goals for themselves. They can decide what they want to do and can plan the steps to get there. You can help your child to become self-motivated by teaching him how to make decisions for himself. This involves: choosing a realistically achievable goal; planning out in detail the steps to accomplish that goal; taking those steps; and modifying the plan if it doesn't work.

Teaching your child to make decisions about what he wants to do should not be limited to large goals. As a child gets older he should be making an increasing number of everyday decisions. You can teach your child to take charge of his life by starting on easy projects such as planning his weekends, or helping to arrange a visit to his grandmother's house or to a special friend's.

Encourage your child to make decisions by:

- Giving him the opportunities to make decisions, and helping him stick with his decisions.

- Praising him for making a choice (even if it's one you wouldn't have made yourself).

- Watching for times when he's actively made a decision or set a goal, and complimenting him for it (for example, when he organizes a picnic rather than sitting around the house on a Saturday afternoon).

Once you have given your child the responsibility for making a certain decision, you have relinquished your right to make that decision. You have also relinquished your right to criticize him for making a decision that you don't approve of.

Likewise, you should never ask your child a question about what to do if you don't want to hear the answer or if there's no chance you will be influenced by the answer you receive from him. Don't ask, *Shall we go to see your grandmother tonight?* if you plan to go anyway and his answer cannot change your decision.

When you really care about the outcome of a situation, you need to limit your child's decision making within the framework you are willing to accept. If you really want to go to a movie, don't ask your child, *What do you want to do tonight?* Instead, ask, *Which movie would you rather see, Movie A or Movie B?* If you don't want to take your child to the ball game (a choice he might make), then don't say, *What would you like to do as a special treat?* Instead, ask your question this way: *On Sunday, we can go to the circus or the zoo. Which would you prefer?* Then, ride with the answer! Allow children their voice in more difficult decisions, too.

Making good decisions is a skill that must be practiced. No one learns to play the piano unless he tries to play it. In the same way, children do not learn to make appropriate choices unless they are given real decisions to make.

Shopping for clothes is an excellent way to give young children some practice in making responsible decisions. However, shopping with children is often frustrating: either they can't make up their minds about what they want, or they glue themselves to the very item that, in your opinion, is absolutely the worst possible choice for them—the chartreuse shirt with the yellow flowers, or the see-through blouse.

The solution? Teach decision making by degrees, by planning ahead. Suppose your young child needs two polo shirts and two pairs of shorts. At the store *you* select four polo shirts and four pairs of shorts, in the right style, price range, and family of colors. Then, let your child choose which two shirts and two pairs of shorts he likes best.

Afterward, talk about the choices he has made—how nicely they match, how you like the style or material. Your child will feel as pleased as you would if you were complimented on the good choices you had made. The clothes will probably become the favorites in his wardrobe. As the child grows older, help him become more independent by assisting him in making a shopping list of what he needs.

Involving your child in decisions increases the chances that he will really make a commitment to them, and carry them out. A good time to reinforce decision making (and sticking to those decisions) is when children go off to an activity or party. You can involve them by negotiating the time when they are expected home. This may solve needless problems later, because arbitrarily telling your child that he should be home from the school play immediately after it is over, when the rest of the cast usually has punch and cookies together, creates an unnecessary problem for the child. Ask your child for information, and use that data to make joint decisions about things that concern both of you. Parents need to know what is happening: *When does the movie end?* or *What time is the party over?* and *What else usually happens?* Going out of your way to gather good information helps you to make good decisions.

Negotiation—the give-and-take process for seeing that everyone's needs are met—is important both before the child leaves the house and when he comes home. Suppose your child comes home twenty minutes late. Your family should discuss what the twenty minutes means. You need to help family members understand that "twenty minutes" is not the real issue—your child's safety and well-being are what's most important. Just as you sometimes come home late if, for example, you are stuck in traffic, your child will sometimes find that the school play runs late, or that someone else is using the phone when he needs to call. Even though the child's pressures seem different from your own, they are still real pressures. The twenty minutes can be explained to your child in terms of your caring, your concern, your worry about when he is late. Make it clear that you're not saying, *Don't have a good time* or *Don't enjoy your friends* or *Don't watch the end of the game*, and especially not *You are a bad person if you are late*. You can't teach kids good judgment overnight, but communication can make this learning stage pass more quickly and smoothly.

When a child has made a good decision, and has carried it out, be sure to reward this growth step. Does he handle himself well in a situation where other kids are putting pressure on him to misbehave? Does he decide to finish his report instead of going to the movies with his friends? Let him know how important those decisions that he made are to you, and that you understand how difficult the decision making was. Convey to him the fact that you are glad to see signs of his maturity. Remember that if you have told your child a decision is his to make, it may not necessarily be one that you agree with. For example, if your child decides, after discussing it with you, to withdraw some of his savings to buy another motorized toy car, and he already has two, it's important to tell him that you're glad he's making decisions for himself, and that he will often in life make decisions that are right for him that others will disagree with—and that's what it means to become independent. Clearly, you would never knowingly allow him to go ahead with a dangerous decision.

Sex Role Stereotypes

Hardly a week goes by without some major magazine or newspaper article describing the life-style of a person or couple who have completely reversed the usual sex roles. As yet, this is "news" because it is so unusual. But the social forces that are allowing these changes are also allowing other, no less important, questions to be asked about the mythology by

which boys and girls have been raised in the past. Traditionally, girls are "nice, sweet, non-mechanical, non-sexual,
emotional beings who are poor at mathematics." Boys are
"manly, logical, rough, tough builders and doers who are in
control of their feelings."

One great thing about the tide of consciousness-raising
that has swept over us in the past decade is that it has made it
possible for boys and girls to expand their roles considerably.
It is not unusual today to see boys not only in cooking classes,
but doing the cooking at home, and girls wielding hammers
and screwdrivers right alongside their brothers. What it
means to be "manly" and "womanly" is changing, so that it
is permissible for boys to show their feelings and for girls to
be assertive and aggressive.

Parents should be aware of some of the stereotypes they
may have about the appropriate characteristics and roles of
boys and girls, so that they don't inadvertently "teach" these
to their children. It's important that boys learn the traditional
female skills of household maintenance so that they will not
always be dependent on someone else to take care of them.
Learning to cook, do laundry, and to keep a level of domestic
order are all important matters. Learning to be in touch with
emotions is essential for all humans, not just females. Sensitivity to the needs of others and the ability to communicate
effectively, while traditionally female skills, are vital for
males as well.

Girls need to acquire the mechanical skills that previously
they had relinquished to males. Knowing how to put up
shelves and hang pictures, make repairs on automobile
engines and mechanical appliances, and repair furniture and
household items can help a girl feel competent and independent. Learning to feel and express anger constructively, to
stand up for beliefs, and to hang tough when someone wants

you to do something you do not believe in are important skills, not just for the male, but for everyone.

Perhaps the most important aspect of sex-role stereotypes is that they functionally, if not intentionally, deprived every person of potential rewards. Not only monetary, but psychological rewards are derived from the performance of occupational and recreational tasks. The traditional division of acceptable areas of interest and employment into "sexually appropriate" halves deprived many men and women of access to jobs and enjoyment to which they were ideally suited and which would have enabled them to make the greatest contribution to human achievement of which they were capable. As a result of new attitudes and the opportunities these afford, children have a wider range of choices than they have ever had.

You can help your children of both sexes to reach their potential by watching out for your own hidden assumptions about what's appropriate for boys and girls, and thinking about how they help or hinder your child's potential. Your daughter will need the help of both parents if she is going to learn not to take the easy way out, or to retreat in tears instead of finding a way to get what is reasonably hers. Your son will need your help in exploring his feelings, and learning that it is not unmanly to cry when he is sad, or to tell someone you love them, when that is what you feel.

When the opportunities arise, try giving tasks to the child of the sex you would not normally associate with those tasks: get your daughter to help put up the storm windows or clean the garage; get your son to help pick out slipcovers for furniture, or to participate in spring cleaning. Praise their accomplishment in non-stereotypical areas and talk about how pleased you are when they expand the list of things they can do well. Most importantly, never discourage an interest on the grounds that it is "inappropriate" for a child of that sex.

If you can learn to encourage them to follow their own inclinations, this will go a long way toward freeing them from the burden of sex-role stereotypes, and help them be happier, more productive adults.

Promoting High Achievement

Some interesting ideas about the home environment that best promotes high achievement come from the University of Chicago's Development of Talent Project. Research indicates that outstanding world-class performers—in athletics, mathematics, the arts, and other disciplines—were usually not child prodigies or geniuses. In fact, they often had brothers and sisters who showed more innate talent than they. What they did have was perseverance to keep studying, and parents who made a fuss over their small achievements and paid lots of attention to what they were learning. Their parents believed in being the best you can, and valued hard work. The parents arranged for extra instruction in the areas the kids expressed interest in, and often they practiced, played, or worked with the kids while they were learning.

You yourself may have a future Olympic star, scientific innovator, or great musician in your house. The best way to encourage him is not forcing him to study or practice, but being supportive of his interest and studies, by arranging for lessons that are fun and challenging, and by spending time with him when he studies and practices. Take him to see achievers in his field and provide reading material about his interests.

One of the major differences between achievers and non-achievers is that the former set goals for themselves, while the latter wait to be told what to do. Achievers decide what they want to do and plan the steps to get there. You can help your child be self-motivated by teaching him the steps of goal achievement.

CHOOSE A GOAL

Sometimes kids plan so many activities that they don't really have time to do any of them well. Others choose things on impulse, neglecting things which are important for them in the long run. You can help by introducing your child to the concept of setting priorities. For the young child, everything is the most important thing to do, and he jumps into whatever he happens to think of first. But as children get older, and competition for their time becomes more intense, they must learn to decide where to spend it. Also they need to learn that there are often things they want to do (go to the movies, see a TV show, play ball) that they won't be able to do because of time or money conflicts with their long-term goals (do well in school, put money away for a new tennis racket). Introduce the concept of priorities to your child by talking with him about a balance in his life between meeting long-term commitments (school, family sharing time, piano/art/dancing lessons) and short-term activities that are fun for him at the moment (playing ball, going to the movies).

MAKE GOALS REALISTIC

The younger the child, the less likely he is to set goals that he can really achieve. The nine-year-old dreams of being a tennis star, or movie star, or discovering a cure for a disease. He may not have any idea that a realistic goal for himself is to be able to return the ball consistently using forehand shots, or to develop good posture, or to do well in math, as a first step to reaching his goal. Help your child achieve his goals by teaching him how to make them realistic.

PLAN STEPS FOR
REACHING A GOAL

Achievers know that things don't just happen by themselves. Achievers make things happen. Teach your child how goals get reached. If the child wants to learn to play a song on the piano, he can plan a series of steps to take him from where he is now to where he wants to be.

Step 1: Play the song all the way through and mark the mistakes.

Step 2: Each day practice one of the difficult parts and correct a mistake.

Step 3: Play the piece all the way through and note any remaining errors. Repeat these steps until all errors are corrected.

Of course, your child is not going to plan out detailed steps for reaching each goal he sets for himself. But if you teach him this process of planning for what he wants, he will know how to do it for his more complex goals.

When your child has successfully reached a goal, help him evaluate the process he chose to get there. Ask him questions so that he will think about what he has done. *What, if anything, would you do differently next time? Was the goal worth the effort? How would you be able to know that in advance next time? Did you have more skills than you thought you did? Could you have planned to use less time? Did you need more time? Did you remember to plan for needed outside resources—equipment, other people, supplies?*

Celebrating Milestones

In order to help a child mature, the parent has to:

- recognize when she's ready for new opportunities,
- give her opportunities to try new things,
- support her while she tries, and maybe fails,
- praise and reward her for success,
- encourage her to challenge herself to try new things.

We like to think of these opportunities for new activities as "milestones."

It is important for the parents to convey to the child their feelings of the importance of the event. This "rite of passage" means that the child, from this day on, is considered worthy and mature enough to handle a new responsibility.

Handing a child a key or getting him a library card may not feel very exciting to tired, busy adults. But events which are paramount to grown-ups may not seem earthshaking to kids. We make a big deal over promotions, and the big game, so it is important to make the child's achievement exciting and meaningful as well.

Milestone celebrations can take the form of a special announcement at dinner, a sign that reads, ADAM CROSSED THE STREET ALONE TODAY; some balloons to decorate the dinner table; party favors; or a fancy dessert to show that this is a special celebration because someone has learned something new, been given an important responsibility, or acquired a new skill.

Before a milestone is reached, plan some activities to get the child ready and eager. In actuality, each of these events marks a rite of passage for your child to a level of greater maturity and is a cause for celebration. You can share your awareness of your child's growth by discussing with him:

- how he has grown in size (what he can reach now that he couldn't reach before),

- how he has grown in his responsibilities (what he can do alone now that he couldn't do before),

- how he has grown in his ability to think and make sound judgments (doing more at home and more complicated work at school).

CROSSING THE STREET ALONE

We want our child to cross the street slowly, and very cautiously, but, if his ball or his friend is on the other side, the child wants to move very quickly, taking the fastest route.

The best way we know to get an extra measure of time is to ask children (and demonstrate how) to *stop, look* both ways and also *listen,* to *see and hear* if a car is coming. Only then should they cross the street. Accent the listening step: it gives an extra second of time that may prevent an accident.

When you are teaching your child about crossing, it is most important *not* to teach him in front of your own house unless you live on the corner. Train your child by your words and your example always to cross the street at the corner.

Practice with your child, going back and forth across the street with him, and then allow him to show you what he will do when he crosses alone.

Be sure to give your child very clear instructions about what streets he is allowed to cross without you, and have him show you which streets he is and is *not* allowed to cross alone.

Teach your child to watch for and follow the directions of the police officer, school safety patrols, and traffic lights; to be especially careful when the weather is bad (because drivers can't see as well and can't stop as quickly on wet or slippery roads). It is recommended that small children not carry umbrellas; they should instead wear rainhats that do not block their vision in any way.

GETTING A LIBRARY CARD

An introduction to the library is one of the greatest gifts you can give your child. Don't wait until your child can read. Going to the library each week for new picture books is an exciting experience and introduces reading and the library to your child at a time when patterns are being formed.

Before you take your child to the library, teach him the correct way to handle books and to behave there:

- Show him how to turn pages gently and from the top.

- Explain that you should never write, draw, or color in a library book, because other people will want to enjoy a clean book when they read it.

- Explain that there is a "being quiet" rule in reading rooms of libraries, so that people who are reading won't be disturbed.

- Teach him that when he is finished looking at a book, he should return it to the same place on the shelf from which he removed it or to the table or cart provided for that purpose.

- Explain that you often have to stand in line in the library to check out books; that you should expect this and be patient.

- Teach him that a library is a place in which to ask questions: when he can't find something he wants, he should ask you or the librarian for help.

You and your child need to designate a special place to keep library books at home. Many libraries do not give you a record of how many books you have taken out. Keeping the books in a designated location may help the child keep track of the borrowed books.

When you go to the library, tell the librarians that this is your child's first library card, so that they can welcome the child to the library. Plan enough time so that the child can wander around without being rushed, looking at books he would like to take out. Direct your child to the section of the library where books for children his age are located, and let him walk around investigating books that interest him. *Allow your child to select* the books that most please him, and go to the desk with him while he checks them out. At home, show your child the place that library books are to be kept and encourage him to read and enjoy them.

CARRYING A HOUSE KEY

Giving your child a new key chain shortly before you plan to allow him to carry his own key builds his anticipation and his sense that this is a significant event. On the day that you give the child the key for the first time, make sure you allot a quiet time to talk, enough time so that you can discuss this milestone without interruption. It is not a good idea to give the child his first key in the morning while everyone is rushing off to school and work.

Carrying his own key has greater significance than just being responsible for the key's safety. It means that the parent feels the child is competent enough to come into the house alone and stay alone for a certain period of time.

Discuss where the key is to be carried—a zippered jacket pocket, or a pocket with a flap or button is preferred. Although we generally advocate putting name tapes on children's possessions, a key is an exception. Never put your name or address on a key or key chain; this way, if it is lost, no one knows whose key it is or the address of the door it can open. Instruct your child not to give the key to anyone without your permission.

Teach him to remember to take the key out of his pocket at night, and help him decide where he will put it. Remind the child to do this the first few nights, until the habit is established. A check list posted in your child's room of the things he has to do to get ready for school in the morning will help him remember to put the key in his pocket when he gets dressed. Stand outside with him while he uses the key to make sure he knows how to use it. Remind your child of your back-up system for whenever he forgets his key (key at neighbor's, grandparents, etc.).

Allowances and Money

Allowances give children the opportunity to learn to handle money, budget, save, plan for long-term projects, and give gifts. There are two main beliefs about allowances, and many points of view in between. One view is that allowances are not earned, and that children should be able to count on their allowances so that they can learn to plan. The opposite view is that all money should be earned, and that children should do chores for their allowances.

Our view is that an allowance is a fixed amount of money, planned in advance and given at the same time each week or month without question. Allowances are not something the child earns, but something that has been decided upon to cover certain types of expenses. We feel it is very helpful for the child to be given the opportunity to earn extra money, but that's an opportunity he can accept or decline based on how much he wants something. (Of course, if the family is dependent on the child's earning extra money for his allowance, that presents a different set of circumstances, which should be carefully explained to the child.)

What happens if you don't give your kids an allowance? You end up with the "give me's"—constantly giving them money on an emergency basis. Since the children have no opportunity to plan, they ask for money on impulse or in emergencies and there is always a crisis. Bribes are not good substitutes for allowances. Avoid offering money in the following manner: *I'll give you fifty cents if you clean your room; a dollar if you get a good mark.* This leads to kids' not doing things unless they get money, and gives them no opportunity to be self-motivated or to take their share of responsibility for running their lives.

Around the age of five or six (when the child has mastered the skills of counting, learned the names of coins and paper money, and developed an understanding of simple addition and subtraction so he can know if he's gotten the right change) is the best time to begin an allowance.

The first step is a planning meeting, for you and your child to discuss what the allowance should cover and when it will be given. To work well it must be a good arrangement for both the parents and the child.

If there is a change in the family's financial situation (unexpected expenses, loss of a job, illness, etc.) and you must change your child's allowance as you are making adjustments in your own budget, explain the reason to your child. Describe the ways other members of the family are helping during this time and offer alternatives, if possible. Perhaps this is the time for your child to get a job or learn to make his own lunch at home instead of buying it at school, for example. The more information you share with your child, the better he can understand the reasons for the change.

Once you've decided together on the time of payment and the amount, stick to it. It is difficult, sometimes, to hand your child his allowance money when he hasn't done things he promised to do. Still, we feel it is important not to tie the payment of allowance to the performance of chores, because that would break the contract you made with him at your planning meeting which was that he would get his allowance regularly. If you need to punish your child for something he has or has not done, restrict television or keep the child home from a social activity, rather than withhold allowance. Your commitment to pay that money on time must be kept if you wish your child to develop money planning and management skills.

A good time to review the amount of money that your child receives is right before the new school year, when you can take into consideration new activities and new things you may want him to handle from his allowance, such as buying lunch. This is when you can teach him that with more money comes more responsibility—like remembering to take lunch money each day—and that more privileges come only with the increasing maturity to handle those privileges wisely.

Parents often ask, *Should I stop my child's allowance when he starts earning money?* We believe that you should continue the allowance if your budget permits. Cutting the allowance penalizes your child for his ambition in getting a job. Opening a child's first savings account could coincide with his first job. We believe that receiving an allowance on a regular basis helps the child learn to develop saving habits. Very young children don't think about the future—they want to use all their money now. But even young children can be taught how saving can help you get something later. The younger the child, the shorter the time must be between starting to save and reaching the goal. Waiting too long diminishes the gratification. By nine or ten, children more fully understand the gratification of impulse control—saving today for tomorrow. But even they tend to "lose it" sometimes. Parents may want to help children save by establishing a matching program—the child saves part of her allowance and the parents match what she saves.

It is not your place to insist that the child save a certain amount of her allowance each week. That makes the child feel that her money is not really her own. She must want to save for something special. A child will not be motivated to save just because adults save. But if the parents show the child that saving is a way to get what she wants, it will not feel like a continual deprivation.

You can provide a role model for saving money: *I'm so happy I saved, because now I can get your bicycle, or take you to the seashore.* Don't always focus on long-term saving—for next year's vacation, or for braces—instead, talk about rewards that are tangible and more immediate.

CARRYING MONEY

It's hard to believe that you have to make a big deal about teaching kids how to carry money. But you do, because they don't know the things that are common sense to you. Explain to your children that no one should know if they have money or not. It should be kept in their pockets, not talked about, not held up and shown to people. This is not show and tell. This holds true if it is a shiny new dime or ten dollars to pay for the class trip. Explain that the sight of their money might encourage someone to want to take it away from them. This needs to be taught to the child in a way that will not frighten him. Instead, teach him this in the context that with new privileges come new responsibilities: being sensible about his property is a responsibility he should begin to develop.

FIRST JOB FOR PAY

When a child goes to get a job, help him look at what he can do. Children don't always know what they can do and are often surprised at the skills they have that are marketable. If a child knows how to clean the basement and the garage from family clean-ups, then he can probably get a job cleaning someone else's basement and garage. If he knows how to babysit with his younger brother or sister, then he can probably watch a neighbor's child for the same amount of time during the same period of the day. If he has learned to clean his fish tank, there may be someone in his neighborhood who is interested in having his tank tended periodically. If he walks and feeds your dog, he may be the perfect candidate to do the same for a neighbor's dog. A special skill or hobby he has learned may be marketable. A young magician can give Saturday afternoon performances at neighborhood parties. A child who is responsible and has a bicycle in good repair can try for a paper route. (The child will need to arrange for a back-up person in case of illness or a trip out of town. Sometimes a sibling or a friend will agree to act as a back-up.)

Look at what your children can do, and help them advertise. Make flyers or announcements to post in the local drug store, corner grocery, neighborhood community center, synagogue, and church.

The next step is to help the child learn to present himself. Help him develop a list of questions he has to ask, for example: *What does the job require? What are the hours? What will I be doing? What is the salary? When and how am I to be paid? Will I have to supply anything on my own* (lawn mower, paint brushes, etc.)?

Also teach your child that before he accepts a job, he should check the family calendar to be sure there isn't anything planned that will conflict with his work schedule.

There are questions that he needs to be prepared to answer as he interviews for the job. Role-play with him by pretending to be the prospective employer. One of the answers that few children know how to give is, *I don't know, but I'll find out and get back to you.* It's important to teach your child that if he doesn't know, he should say just that.

He should be able to talk about his job-related experiences: *We do family clean-ups twice a year, and I have helped for four years. Yes, I'm responsible for walking our family dog and feeding him.* He should be able to answer the question, "How much do you think you should be paid?" An important piece of training is to teach the child to tell the truth. It's very tempting to stretch the truth in the interest in getting a job, but if the child hasn't the skill or information he's being asked about, he needs to say that. If appropriate he can also say that he believes he can handle what needs to be done or is willing to learn how to do it.

Rejection is something we all have to face, so it is important to have your child realize that he may not get the first job (or first ten jobs) he applies for. Applying, getting rejected, and reapplying are part of job hunting. Help your child develop a realistic set of expectations about job hunting.

If there is no work available outside of his home, there are still some alternatives for the child who wants to work. You can contract with your child to do a special job at home. And then, as much as you're able, follow the same steps as you would with an outside person. Decide what has to be done and what the time schedule will be, whether he is working by the hour or for a flat rate, what he is to accomplish. There must be an understanding about how this job relates to his allowance.

Another alternative for the child who wants to learn something, even though there is no on-the-job training around, may be apprenticeship without pay to someone who can teach him a skill or craft. This may require your making a contact with someone with expertise in a given field. The parent may or may not decide to subsidize the child for this "work." A neighbor's child started learning to string tennis rackets when he was eleven, and within a year he was doing it for pay. Because of the child's interest and commitment, his parents invested several hundred dollars in a stringing machine. The child paid back his parents' investment, and he is now in business for himself. Another child, who went fishing with his father and grandfather for many years, learned to make lures for them. Others expressed interest, and it has grown into a thriving business.

Another alternative is doing volunteer work to build up his contacts and work experience. Community action projects, political campaigns, and ecology events need people to do many different chores.

Getting a job, like getting many things in this world, is as much a function of perseverance as it is of having particular talents. Making contacts, talking to those contacts about what you want, and continuing to plug away seems to pay off, for both adults and children.

BEING A WISE BUYER

Kids can be really good detectives. Once they understand what to look for to be wise buyers, they can check for things like open packages, leaking containers, foul-smelling food items. They can investigate things like "is bigger always better?" Kids tend to think that bigger *is* better, so it's the parents' job to set concrete examples to help kids learn how to get the most for their money. For example, if one kid wants to buy a one-ounce candy bar for five cents and the other kid wants a two-ounce candy at twelve cents, the parent can help the child start thinking about dollar value, to determine if bigger is necessarily better. The concept of ounces and of pounds equaling money is excellent companion learning to what kids are getting in school. Also good is the topic of how much money you give and how much change you get back.

Your child probably sees many toy commercials and buys items he has seen on TV. We believe it is excellent training in developing good judgment for the child to play detective when he gets the toy home. Ask him how the toy measures up to the TV ad. Is it as large as he thought it would be? Does it jump as high as he thought? Does it go as fast? Stop as quickly? Is it as much fun? If not, why not? In this way, he can make better judgments next time he shops for a new toy.

Even children who can't read can be taught to compare features—this toy has a whistle, this one doesn't. And, as money has to stretch further and further, it is never too early to start children thinking about wise shopping.

If an item should have a warranty or guarantee, does it? These words are interchangeable. They stand for a printed statement given to the buyer of a product by the seller at the time of the sale, and they spell out certain qualities or performance standards of the product. They also state what will happen if the product doesn't meet those standards, such as repair, refund, or replacement. What is guaranteed (the whole thing or certain parts)? For how long is it warranted? What remedy is promised? What must the customer do to get what is promised? For example, if you bought a bike and a week later it needed to be fixed, what would your warranty cover? Would it cover only certain parts of the bike or the whole bike? Would it cover labor? Would you have to pay for shipping it to the repair station?

Scholastic Development

School is the child's major job and his top priority. Making that point very clear to children allows them to focus on the most important aspect of their world. The emphasis and respect which adults place on school and school-related activities serve as a model for children's own feelings regarding school.

Enhancing a child's learning is clearly the parent's option. Extra-curricular activities can strongly affect your child's education. Nature walks, visits to museums, movies, theaters, zoos, historic areas, special events, exhibits, and tours are all ways in which children obtain information. Shared activities, such as cooking, fishing, and woodworking, add knowledge plus a feeling of closeness.

Your participation in school activities demonstrates to your children that you are involved with the most important and time-consuming part of their lives—school. Volunteer to take part in book sales, bake sales, parent-teacher organizations. Fathers and mothers are often needed to work on committees, run fairs and carnivals, go on class trips, and lead study groups. Working parents will probably have to choose carefully the events in which they will participate, because time will often not be available for all they'd like to take part in. Discuss with your children which activities are most important to them and decide together which you will attend and take an active role in.

There are also many ways to enhance learning without leaving your home. Bringing books from the library, searching the TV schedule for worthwhile programs, noting newspaper articles or magazine stories, and sharing your own wealth of information all help enhance your child's learning.

Encourage your child to read both fiction and non-fiction books. Subscriptions to periodicals written for their age group make entertaining and informative gifts for children.

When parents talk about reading, the question they almost always ask is *What can we do to help our children learn to read or become better readers?* Although the answer is different for each family, there is one sure thing: parents have tremendous influence over whether their kids become readers or not. Every time you read, you act as a model for your child. Every time you read to your kids, you help them develop an appreciation for books. Visiting the library, buying books, encouraging children to tell you about the books they are reading, and asking questions about what they're reading all help motivate them.

Selecting the right books for young children is often difficult, even though there are so many good ones. Some resources are your school librarian, your child's teacher, the public librarian, and book reviews in newspapers and magazines.

Praise your child for reading. Encourage his interest in a special topic. When he settles down with a book, respect his need for quiet or privacy and do whatever you can to make your child read comfortably and happily. When your child is reading, don't interrupt him to ask for help with a chore or to answer the door, unless it is absolutely necessary. Let your child understand that you value his reading time. Help your child develop a personal library by creating a special place in which to keep his books. You can encourage your child to read by having the kinds of books he likes easily accessible around the house.

HOMEWORK

All of us would like our children to be as successful in life as possible. One of the main routes to success in our society is doing well in school, not only by mastering content, but also by mastering the skills that are important for reaching goals: good organization, getting things done on time, perseverance, ability to put up with frustration, working well with others, decision-making ability. Also, of course, getting good grades opens advanced opportunities and career goals.

As parents, you probably do not spend more than half a day a year with your child in her school classes. Your primary route to understanding and affecting how your child is doing in school is being knowledgeable about how she's doing with her homework.

Children plus homework often equals frustration. When parents feel that their kids are not meeting their responsibilities as they should, they tend to get upset. It's important to remember that knowing how to do homework is something that children must master—it doesn't come "naturally." So, invited or not, your job is to help your child learn to get homework done, and done well, in a reasonable amount of time.

A question parents often ask is *How much should I help?* We believe you should provide encouragement, be a listener when asked, and, of course, provide resources like dictionaries, encyclopedias, and training in how to use the library. It's not helpful for you actually to do any part of your child's homework—get library books, look things up for her, edit or correct spelling or grammar, unless you are encouraged to do so by the teacher. Many parents do proofread final reports, pointing out misspelled words and having the child look them up to correct the spelling. Also, many parents will type a child's report for her, but if you do this, we feel you should type it as the child gave it to you. Again, you might ask a question or suggest she look up a misspelled word, but do not edit.

Find out the teacher's position about homework, and follow it. Some teachers may encourage parental help and not care who types the child's paper. Others may want the child to do all the work herself. The beginning of each school year usually brings a new teacher into your child's life and therefore a new set of rules and expectations.

Help your child see the relationship between your work and hers. School is the child's main job, and homework is part of that job. When the concept of homework is presented this way, children grow to understand that it is something they have to do, every day and on time, just like a job. if you are frustrated by your child's disorganized or haphazard homework patterns, you can build as much structure into your system as you need:

- Get your child a book in which she'll record all school assignments.

- Set up a specific place for your child to do homework. The child must know it is the place to do homework, a place to spread out and not be interrupted.

- Plan a strategy for problems that your child cannot solve, or questions that she cannot answer. She might place a paper clip on the page or paper next to the trouble spot, leave space, and go on to the next question. Or she might set aside the homework for that subject and complete assignments for other areas of study. Whatever strategy you choose, make sure your child knows you are interested and willing to help.

- Check her work to be certain it has been done and done on time.

- Decide with your child on a specific time each day for homework. If possible, pick the same time each day for homework. If that cannot be done because your child has different after-school activities and lessons on varying days, set a specific time for each day of the week.

- During homework time, permit no interruptions—no phone calls, no walks to the refrigerator for a snack, no TV—nothing to break the mood and decrease efficiency. Have breaks at predetermined times or a specific number of breaks per homework session.

When your child finishes her homework assignments on time, she will have a sense of success. No longer being rushed to hand in incomplete papers and not forgetting tests or projects anymore, she will feel better about school and herself.

It is important to praise your child when you see her being conscientious about getting her work done. It is also important to be available to help when help is needed. Let your child know very clearly that you are there to be supportive and helpful and to answer questions.

Frequently there are particular little sets of facts that kids have to memorize which they just can't seem to master—for example, multiplication tables, some combinations of numbers, or certain grammar and punctuation rules. A game can be made out of tedious, but necessary, memorization. Put the problem, rule, or whatever on a piece of paper posted on the refrigerator. Use it as a visual cue and quiz the child whenever you are in the kitchen together. Try to make it fun by working it into the conversation at unexpected times. Learn to laugh about it.

Remember, the home environment contributes a great deal

to your child's accomplishments at school. Following the classwork day by day, and asking to see any papers that the child gets back allow you to stay in close touch with your child's academic progress. Taking the time to look through textbooks and other school materials may give you ideas for topics for family discussions. These conversations will enhance the classroom learning experience.

HIRING A TUTOR

Parents should monitor a child's day-to-day progress so they can be alert to things going very well (to share in the enthusiasm and excitement) and things going badly. If a particular subject continues to give a child problems, consult the teacher before it becomes overwhelming. If it is documented that the child is indeed having a difficult time in spite of extra help from the teacher, perhaps a tutor, on a short-term basis, is the answer.

The school will probably have a list of tutors who are experts in various subjects. When the child conquers the difficult material, he will be relieved, and his new self-confidence will encourage future successes.

Tutoring does not have to be reserved for remedial work. It can also be a source of enrichment for subjects of interest to your child which are not taught in school. We've known second-grade kids who through tutoring have developed a lifelong enthusiasm for Greek mythology, mime, literature, magic, and other subjects.

REPORT CARDS

The principal measure parents have of their child's achievement at school is the report card. As inadequate as it may be, it is often the one guide you have to your child's scholastic progress. Report cards are usually given out a few times a year, and these become the times that parents focus on the child's achievement in school. However, a day-by-day, week-by-week awareness of the child's accomplishments will cut down on surprises from report cards, because both you and your child will constantly know how she's doing in school, and will shift the focus from *evaluation* to the learning experience itself.

At report-card time it is helpful to keep your child's academic growth in balance with other areas of growth. Everybody is above-average in something. Encourage the child who is academically outstanding to develop socially and athletically so that she doesn't become one-sided. It is important for the child who is average or below-average academically to develop other strengths so that she can be outstanding in her own specialty.

Keep grades in perspective with everything the child is able to do in school. The child who works hard to achieve a B grade and is active on the student council, or is a project leader, or whose painting won first prize in the school art fair, deserves to be rewarded as much as the child who gets all A's. This is not to say that the child who gets B's because of poor work habits does not need to improve, but it does point out that each child is an individual. Your job is to help that individual develop as fully as possible in all areas of human growth.

A good report card is a tangible symbol of your child's progress in her classwork, social behavior, and work habits. If your child has successfully applied herself with great diligence to a difficult subject, it is important that you recognize the significance of any improvement and tell her how proud you are of that specific accomplishment. Spending extra time doing something your child particularly enjoys is a good way of expressing your pleasure. An unexpected gift of your time rather than a material reward can give special meaning to a job well done.

A bad report card is not necessarily made up of C's, D's, or failing grades. It is one that shows your child is not working up to her potential. A child who is working as hard as she can should receive equal compliments for getting C's as the child who brings home all A's. The marks on a report card should never be a surprise to either you or your child. If you are shocked by your child's grades, it means you have been missing signs that have been there for a long time. Thus it is important to establish a communication system between you and your child, so that she can comfortably tell you about any school problems while they are still small problems.

When a child understands that she can tell parents about a school problem, the parents can become partners in seeking a solution. A child may need extra help from the teacher, a parent, an older brother or sister, or an outside tutor. New work that depends on the mastery of previously taught concepts should not be allowed to explode into a continuous sense of failures and frustrations.

Poor conduct marks require a discussion between parents and child that allows the child to define the problems as she sees them. Help your child understand the importance of self-control, and explore the possibility of changing seats, improving study habits, or paying more attention in class. A child is likely to do better in a class when she is attentive and interested.

Follow up these discussions by meeting with the child's teacher, reporting the teacher's suggestions and evaluation of the problem to your child. Work out a plan with the teacher to enable your child to improve, and develop a check-up system that allows you to follow her progress.

CONFERENCES

Many adults don't go to their children's school conferences because they are still intimidated by memories of their own schooldays. Sometimes parents go to school conferences with a great deal of anger because they feel the teacher doesn't understand their child. Or, if the child got a bad mark, the parent gears himself up to charge in and "straighten it out." This attitude sets the stage for trouble.

The following nondefensive behavior helps resolve conflict:

- Ask questions and then listen to the answers without interrupting or arguing. A good beginning might be, *I'd like to hear what you saw happen yesterday.*

- Reflect back accurately and sympathetically what you have just heard the teacher say. *So you feel John started the trouble yesterday.*

- Share only the facts. *This is what Julian said. This is what I saw.*

- Be supportive of the teacher's feelings. *This must be tiring for you, upsetting for you, I appreciate your taking the time to help us work this out. . . .*

Your child's teacher does not see your child as you do, because he sees the child in a different environment. When you and your child's teacher meet, you're conferring to share the wealth of information each of you has about the child. It is important to listen with an open mind to your child's teacher. Then, if you think there has been an error in judgment or something missed, this is your opportunity to explain or give extra information.

A parent helps to set the climate for a parent-teacher conference by being prepared to use the allotted amount of time in the most productive way. Ask your child in advance about any questions he needs answered or anything he doesn't understand or is having trouble with. If there are back-up pieces of material—a test whose grading you question, home-work assignments, or anything that puzzles you—take them with you.

Make a list of things for which you wish to praise the teacher—positive results of the time that this teacher has spent with your child. *Michael told us about your taking special time to help him with his long-division problems.* Or *I've enjoyed reading your comments on Gary's compositions.* Positive reinforcement works as well with teachers as it does with your child. Thanking teachers when they do things that you would like them to do more often increases the chances that they will.

The most important rule for parent-teacher conferences is that defensive behavior breeds defensive behavior and respectful behavior generates respectful behavior. Your goal at the meeting is to obtain more information about your child's school situation. Encourage the teacher to talk about your child by asking questions; then keep quiet while the teacher answers. Repeat back to the teacher what you understand he has said, particularly if it is something you'd rather *not* have heard. Encourage the teacher to talk more by asking for anything else that seems important about your child. Ask about your child's strengths and about the things the teacher thinks the child should be working more on.

Here is a common hassle that can easily be avoided. Paul's father and Paul's teacher were having their conference. The teacher said, *Paul talks too much during class.* Paul's father, who had been a very good student himself, and who took great pride in Paul's good manners, said, *He has very good manners at home, I can't believe he would be rude in school.* This is a blaming statement aimed at the teacher. This sets the stage for a useless and needless disagreement between father and teacher—the teacher didn't say Paul was rude.

If Paul's father did some "paraphrasing" he could help

understand exactly what the teacher had on her mind, and Paul might benefit. Paul's father could say, *I'd like to know more about Paul's talking too much during class.* In this way, Paul's father can learn exactly what the teacher is trying to say. It might be that she sees Paul as a real leader, but that he needs help learning exactly how and when to show that skill. Or it might be that she thinks that Paul has difficulty sitting still for long periods of time, and may need special activities. Or it may be that she is upset with Paul for something else that the father can clear up. The point is that unless the parent listens and helps the teacher to talk—rather than closing her off by being defensive—neither the parent nor the teacher will be helping the child.

If there is a need to check up on your child's behavior, study habits, handing assignments in on time, or whatever, plan with the teacher on a time to meet, talk on the phone, or touch base by letter. If you check in with the teacher by letter, be considerate of the teacher's time. You'll increase your chances of getting information by asking questions which the teacher can answer with a simple yes or no: *Is Paul getting his assignments in on time this week?* By working together, you and the teacher can help your child do the best he can.

It is important for the parents to accept the fact that, at this stage, the child is engaged in a learning process, and he will therefore make mistakes, do things only partially right, and not behave as if he already had fully developed skills and knowledge. Learning is what growing up is all about. If the child already knew everything, he wouldn't have to be in school. Parents must be able to accept their child's mistakes, his falling back as well as moving forward. This does not mean that you should encourage your child's failure. It means that you can separate your love of your child from the mistakes of the day. Help your child realize that doing something wrong is something that happens to all of us; that the mistake must be corrected, but that it doesn't affect his over-all relationship with you.

It is important that you tell your child in a clear, construc-tive manner any information that the teacher has given to you. Remember to tell him the good things the teacher said about him, as well as the points that need some work. Try to develop a plan with your child that will help him overcome his problems.

If your child is talking too much, make a simple "shush" gesture when you say good-bye in the morning; put your fin-ger to your lips and, with a big smile, say *Remember* and *Good luck.* This is a positive way of beginning to solve the problem. If your child has a habit which is particularly hard to break (e.g., getting out of his seat, talking while the teacher is talking, or daydreaming in class), some type of behavorial conditioning might be helpful. You can work with your child at home to make sure he clearly understands why that behavior must change. (For example, demonstrate that talk-ing when someone else is talking is annoying by talking when your child is talking, and then point it out to him.) Ask him to count the number of times he behaves that way during a par-ticular day or class period and write that number down. Then, that night, ask him to set a goal for reducing the num-ber. Talk with him about how important it is that he not cheat himself by doing a dishonest count when, the next day, he tries to get the number down. You will be surprised at how quickly bad habits begin to disappear if you pay attention to them. Be sure to explain to your child any follow-up system you have with the teacher to monitor his behavior.

Meeting New People

All of us sometimes feel ill-at-ease when we have to meet new people. This shy feeling can be lessened if children learn how to meet new people at an early age. Like mastering the use of the knife and fork, introductions and responding to them become natural and comfortable with practice.

The easiest way to learn how to respond to an introduction is within your family. Introduce father to son, brother to sister, mother to daughter, and so forth.

Show your child how to shake hands firmly and say, *How do you do? Pleased to meet you,* or some similar phrase. Show him how to look directly at the person he is talking to. Encourage children to say something as a bridge, or conversation starter. School, sports, holidays, hobbies, the decorations in a room, an interesting toy or game or movie are all good topics.

Taking your child to the home of someone he hasn't met before can be upsetting for him. A quick, easy strategy that might help to reduce the tenseness of the situation is to call the new people on the phone a few days in advance and let your child talk to them. Hopefully, in the course of conversation your child will learn something about the house, the neighborhood, and the people. Perhaps there is a pet, a special room, or a musical instrument that the child will look forward to seeing. In any case, the new place and people will seem more familiar.

Your child may feel particularly shy with strangers. To help overcome this, teach the child to focus on the other person, instead of worrying about his own feelings. Help your child think about and talk about what the other person is interested in or concerned about. Encourage your child to be supportive of others—to give praise for things the other person is proud of. Concentrating on making the other person feel comfortable will take your child's mind off his own shyness.

Values

The thing to keep in mind when teaching your children values is that seeing is believing. What your kids see you *do* is going to make an impression. What you *say* your kids should do, probably won't. Values differ for each of us, of course, but whatever you would like your kids to value will seem valuable to them only if they see you valuing it, by living it! If you want to teach respect for others, don't push in front of people in line at the supermarket; tell your children that being fair to people is more important than the thirty seconds you'd save by getting there first. Telling the waitress that she didn't charge you for the soup you ate will teach your child honesty and fairness more effectively than hours of lectures will. Admitting to your child that you were wrong does more than repeated discussions about how he should not be defensive when you correct him. Your telling the truth (especially when it isn't easy) will be a more memorable experience for your child than years of your saying, *You should tell the truth.*

"Honor thy father and mother" will best be brought home to your child by the way you treat your own parents, in-laws, and other senior family members.

Reward your kids when they do things you value. For example, if your child tells you immediately about breaking a window, or failing an exam, or sneaking into the movies, or shoplifting, make it clear to him that you very much value his telling you about it honestly, even though you do not approve of what he did.

Whenever your child does something that takes guts, he is probably standing up for some value. You'll help your child develop his own standards much more effectively by watching for those instances and praising him, than by just criticizing him when he does wrong. Think about how you would respond in a similar situation. Which will affect you more, someone's saying to you, *You shouldn't cheat on your taxes*, or *It really was terrific that you pointed out to that waitress that she didn't charge you for the soup*.

Criticizing your child's values is like telling him he is a bad person. It decreases the chances that he will tell you about something he's concerned about that could possibly elicit criticism.

Are we saying you should never correct your kids? Of course not! But as your child develops values, attitudes and feelings about things and people, it's important for you to keep an open line of communication with him, so he will want to talk with you about things he's concerned (or guilty) about.

Set up a supportive climate for talking, while at the same time being very clear about how you feel about your child's activities. For example, if your child tells you he sneaked into a movie with his friends, first tell him that you value his being honest with you. Then apply appropriate punishment for the illegal activity—but do not criticize your child for being a bad person.

LYING AND STEALING

Children lie for a variety of reasons, and before you can start to correct lying, it is important to understand the child's reasons for being dishonest. He may be telling "little white lies" because he hears you do the same. Or he may be lying because he did something he considers so bad that he can't admit it. He may be lying because he wants your attention, or to avoid loss of face, or to get his little sister in trouble, or to impress somebody. The same is true for stealing: first find out what is going on in the child's mind.

Even though the question parents most want answered when they find their child is lying or stealing is *Why did you do it?* that's the one question to avoid asking. For most children (and most adults) it is unanswerable, so the answer will be either, *I dunno* or a long, impassioned excuse, *Jimmy made me. See, he said that if I didn't do . . .*

It is important that the child return any gains he has gotten from the lie or the theft. Help him to do this in a manner that lets him know you expect him never to take things which don't belong to him or lie again. *Return the ring to David because it's his, not yours. The book has to go back to the store—let's go do it now and apologize to the store's owner. You took George's baseball glove and damaged it: how do you plan to repay him?*

When you know your child has lied or stolen something:

- Do not treat the situation like a major crime. Insist that restitution be made, but don't treat the child like a criminal.

- Confront the child with your facts. (*You took Charlie's shovel.*) Don't try to entrap him into confessing. (*Where did you get that shovel?*) Don't ask him questions you already know the answer to.

- Do not insist on a confession. Instead, insist that the act be put right.

- Once restitution or punishment is completed, never bring the topic up again. Adults are not tried for the same crimes twice, neither should children.

- Make sure that your child knows you still value and love him as a person, even when you don't like what he's done.

- In the future, reward honesty. Notice when your child has told the truth in a difficult situation, and tell him how pleased you are with his honesty. Also, acknowledge the child's right to have feelings that you don't approve of; don't force him to lie to win your approval. If he hates his teacher, don't say, *You know that's not nice.* If he tells you he'd rather go to the movies with his friends on Saturday than visit his aunt, don't tell him he ought to feel differently.

Encourage your kids to talk to you about the thing they want—a new blouse, a bike. By putting "it" into words, and expressing your sympathy (*I know you'd like to have it; it's really pretty, but it's not possible in our budget right now*), you'll decrease the chances of your kid's acting impulsively (shoplifting), and again you'll increase the chances of his talking about what's important to him. You might also say, *Would you like to plan to get it for your next birthday?* Or, *if you want to save for it, I'll match what you save.*

CITIZENSHIP TRAINING

Within the last decade some major development programs were launched in the schools to teach children citizenship. Many of these programs utilized innovative and educationally sound methods for helping kids come to terms with such important issues as abiding by the law and how to work to change laws. Children were encouraged to understand what it feels like to be the victim of a crime, as a means of increasing their motivation toward reducing personal crimes, and to decrease their tendency to see a robbery victim as an object who has no feelings.

For the most part, these citizenship-training programs were removed from school curricula, so if your child is going to receive education in being a responsible member of the community it is probably going to come about through your teachings and your example. Some of the topics that you may want to cover are: voting, jury duty, following the laws of the community, participating in community activities such as clean-up days. Teach your children how to get help if they see a problem, obey local ordinances about pets, and have empathy with the victim of a crime.

Talk to your kids about the activities you engage in to support your community: *I don't really like paying taxes, but taxes pay for our fire station and street repair, and that's good for us and for everyone. Your father is taking Mrs. Smith out shopping because she is too elderly to go alone. Your older brother is running in a race on Sunday to raise money for a local charity. The adults on the block are participating in a citizen watch to keep the neighborhood safe.*

Take the time to talk about community issues with your kids, so that you can teach them about channels for making change. They need this instruction to fight off the prevalent myth that "you can't fight City Hall." Show them how they can write letters to newspaper and magazine editors, members of Congress, local politicians, and consumer groups; they can sign petitions and raise issues around the home that will be of interest to the entire family, perhaps enlisting the aid of their parents in a campaign to change something. Sometimes they will get a response to their letters, but not always. However, their reactions will be noted by the decision makers. It's important to tell your children that only by participating will they make their voices heard.

SWEARING

Children swear for a variety of reasons, depending on their age and stage of development. Younger children are interested in words related to bodily functions and in words which get a lot of attention. You can say things like *That is not a word I want you to use, That is not a nice word*, or *That word is called swearing, and that's not polite.*

When the child gets older, swearing may become part of what he does because the "other kids" do it. He may even use words that he does not know the meaning of, because they seem to command the respect or admiration of his peers. At that time, you can introduce the concept that as he gets older, he'll be moving into different environments and learning things different from what he learns at home.

Swearing does serve the function for many of giving a sense of release in an intense situation, and may even prevent acting out physically. If you use swearing in this mode, rather than being angry with your child if he does the same, you might work with him on other ways he can find to express his anger or hostility.

Experts seem to agree that parents who don't want their children to swear must be consistent about not swearing themselves, and that although they need to be firm about insisting that the child not swear they should not overreact if she does on occasion use inappropriate language.

Kids in Restaurants

Some restaurants are designed to be welcoming to kids. They are decorated in bright colors, have easy-to-clean tables, chairs, and floors, and offer special foods and decorations which appeal to kids. Most of the quick-service restaurants are of this type.

Other restaurants are designed for adult tastes. These are slower paced, have linen tablecloths and napkins, offer more sophisticated food choices, and have a clientele that is there for a relaxed dining experience. And, of course, there is a whole range of restaurants in between.

Your children should be exposed to both of these types of dining and should learn how to behave appropriately in each, both for your sake and for theirs. When you want to eat out, think about your child's attention span. How long he can sit still dictates what kind of restaurant you'll want to take him to.

Going out to eat is a wonderful opportunity to expose your child to new foods that he may not get at home. Make the assumption that your child will like everything, at least enough to taste it. The child who ordinarily says, *I don't like fish*, may taste it in new surroundings, prepared in a different way. He may still hate it, but he may like it. Don't insist that your child eat anything he says he doesn't like, but do strongly encourage him to taste everything at least once.

Often parents are embarrassed about their child's table manners when they take him out to eat. Children will eat the same way outside as they do at home, and a restaurant is not the place to teach manners for the first time. If the child shoves the whole roll in his mouth or eats with his fingers at home, he'll probably do the same in the restaurant. So, in your daily meals at home, correct any table manners that you don't want to show up in a restaurant.

A restaurant should not be a battleground. The fact that you are probably paying more for a restaurant meal than one that is prepared at home is no reason to force the child to eat what he doesn't like or to finish everything on his plate.

If you plan to go for dinner to a formal, slower-paced restaurant, have a rehearsal at home. When you sit down at the table, instead of serving dinner as you normally would, you can say something like, *If we were at the restaurant we're going to next week to celebrate Aunt Rose's birthday, we would first tell the waiter what we wanted to order from the menu. Then, we would have to wait while the chef cooked our dinner. This might take a while, so let's talk quietly while we wait.*

Explain that the waiter will clear away the dishes between the courses, and there may be another wait between courses. When the bill comes, if the child is old enough, you can show it to him, and let him see how you calculate the tip.

To help children learn to order according to the foods they would enjoy, as well as being appropriately priced, start with asking the youngest child to tell you two things he'd like. Then, if both are okay, ask him to choose his favorite. If one of them is too expensive, or takes too long to prepare, you can choose the other. Also, have the child learn to speak directly to the waiter when everyone is giving the order. Teach him how to give his order clearly.

Decorating Your Child's Room

A clear and practical measure of your child's growth and maturity is the way his room looks. Switching from small beds and baby blue or pink to decorations that fit the child and express his interests and personality helps children think of themselves as more grown up.

Inexpensive materials such as carpet remnants, a can of paint, imperfect sheets for curtains and spreads, cinder blocks and pressed board for book shelves, and lots of creativity can make a room look really exciting.

Kids don't care if it is convenient—climbing a ladder to a bunk bed, pulling out a trundle bed, or pulling back curtains before they can snuggle does not seem to bother them. Creating a unique sleeping area is really a plus.

Remember to have plenty of lights—kids like it bright. And it is especially important to have proper lighting in the sleeping area (for reading in bed) and in reading-studying areas. Storage areas should be created for clothes, books, sports equipment, and collections. A strong board attached to the wall with hooks can hold tennis racquets, lacrosse and hockey sticks—things that adults are always tripping over—and a shelf can hold balls, helmets, and so forth. An open shelf can hold all the little cars or dolls that always get underfoot when not in use, and allows kids to reach what they want. Besides good light, work-study areas need enough space to hold books, papers, pencils, and supplies needed for school each day. Encourage the child to put things away in the same place each day. This will save loads of time looking for lost or misplaced school-related materials.

A bulletin board to hold important papers, invitations, tickets to plays, pictures of favorite stars, sports heroes, and odds and ends, avoids clutter, can look attractive, and keeps things organized. Leave lots of open spaces for your child to spread out and play in his room. Involve the child in choosing colors, styles, and arrangements, and in doing the work to make his room attractive, enjoyable, and functional.

Growing and Giving

Give your maturing child the opportunity to learn to give. When growing children want to buy a present, or do something special for a parent's birthday or a holiday, the other parent should help them learn that sometimes the gift of "yourself" is better than something from the store. Teach kids to try to put themselves in Dad's place for example. What did he say he wanted recently? Soup like Aunt Madeleine makes. To see his old friend Jim. More flowers in the garden. Time to see the Liberty Bell or the Natural Science Museum.

Perhaps you can help your child arrange such an experience for the other parent—a "happening." It takes time and effort, but not lots of money.

Consider a movable feast—a basket packed with fresh fruit, fresh rolls, and some cheese on the way to visit someplace Dad wants to see on his birthday. Or make the soup that Aunt Madeleine makes. Or call Jim and arrange for him to visit as a surprise.

This is particularly important and sometimes difficult when a child's parents are divorced. It is helpful for the child if the parent with whom he lives makes sure that communication lines are open to the other parent. Just as you took pains to assure your child that the arguments between your spouse and you had nothing to do with him, you should assure him that the good feelings which may exist between him and his other parent are fine. They don't mean that you are a bad parent, or that the child likes his other parent better than you. Thus, regardless of how you feel about your former spouse, it's important to teach your child to reach out to his other parent; to remember birthdays, Father's or Mother's Day, holidays, and to send a card, make or buy a present, and to continue to do whatever was the tradition before the separation.

Chores

In pioneer days, chores were what everyone did to take care of the family, and all hands were vital to get done what was needed for survival. Much later, in a different economic climate, chores were assigned to children as part of their training in character development—children cleaned their rooms because it was "good for them," because it fostered a sense of responsibility.

Today, economic factors are again making it necessary that all members of the family do things around the house— because they are needed to sustain the family's life-style. This is particularly true in households where there are two parents working outside the home, or in single-parent households. Even if both parents are not working, they may participate in many activities that keep them so busy that extra help around the house is useful and welcome. Even if the family employs household help, the children still should be given responsibility for and taught some domestic tasks.

There are a variety of reasons for youngsters to be taught

household skills early. First, unless boys are taught some of the traditional "female" skills like cooking and homemaking, they don't learn them. Likewise, unless girls are specifically taught, they are deprived of essential skills such as handling tools, and being able to make minor repairs around the house.

Second, with more and more parents working out of the home, there are fewer opportunities for children to be taught the tasks they have to do to help around the house. This means that at the very time that children are needed to do the tasks that in previous generations the non-working mother would do—such as cleaning, laundry, shopping, cooking, and so forth—there may be no role-model at home to demonstrate how to do those chores properly.

With growth comes responsibility as well as freedom. Chores are part of that responsibility. Talk to your child about the fact that the house looks nice only if everyone helps to take care of it, and that if everyone does a little bit, no one gets stuck having to do a lot of chores.

When you talk with your child about doing chores, help him to learn that there are really two parts. One is doing a good job completing the chore itself, and the other is establishing a favorable climate, so that everyone has as good a time as possible doing the work. It is unpleasant to be working with someone who is grumpy. So, teaching your child to make chores fun, or at least to do his work with good grace, is an important part of his learning experience.

Family discussions about chores should include some talk about building good day-to-day habits. It is just as easy to put something in the right place as the wrong place, and much easier to live in a clean space than one that has piles of accumulated toys and clothes from days of activities. Teach your child to check each time he leaves a place he has used to be sure it is in good shape. As a parent, you need to make sure

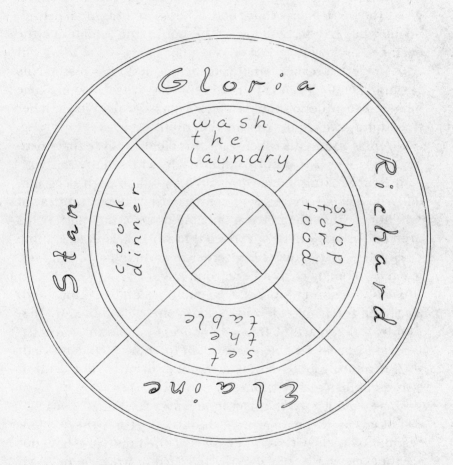

that the child has a place to put the things he is using and that you keep your part of the house orderly and neat as well.

In order to have the house run smoothly, and have adults and kids do what is expected of them, summarize on a chore chart the discussions that you have had at a family meeting about what has to be done in the house and which chores each person is going to do on a regular basis.

To prevent a revolution at your house, develop a method of assigning chores that is fair to everybody. The decision as to what has to be done should come from a basic plan devised by the adults with input from the children.

Parents often talk about the problems they experience because their kids don't communicate with them. You will find that working alongside your kids, while each does his daily household chores, will create natural opportunities to talk about what each of you is doing or thinking. Both children and adults will be surprised that work doesn't seem like work when you're doing it together to accomplish a goal and learning to enjoy each other's company.

Weekly cleaning jobs, like vacuuming and dusting, and sweeping the front sidewalk, should also be planned by the family. It is important that no one feels he has the hardest, longest, or most terrible job to do all the time. You can avoid this by rotating jobs, so that everyone gets a turn at the hard jobs as well as the easy ones.

There are big jobs that get done only a few times a year—cleaning out the garage and the attic, getting the garden ready. If you expect every member of the family to show up for the big cleaning day, be sure to schedule it well enough in advance for everyone to plan on it. Don't forget to put it on the family calendar.

Have the equipment and supplies that you need ready, and help everybody learn that pitching in gets the job done quickly. Even very young children can do something to be help-ful—bringing clean rags, taking away twigs and branches, cleaning up a special corner of the attic or garage where there is nothing heavy or dangerous. Try to make it fun. Create a "do-it-yourself" sandwich buffet with fun things to eat, and put on some music while you're working. Days like this build special feelings of community and create good memories. When you have finished, do something to celebrate the accomplishment—go out for ice cream, dinner, or a movie together.

What should parents do if chores aren't carried out? When your child hasn't done something he said he was going to do, the first step is to find out why. You will want to take different steps if he just "didn't feel like it" or "didn't remember," from those you will take if the job he agreed to do turned out to be bigger than he realized, or one for which he didn't have the time, skills, or knowledge.

Continual "didn't remember" or "didn't get around to it until too late" can be cured with a note on the bathroom mirror, where everybody looks, reminding TODAY'S THE DAY THE TRASH GOES OUT! Ask your child if he wants you to remind him when his chores are due, until he can remember by himself. Tying a chore in with something that happens regularly may help—for example, doing the vacuuming before going to sports practice or choir rehearsal.

It may help to review the process at your family meeting, particularly when you can praise the behavior of those whose chores went well. You can also teach your children to nego-tiate at your family meetings. For example, if Robert really hates vacuuming, and Lisa doesn't like setting the table, they may agree to swap those chores.

On the other hand, if the situation is that reality has caught up with the child, and he finds that he doesn't have enough time to do all the things he needs to do, he may learn that he has to change his schedule. He might choose to get up half an hour earlier on Wednesday and Friday to do his chores, or to fit in chores in short spurts in previously unused time. Keep an eye open for any skills you might help your child develop so that he can do his chores more efficiently and easily.

When household jobs are divided up among members of the family, they will not all be done perfectly. A seven-year-old is not going to make his bed the way you would and a ten-year-old is not going to leave the kitchen spotless. Therefore, adults have a choice: they can either do all the chores themselves, or they can have the children help and accept the level of performance that the child achieves. There is a difference between showing a child how to improve or learn something more about doing the task he is involved in and nagging or criticizing.

Establish priorities about what is the most important part of the job, and if the child does that, make sure you praise him for that instead of critizing him for the bits that are not done as well.

Don't always insist that chores be done immediately. Instead, say, *By the time you go to bed* or *By the end of the weekend*, which gives him some flexibility.

Remember, it's unreasonable to expect the child to be as organized, neat, and careful as an adult. Sometimes, changing expectations helps things flow better; if you expect your young children to do their chores twice as slowly and half as well as you do, half your frustrations might disappear.

LAUNDRY

The transition from an adult doing laundry for the family, to children doing their own laundry, will only happen if you plan for it. Often this comes about just because children take on more responsibility as they grow older, or the need will arise if parents work outside the home.

There are two ways we know of to manage laundry. One way is to have one person become responsible for the family laundry for one week at a time, and the second way is that each person is responsible for his own laundry. Doing your own wash is one of the clearest ways to illustrate what happens when responsibilities aren't met. If the laundry isn't done, then when twelve-year-old Neil needs a clean shirt for the band concert, it just isn't available.

No matter which method your family chooses, they both require a period of time to learn how to do laundry. Show your children how to properly sort the clothes, place them in the machine, add soap (softener and bleach), time the load, etc. Give children information on how often the laundry should be done. Plans should also include how the laundry gets to the washing machine. (For example, does each person bring his own laundry down and sort it, or does the "laundry person" have to collect it?) How does the laundry get back up to each person's room? Who folds?

There are times that every system breaks down—crunch times—and provisions need to be made for this. Perhaps the parent who is on laundry duty has an unexpected late meeting on laundry day, or the child responsible for handling the chore has a major exam or report due the next day. When times get really tough, everyone just has to help!

KIDS AND THEIR CLOTHES

Hang it up! This is one of those tasks that seems almost impossible to get kids to do. No amount of talking, telling, or showing makes kids hang up their clothes automatically. Tell the kids that *the clothes have to go somewhere and it is*

*just as easy for them to get put in the closet on a hanger,
as under the bed.*

One system you might try to help your children learn is that
when they take off a piece of clothing, it should go one of four
places:

- in a laundry basket or hamper,
- in a place for things that need to go to the cleaners,
- in a place for clothes that need repair (button, seam, zip-
  per),
- wonder of wonders—hung up in the closet.

So try asking, setting a good example, reminding when necessary, and most of all have patience until the kids get the
"hang" of it.

Going on Their Own

As children grow, we want them to be responsible and independent. Unfortunately, in today's world safety imposes certain restrictions on children traveling alone. With this in
mind, we suggest the following precautions as your children
begin to do more things on their own.

Encourage your children to walk in groups, and teach them
to avoid deserted or dark streets and alleys. Point out to them
that it is not good to take shortcuts through empty parks,
playgrounds, or schoolyards. Have your child make a habit of
calling you when he gets to his friend's home, just to say he's
there. Figure out the best routes for the child to take to places
he goes on a regular basis.

It is necessary to take the time to teach your children how
to take and behave on public transportation, whether it is a

school bus or city bus, trolley, or train. Explain clearly that the child should sit up straight back in his seat. If a vehicle stops suddenly, the child who is leaning forward can be easily thrown into the seat in front of him, increasing the chances of injury to his teeth and face. Teach your child not to talk to strangers, but to ask the driver any important questions. Your child should be taught his name, address, and telephone number at a young age.

If you live in an area where commuting is part of your way of life, you should familiarize your child with this kind of travel. Show your child how to use a timetable when he's old enough. Also, tell him about the information desk at the station where he can find out when the trains or buses are running, and that you can call the station to find out about how to get to a particular location.

When the child is old enough to take public transportation alone, think about where he will wait for the bus or train, both going and coming. Are the areas where he will wait safe and well lit? Think about the route the vehicle will take. Is it safe for the child to be traveling through these areas alone? Think about the walk to and from the bus stop or train station. Is it safe? Is the trip normally traveled by your child on weekdays equally safe on weekends, holidays, or at night? If you have concerns, reconsider the trip. But if all of the above check out, then you can begin to train your child to go alone. It is vital that you show him where to wait for the bus or train and how to pay. Teach the child exactly where to get off; tell him what landmarks to look for and when to begin moving toward the door. *When you pass the yellow gate, it's time to walk to the door.* Children who know how to get on buses may be concerned about whether they will be able to get off the bus at the proper stop.

When your child makes his first trip alone using public transportation, have him met when he gets off or have him call you to let you know that he has arrived safely. (If you are like many parents, the first time he travels alone you will nonchalantly wander around the house and glare at the phone until it rings and you hear that he is safe.)

We suggest a three-step plan for introducing your child to traveling alone.

Step 1: You take the child with you, but let him tell you all the steps of the trip.

Step 2: The child takes you on the trip with him. He pays the fare, he handles getting on and off at the right places, and directs the walking to and from. But you are there, by his side, as a support and reminder if he forgets.

Step 3: The child goes "alone" but you go the same route at the same time. You pretend that you are strangers. Of course, if the child requests another come-along time, you may need to adjust to his needs.

SAFETY ON
THE STREETS

Sometimes the things that are most important for us to discuss with our children are the very things we keep silent about. That is usually the case when the topic is something we ourselves are most concerned about. The possibility of our child's getting hurt by someone often makes us so apprehensive that we push the idea away from our consciousness. But this is one time when ignorance is not bliss. Your child needs to know what to do in the unlikely, but possible, event that he is approached by someone who means him harm. However, he needs to learn about it in a way that will not make him apprehensive about going about his daily life.

Focus on a balanced picture. Start by making a bridge to something the child is familiar with—the concept that some people have physical illnesses. *Remember when Margie was sick with the measles? Margie did not look normal with all those spots. Audrey broke her ankle, and didn't walk normally with her cast on.* Move on to the concept of mental illness: *Some people are not normal in the way they think about the world and the way they act. Some physical illnesses can't be seen from the outside (like a sore throat) and some mental illnesses can't be seen from the outside either.* This sets the scene for telling him that under no circumstances should he go in a car with a stranger, take gifts from a stranger, or give personal information to a stranger.

Emphasize that there are lots of areas in his life where being with people brings him great joy, and that being open and responsive to friends and acquaintances is a large part of the fun of life. But he must know who someone is (through an introduction from a familiar adult or child) before he can make friends.

The following tips from Pinkerton's Security should be shared with your children:

- Always travel in groups or with another child.

- Stay close to others when walking to and from school or at play.

- Never talk to, walk with, or get into a car with a stranger.

- If a stranger tries to touch you or grab you, yell, and run in the other direction. Tell a responsible adult as soon as possible. Try to remember what the stranger was wear-

ing and what he or she looked like. Compare the stranger
to someone you know: Is he taller than Daddy?

- Take the same route to school every day.

- Call home whenever you'll be late.

We recommend teaching these rules to kids as soon as
appropriate, but not all at once. It's important to balance your
kids' safety with the development of their confidence that, on
the whole, the world is a pretty nice place to be. So, you might
want to talk about going to and coming from school in a group
with your child when he first starts going to school alone; and
you might want to discuss strangers with your child and several of his friends, where you can have them role-play with
you as a stranger asking them to get into the car, offering
them candy, saying a family member was hurt, and so forth.
These are excuses for getting the child to come with the adult
and should be pointed out to the child as such. Letting them
practice in a group what they would say and do is a good idea,
because the kids can talk with each other about it, reinforcing their sense of mastery about it while drilling safety procedures into routine behavior.

It is vital that you impress upon your child that there are
safe people to go to when he is out of the home and has a
problem. You can help your child get comfortable with the
idea of talking with a police officer by role-playing various
situations with him (losing bus fare, being lost). Also, it's
important to teach your child to tell you about what has happened if something upset him while he was out. You can role-
play these situations with him too (someone has been hang-
ing around the schoolyard whom he has never seen before,
someone asked him to get into a car, someone wanted to give
him candy or a toy, an adult he did not know wanted to hold
his hand in the movies). Teach your child how to use police

emergency numbers on both residential and pay phones so that he can get help when he is at home or out.

CHILD MOLESTING— NOT ALWAYS A STRANGER

Unfortunately, a large percentage of the time that a child is physically molested it is by someone whom he knows, rather than by a stranger. Often, the child has some warning, that is, the person (a relative, neighbor, or acquaintance) approaches the child a number of times, making suggestions or gestures which in some way embarrass or upset the child. Thus, it is vitally important to your child's mental and physical well-being that you not only encourage, but actively teach your child to come and tell you if anything ever happens between him and another adult which embarrasses or disturbs him in any way. Children generally respect and trust adults, and they may feel they are doing something wrong by telling their parents something about another adult. Impress upon your child that he can tell you anything.

Children intuitively sense when parents have difficulty talking about sexual issues, and often they interpret what happened to them as somehow being their fault. Because they feel they should not tell their parents what happened, they do not get the matter put into proper perspective for them, and they live with a burden of guilt that can affect them for years, perhaps seriously. Tell your child that he did nothing wrong and that it was very right of him to come to you and tell you what happened.

By encouraging your child to talk to you the first time an adult does something which upsets him, you can either put the incident in a better perspective for him if it is not a serious matter, or help head off a problem before it can get serious.

Since child molesters are not identifiable as a group (they can be rich or poor, well educated or uneducated, well dressed or raggedy, relatives or strangers), the only way your child can spot them is by their behavior. Therefore, it is important to be open with your child and teach him that there are different kinds of touching that are acceptable from different kinds of people. Affectionate touches from those in the family who love him and whom he loves are different from those same kinds of touches from other people. Tell him to come talk to you if *anyone* tries to touch him inappropriately or in any way that makes him feel uncomfortable.

Be aware if the child:

- gets upset when told of someone's impending visit,

- gets upset when told he will be left alone with someone,

- becomes rebellious in the presence of a particular adult,

- suddenly develops a rebellious attitude toward someone with whom he had had a good relationship.

These may be clues your child is trying to give you to an existing problem.

CAB MONEY

There are some situations in which a child may need to leave the place he's at even if no one is at home—for example, if he's at a party or other event and feels uncomfortable in the situation and wants to go home.

To take care of these unexpected situations, leave cab money at some jointly agreed upon place in the home, and tell the child where it is. Also, teach the child how to call for a cab so that he always has the security that he can take himself out of an uncomfortable or dangerous situation.

Sleepovers

Sleepovers give your child another view of the world—an awareness that not everybody does things as they are done in your house. Sleepovers can start for a child at an early age, although your best guide is the child's request. If your child is very young, tell the adults who will be caring for her what her nightly routine is: does she get read to, does she sleep with a light, does she get tucked in, does she sleep with a stuffed toy? Also, make your child aware of the household routine of the home she'll be visiting so she won't be surprised.

The first sleepover may be different from what your child imagined, so you should be prepared to come get the child if you get a tearful phone call at midnight. The issue to be dealt with here is separation. Learning to master being away from home and parents is an important experience for your child. But separation almost always brings some anxiety and some sadness with it, so be prepared to be soothing. Talk about the good things that will happen, and be prepared to listen to the fears and anxieties without making light of them. *Of course you're a little worried about sleeping away. Most people are a little nervous the first time. Aunt Ruth is really looking forward to baking your favorite chocolate cake with you, and cousin Gail is so excited about playing her new game with you tonight.* Involving the child in preparations for the sleepover helps as well. *What pajamas should we pack? Do you want to take your yellow jacket? What game and book do you want to pack?*

When your child gets home, give her plenty of time to talk

about the experience and how she felt. Don't intrude, but do listen to see if she was lonely or happy, and if she is interested in doing it again.

If your child is older, and is hosting a sleepover, make sure you sit down together and discuss the rules: how many people, what they will be doing, what foods will be served, where, and what the budget will be for the food. Then, relax and try to have a good time staying awake all night, because the guests probably will.

Overnight Camp

Going away to camp should be a mutual decision. Any child who is old enough to go to overnight camp is old enough to be part of the decision-making process. Decide together what the goal is for the summer: have a good time in a new environment; attend a special interest camp for drama, music, sports, computers; lose weight; develop wilderness skills or outdoor knowledge unobtainable in the city or suburbs.

Within these different kinds of camps, parents should decide how much time the child will spend at camp (usually one week to eight weeks, depending on the camp). Look for the camp that best suits your child's level of interest and personality, your price range, and the desired location.

Camp advisory services can be found in the yellow pages of the telephone directory. There is a guide to summer camps published by Porter Sargent Company, 11 Beacon Street, Boston, Massachusetts 02108. This guide lists some of the summer programs available and gives basic information about them. There is also the Parents' Guide to Accredited Camps in four regional editions published by the American Camping Association, Bradford Woods, Martinsville, Indiana

46151. Each guidebook gives comprehensive information about camps accredited by the association. Also there may be excellent local sources of information. Check your community centers, Y's, churches, synagogues, and Chamber of Commerce for additional camp information.

Your child may come home with camp suggestions she has gathered from talking with her friends. Talk with the parents of your child's friends if their children have been to overnight camp; also talk to the children. You can gain good first-hand information this way.

When you have your list of possible camps, you will need to do careful research about the specific camps you are considering. Things you'll want to learn about include: the philosophy of the camp's director, the activities, the facilities, the qualifications of everyone working at the camp, the counselor/camper ratio. When you ask about the size of the staff, remember that staff is not limited to counselors—it can include kitchen, medical, and administrative personnel. When you speak to the director of the camp, ask for the names of the families of past campers who live in your area (both those who had a good time and someone who went home partway through the season). Call the families of these campers, and ask lots of questions: What the child did; how the camp was different from what they expected; whether they would send their child again; what parts the child liked best and least; what the child said about the activities, the counselors, the facilities, and so forth.

The next step is to set up an appointment with the director or a representative of the camp. Your child will probably have questions of her own to ask at this meeting: *What do we eat for breakfast? Must we participate in all activities? What do we wear? What do the bunks look like? What time do we go to bed?* Afterwards, you and your child will sift through all the information you have, then share feelings, concerns, and hopes to make the best mutual selection possible.

Most children and their parents suffer some feelings of loss and sadness when the child leaves for camp. These feelings range from slight to overwhelming. The possibility that the child will feel homesick should be discussed even before the child leaves home. Knowing that other kids have these feelings, that they are perfectly natural, and that they will probably pass in a few days will be comforting to your child. Knowing that the family is always there as a support is very important. Make sure the child always knows where she can reach you while she is away at camp.

Apparently, the parents' own fears of separation have a lot to do with the way the child will feel. Naturally, you are going to have some concerns, but these should not be conveyed to the child because they can give her the message that she should feel bad, too. Talk to the child about the positive aspects of going to camp.

Getting letters from home may be one of the highlights of the camper's day. It's important to write because the mail is your primary contact with the child who is away, and her primary contact with you. A few days before she leaves for camp, start sending her mail. It will be a good feeling to get to camp and find mail waiting for her. When you write:

- Don't convey any of your fears or apprehensions.

- Don't make a big issue of the fact that you miss the child.

- Don't write about all the good things you're doing at home that she is missing.

- Use fun stationery.

- Ask a lot of questions about your child's life at camp.

- Ask specific questions about your child's special interests.

- Don't be formal or stodgy.

- Send cute cards, cartoons, books, magazines, new barrettes, a fun T-shirt, and, within the camp's guidelines, some goodies.

- Tell her you love her and that you're looking forward to the parents' visiting day.

It's important that both parents write. Sometimes it can be in the same letter, sometimes it should be individually. This says that both parents care. If allowed, a surprise phone call is a nice treat. Encourage your kids, before they go away, to gather their friends' addresses, so they can write to them. If there are some people your child must write to, explain why this is important and make up an address book with labels in the back already addressed for these letters. Make writing simple for her, because she will get caught up in the camp activities and time will slip by before she knows it. Expect that you will have to remind her about her "have to" letters.

If an important birthday falls while she's at camp, take her shopping before camp to buy a card. Let her sign it, stamp it, and pack it in her trunk. A week before the birthday, remind her to mail it. Children have more fun writing letters if they have interesting stationery to write on. Buy your child small writing paper with cartoons or pictures for use at camp.

Many parents experience a regular progression of feelings ranging from sadness (when the child first leaves for camp) to excitement about being able to do things they can't do when the child is at home: start a diet without having the kitchen stocked with the kid's goodies; go out to the theater; have romantic dinners; take a summer course; join an exercise class; brunch with a friend; garden; eat meals when you feel like it; eat exotic foods. Even having just one of several children away means less cooking, cleaning, car pooling.

It takes as much as several weeks for some parents to be able to enjoy the change, but planning in advance to enjoy your time alone is an attitude worth cultivating.

Pets

Before you decide to get a pet, think through with the child what his day is like now and how it will be different if you have a pet that needs care. Do an imaginary walk-through of what it will be like when the pet comes. For example, in the morning, ask your child to pretend that you have a dog. *Do you have time to walk it now?* After school, say, *Now is the time to feed and walk the dog and buy more dog food. Do you have time to do it?* This allows both of you to see where the "crunch times" will come, so you can determine that someone will always be available to take care of pet-related chores. Pet care can be scheduled and treated like any other household chore.

It's the parent's responsibility to become informed about the proper care of a pet and the financial outlay which will be involved. Get some books or pamphlets, call a vet, and talk to your local society for the care of animals so that you will know exactly what is involved. The conditions for adoption of a pet from a shelter may include that you pay for it to be altered and have its shots.

The decision about what pet to get has to be a joint one. So don't buy an animal just because your child likes it. For example, if you can't stand the idea of feeding live mice to a pet snake, or can't abide cleaning up in the street after an urban dog, think about alternative pets for your family.

Provided they are in good health, cats need little care. Frequently, two kittens are easier to raise than one, because they keep each other company and do not become dependent on people for constant stimulation. Fish require a minimal amount of daily care.

Through TV and movies, children often falsely attribute human motivations and feelings to animals. They think that pets smile when they are happy, and that pets feel sad, disappointed, and so forth. It is important that children learn that pets have characteristics of their own and have needs different from those the child wishes they would have. Birds cannot be squeezed and cuddled, fish need to live in water— *You can't take your goldfish to bed with you.* Exposure to pets helps children realize that not every living thing wants what the child wants, and that different animals (and people) need and express love differently.

The young child may be overwhelmed by the differences between what he imagines to be true and reality. In the classic story, Lassie takes care of the family and herself. In real life Lassie messes, has to be cleaned up after, has to be walked, gets sick, and needs shots. The young child may not know what it means to take care of a pet even though he pleads for one, because his understanding of what is involved may come from his fantasies about animals, not from any experience in the actual daily care of an animal. Because pets often do not meet the child's expectation that the animal will be a friend or companion, the child tires of the pet.

Besides the obvious appeal that animals have for most people, children may ask for a pet for various reasons. Maybe their friends have pets or they may want a new animal to replace an old pet. Sometimes a child may want a pet because he has little human companionship. If you sense this may be true for your child, it may be important to focus on that issue. The child may really need help in learning to socialize effectively with other children.

It usually works out better if it is understood from the beginning that the pet belongs to the whole family, even though it may be in the child's room most of the time and the child may be its primary caretaker. Children are not as consistently responsible as adults, and although you may assign pet-care chores to the child, the ultimate responsibility for the animal may rest with the adults until such time as the child can handle the pet's needs entirely on her own. She may be well into her teens before she can handle a pet herself.

You Can't Do It All

This chapter has covered a wide range of things you can do to encourage your child to accept more and more responsibilities. We've presented a smorgasbord of things you can choose from, rather than a full-course dinner that you should totally consume. Clearly no parent can do all these things all the time and no family will have perfectly behaved kids who always do all their chores or perfectly behaved parents who never lose their tempers and whose houses are always models of efficiency and neatness. In fact, the pressure to be that perfect would create exactly the kind of frazzled climate that this book is trying to help you avoid. So, use this chapter when you need it, as a resource to dip into for specific ideas for particular situations that are difficult in your house. Use it to make things easier for you.

We've presented some of the things you can do to encourage your child to accept a wider and wider range of personal responsibility. But this process takes years, and there will be wide swings in his ability to accept responsibility for his behavior, his health, his room, his chores. During this elementary-school period, the child will move back and forth between wanting you to take care of him and wanting to do things for himself. Research indicates that independence is not achieved through forcing the child out of the nest, but by assuring him of your support for as long as he needs it. At the same time you should step back when he does things differently from you, on his own, in his own way, making his own mistakes. As the child of this age matures, he will often revert to the behavior of younger ages, particularly at times of stress—when faced with a new school or a new sibling, for example. Recognizing that this regression is a temporary stage in his continuing development rather than backsliding will help you both.

No one is ever too old to be nurtured, to feel the pleasure of a pat on the back, or to enjoy the security of having a caring, ever-present family.

Handling Fights
When Parents Argue
Criticism
Adoption
Confidentiality/Embarrassed Kids
Apologies
Punishment and Discipline
Peer Pressure
Common Problems
Siblings
Moving
Fears
Drugs, Alcohol, and Cigarettes
Divorce
Sex
Death
Failure
When Mother Goes to Work
Networking
Caring for People and Showing It

5
One-on-One

This chapter deals with the times you share with your child person-to-person. The times of pure pleasure and treasured companionship usually don't need elaboration or explanation. They happen, we enjoy them, and we store them away in our bank of wonderful memories.

In contrast, the one-on-one experiences we participate in to promote growth and development in our children and ourselves are often more difficult. They concern us a great deal, and they leave us wondering if we "did it right." This chapter contains techniques that may be helpful when you find yourself in the hard, uncomfortable, even scary situations when you don't know what to do or say.

Handling Fights

Most people think of fights as the result of two people's having irreconcilable needs (like two people wanting one pencil). But rarely is that what a fight is about. Frequently a "fight" occurs because two people are trying to solve two problems at the same time. If you could get both to agree on who was going to go first and who would go second, and then try to solve each person's problem separately, most fights would be resolved easily in a way that would meet everyone's needs. Furthermore, it would be a "win-win" solution in which both people win, as opposed to a "win-lose" solution.

It's important to teach your kids that disagreements are different from fights. People can agree to disagree, and that's fine. You can hate spinach and your son love it, or vice versa.

If you want to encourage your child to develop her own opinions, even if they disagree with yours, it will help you to realize that there is no such thing as a true, or correct, opinion. By definition, an opinion is a judgment about something. Opinions are therefore different from facts (which are either true or false and can be verified).

Fights over opinions can go on forever. (*The seashore is better than the lake. The lake makes a better vacation place than the seashore. No it doesn't! Yes it does!*) Since it is hard to have an argument over facts, one way to de-escalate a conflict is to move away from opinions and get the facts on the table.

Opinion: You're seeing too many movies.
Fact: You went to the movies twice this weekend.

Opinion: You're not paying enough attention to your school-work.
Fact: We agreed that you are to spend an hour a night on your homework. Last night you spent only half an hour.

If you and your child merely have two different opinions, arguing will only solidify both positions and take you further apart. If this is the case, try to compromise. (*You like the red blouse and I like the green—that's okay. I'm sure we can find a different blouse that we both like a lot.*) Or maybe the discussion will have given one of you new insight. Maybe you'll change your mind or your child hers.

If the discussion goes back and forth more than twice (discounting each other's viewpoints), that's the time to agree to disagree and try to find a different solution.

If a disagreement is over facts, stop fighting and go get the facts. *Everybody in the class is joining the swim club.* Here, the parents' job is to check the facts. *Is* everybody joining? Will your child be the only one left out? Or is "everybody" merely three of your child's friends?

Sharing facts helps your child understand your new point. For some reason, something tends to keep parents from being really straight with kids and sharing facts which would help them understand what's going on. Tell your child, *I'm concerned about your walking home in the dark after swimming,* or whatever the facts are that make you feel you can't grant your child's request at the time.

If you have a beef with your kids, don't attribute the problem to your spouse. Don't say things like, *Your mother won't like that!* or *Just wait till your father gets home!* Attributing your feelings to your spouse causes problems because the children can't clarify things with you about how you feel— you've instructed them *not* to talk to you but to talk to your spouse instead. This imposes your feelings into the relationship between your children and your spouse, possibly interfering with the good things happening between them.

When Parents Argue

All parents quarrel from time to time, and it is important that you, your spouse, and your kids know that this is perfectly normal. Hiding quarrels from your kids (by seething silently inside while pretending that everything is okay) is almost impossible. Kids can almost always sense when there is something negative happening between their parents, and if they also sense that you don't want to talk about it with them, they will be in a difficult situation, unable to get a proper perspective on it.

When your child is upset by hearing his parents fight, and he asks you to stop, reassure him that arguing or fighting from time to time is natural in a relationship, and that it has nothing to do with him, he did nothing wrong, his parents both love him, and they love each other. An apology may be in order if your argument disrupted the child's activities. *We're sorry if we disturbed you when you were studying.*

Sometimes, children will understand what is happening if you draw an analogy to their fights with friends and siblings. *Everybody is not going to get along with everybody else all the time. But eventually you make up.* In the end, genuine love between you and your spouse and toward the kids—expressed by direct communication and by being able to joke about the subject of yesterday's quarrel—reassures the child that things are basically okay at home.

If your quarrel is about the child (should he have the new bike or not; should he go to camp or not), if you or your spouse could look bad in the child's eyes, or if the fight is particularly bitter, it may pay to find a sitter to stay with the children while you and your spouse go for a drive or walk to finish arguing it out. If appropriate, you can tell the children, *We are going out, because we want to have some time alone to settle what is bothering us.*

Fighting about the children is one of the most common forms of marital discord. And, since the issue is apt to cut to the core of values that are very important to both parents, coming to agreement may not be easy. Very often disagreements about kids arise because we, as parents, tend to behave toward our children the way our parents behaved toward us. Was it difficult for your mother to express anger? Did she tend to keep her negative feelings inside? Did your father express his anger by withdrawing, sulking, walking away, yelling? You might repeat your parents' behavior patterns with your own children. Our behavior is shaped, in part, by what happened to us when we were at the same stage of development as our children are now. When you were six years old, were you angry with your baby sister because in your opinion she got away with everything? If so, you might tend to be especially angry with your wife if you think she is spoiling your daughter. If you were raised in a household where the children had to earn everything they received, you may want to raise your children in a similar environment.

Your values were formed early in life, and you will probably strive to pass them on to your offspring. But you and your spouse may have been raised quite differently, and you will therefore find it necessary to iron out some conflicts about child rearing. Settle your differences by talking about them *before* you are faced with them. One way to do this is to set aside some time to talk with your spouse about your family histories. Consider as many important issues as you can: chores, friends, discipline, homework, allowances, working, handling money, expressing feelings. After you have a list of major items, each of you should clearly say how you felt then, and how you feel now about the way you were treated as a child in these matters. After you each thoroughly understand your own and the other's position, it is time to reach an accord as a couple. When there is disagreement about serious issues, outside advice may help. Sometimes talking with other parents with whom you both have a good relationship helps—allowing you to air your feelings and hear other viewpoints. A meeting with a professional of your choice may prove constructive. It can be a pediatrician, a minister, a priest, a rabbi, a teacher, or a mental-health professional— anyone whom both of you trust and respect and with whom you will be comfortable talking.

If you are undecided about how you will handle child-rearing issues as a couple and you get caught off guard, you will fight at the very time you need to be in agreement to tell the child what he can or cannot do. If you are unable, or unwilling, to settle on ways to handle different situations, the child may learn to play one parent off against the other.

Criticism

Criticism is generally a synonym for pointing out to someone why he isn't doing the right thing. The goal of criticism is to change someone else's behavior. Telling someone he's wrong may seem like the most straightforward way to get him to change, but that's not always the case. Why not? Because people have feelings, and if those feelings get hurt, people start paying more attention to protecting their feelings from further assault and less to correcting their mistakes.

Every message has two parts—a person component and a topic component. If a criticism focuses more on the person part of the message (*You dummy. Everyone knows better than that.*), the listener starts focusing on himself, not on the behavior that provoked the criticism. However, if the criticism focuses on the topic (*You bought white bread, but I asked you for whole wheat. What would you do differently if you were doing the job over?*), then the listener will not feel threatened, will not need to defend himself, and he can focus on changing the inappropriate behavior. In summary, when you are about to criticize your child, try to criticize his behavior, not him as a person.

Is this always possible? No, not always—because often, when our children do things wrong, we feel angry, and when we're angry we say angry, irrational things.

Some suggestions for giving criticism:

- Pick the right time and place: never in front of others. (In an emergency, take the child aside.)

- Share your data: *Your bed was not made this morning.*

*You have interrupted me three times in the last four
minutes. You did not get home until 9:30, and you had
agreed to be in at 9:00.*

- Find out what really happened, by asking: *What happened? Tell me about it.*

- Share your feelings, if appropriate, and be straight: *I'm
very angry. I'm feeling disappointed. I'm feeling
annoyed.*

- Negotiate a change in behavior, or set rules if you feel
that's appropriate. *We're agreeing that your bed will
be made tomorrow, and if not, you will not go out after
school.*

- Support your child's efforts to change: *I know chores
aren't fun, and I'm glad to see you trying to do your
share. I know how hard it is to wait to talk—I don't
even expect you to remember all the time—but I'm
glad to see you try.*

We all expect parents to criticize their children, because
one of a parent's roles is instructor. But, as in so many other
areas, one of the strongest forces in your child's learning to
take criticism gracefully is how he sees you taking it. For
example, a woman spoke to her children about continuing to
read when she was talking to them. She said, *I feel bad if you
read when I'm talking to you, because I feel you don't care
about what I'm saying.* The kids understood, and they tried
to change. A few weeks later, one of the kids tried to say
something to his mother when she was deep in a newspaper
article. He said, *You're doing just what you told us not to
do.* Fortunately she was able to pull herself out of the article
enough to realize that she should reward her child for taking
criticism well and for giving it straight. She said, *You're*

absolutely right. I can see how easy it is to get engrossed in reading and how hard it is to put it down. I apologize. What did you want to tell me?

Adoption

Adoption is a difficult topic for both parents and children. Many parents treat it as a secret, and live in fear that their child will somehow think less of them or of himself if he finds out that he is adopted.

Our best information leads us to believe that to the extent that the truth is withheld from the child, to that extent do you have potential for problems. The child who senses your discomfort with the facts of his adoption may draw the conclusion that you are uncomfortable *because* there is something wrong with him or his real parents or the facts of his birth or that there is something that you are ashamed to talk openly about.

It seems to be easier all around, on the child, the parents, and the rest of the family, if the facts of the adoption are acknowledged as simply as the fact that he is a boy and his sister is a girl. No big deal needs to be made about the adoption, but it is acknowledged openly among all family members from the time the child learns to talk.

In addition to creating confusion in the child if he feels you are withholding something from him, you expose him to the danger of the taunts of other children, who may not even know what adoption means but who sense that it is a good weapon to cause hurt. We've heard of tragic cases of children overhearing their parents talk about a classmate's being an adopted child, and then teasing the child who had never been told the truth by his adoptive parents.

It is important to prepare your child for the day when another child taunts him with *You're only adopted; you're not real.* To develop a sense of pride in your child about being chosen, you can say things like *There are two ways that people come into families—they are born into them or they are chosen into them—and we chose you.*

Help your child to feel confident that he is special because you chose to bring him into the family and you continue to be glad you chose him.

Also, you might talk with the first or second grader about name calling, and explain that sometimes when friends get mad, they are likely to express their anger by calling the person names. They pick on whatever is different, so a thin child might get called "skinny," and a child whose parents have a lot of money might be called "spoiled," and you might be called "adopted."

The younger child will probably not ask deep questions about his "birth" mother or father. If the child asks, you can simply explain that his birth mother couldn't keep him because she was too young, or still in school, or didn't have enough money to take care of him properly or whatever the situation was, and that she wanted him to have a good home. Later, when the child starts asking deeper questions about how he came to you, you can explain more fully that the agency wanted to make very sure that he had a good home, and that you had to work very hard to get him, and that you chose him out of all the other children and wanted him in particular to come to live with you.

Parents should be careful to be guided by the extent of the child's question. In your anxiety about the topic, you may dump more on him than he is ready for. Your child will probably tell you what he wants to know by the questions he asks, and if you're not sure, you can answer simply, and stay alert to see if there are further questions or if he is satisfied.

The older child may use his adoption as ammunition against the parents when he is angry about being told to do something he doesn't want to do. *I don't have to do what you say because you're not my real father!*

The father's answer should be *Yes, I am your father because I love you, I take care of you, and you live with me. And you are my child.* Accept his feelings of anger. *I know you're angry with me right now, and anger happens in all families.*

It is important to note that there are two issues here for you, the parent: one is that the child is testing to determine his place in the family and your commitment to the role of his parent. The second is the issue of the child's using his adoption as ammunition to "get away" with not carrying out his responsibilities—just as every other child tries to do. Insist that your adopted child carry out his responsibilities in the same manner as you would insist that any child do. This is made difficult if you feel guilty or ashamed about some aspect of adoption. If so, perhaps talking about it with other adoptive parents in a support group, or with your pediatrician, or a counselor or psychologist, might help you become more comfortable. What is important is that you not let your child manipulate you by his anger about being adopted into treating him differently than you would treat any other child.

Confidentiality/ Embarrassed Kids

An important issue for kids is confidentiality and trust. If your child has told you something in confidence, try not to betray that confidence. Trust lost at that level is hard to rebuild. If you do occasionally slip, an apology helps. Kids get terribly embarrassed if you tell your friends or relatives about the "cute" things they said or did. An eight-year-old boy was made miserable because his mother chatted with a friend about how "sweet" the boy looked in his new shorts and what adorable legs he had. The friend's child—a classmate of the boy—overheard the conversation and labeled the boy "adorable legs." It took the embarrassed little boy weeks to shake this hated nickname in school.

Respect your child's privacy. Don't read things the child has written if they are not meant for your eyes. Don't talk about your child with his friends or try to pump them for information that your child has not chosen to share with you. Don't tease your child in a way that might embarrass him, especially in front of his friends.

Although kids are small in size, they are frequently large in sensitivity. They embarrass remarkably easily, although they may not have the verbal facility to let you know about it. Because we sometimes don't know the norms of a child's world, we may inadvertently do things which embarrass her.

Some things that embarrass kids are preventable, however. Basically, children want the same things from you that you want from them. They want you to be appropriately dressed, for example, wearing the "right" clothes to the school play (not zooming out of the house in the clothes you were cleaning the basement in); not wearing pajamas or undershirts when friends are coming to visit; not being radically different from other parents. Your kids would like you to have respect for their activities. You want your kids to dress appropriately for synagogue, church, visiting your friends, and school; they want you to dress appropriately for their important events as well.

Kids also want us to be appropriate in speech—which again means not being too different from the norm: not talking louder than the other parents during the intermission at the school play, not being abusive to the umpire at the ball game; not using inappropriate vocabulary at a child's activity. Never use public events (school activities, another child's birthday party, the skating rink, or the bowling alley) as a time to improve the child (*your hair isn't combed; your clothes don't match; why did you talk so softly*).

Kids want their parents to be dependable. If you've promised to bake brownies, take part in the school fair, be an aide on a school trip, chair a committee, or just show up, do what you said you'd do, and do it on time.

If you embarrass the child, he may not tell you so, but he will gradually pull away from communication and closeness with you.

Apologies

Play practice ended at 3:30. At 3:30, you are still stuck in traffic on the expressway. You don't arrive until 4:00. All the other kids are gone, and your child is upset. He says angrily, *You were supposed to pick me up at 3:30. Everybody else's parents showed up on time. How come you always yell at me when I'm late?*

You're angry yourself. After all, you've been sitting in traffic for forty-five minutes, and now your kid is being fresh. Still, the only thing at issue in this situation is that your child is right—you were late, no matter how many good excuses you have. If you ever want your child to learn to apologize when he is wrong, you have to be able to do so when you are in the same, tough situation.

It is important for people to be able to say, *I'm sorry, I made a mistake*, when they did make a mistake, without feeling put down. Don't start off by listing your excuses, or pointing out that you did start out on time. Your first step should be a clear *You're right! I'm sorry I'm late.*

Sometimes you may decide that you did something wrong concerning your child only after you've thought about it. Leave a note in the child's room, take the child for a walk— away from family distractions—and say, *I'm sorry.*

Just as important, you have to help your child learn to say, *I'm sorry*, to you, and to help him recognize that none of us is perfect. No one is able to do what everyone else expects all the time. Being able to say, *I'm sorry*, without feeling over- whelmed by guilt, is an important part of a child's develop- ment, and vital to healthy interaction with the outside world. Mistakes can often be corrected by being direct, saying you were wrong, and trying to make amends for any damage.

Remember the principle of positive reinforcement. If your child apologizes for doing something wrong, you have two choices: you can say something nice about the apology, or you can say something critical about what he did wrong in the first place. If you want to encourage him to be straight about apologizing, you must take the time to reinforce that behav- ior. Say something like, *I'm very glad you apologized. I don't like the fact that you forgot to stop at the store again, but I do appreciate your apology.* This helps the child understand that you feel good about his owning up.

Punishment and Discipline

Just as adults know that they will probably be punished by fines and license revocation if they continually break traffic rules, so your children should expect that unacceptable behavior will be punished.

For better or worse, chances are good that you will punish your children the way you were punished. What we *know* is what we *do*, because we are most comfortable with it. So, it may be helpful for parents to discuss with each other how they were punished as children, how they feel about those methods, and which of them they will jointly apply to their children. There is no single right way to punish kids. A parental outburst which is soon over and which clears the air might be better for the child and the parents than a climate of suppressed anger and disapproval which lasts for days and leaves the child fearful about when the ax is going to fall.

Something that is frequently effective is removing the child from the situation in which he is misbehaving. This can be used at meals, when food fights start or when table manners do not improve after continuous instruction. Children can also be asked to leave family discussions (for constantly interrupting) or social gatherings (for inappropriate behavior).

In school settings, this type of punishment is called "time out." The child is taken away from the activities the rest of the children are doing, and left alone in a designated place to think about what has happened and what he wants to do differently next time. If you give your child a time out, don't send him into a situation which is rewarding. For example, don't send him alone to his room if that's where his favorite books and games are, or to the den if that's where the TV is. Some parents send the child to a special "time out" place or chair when he breaks a rule.

The amount of time that you leave the child alone is important. We believe it is best to leave him there for just a few minutes, and then to discuss with him what has happened; why you were upset, what rule was broken, and what he (and you, if appropriate) can do to avoid its happening again. If you leave him alone too long, you'll lose your chance to make an impact, because the incident will become too distant. Some parents allow the child to set his own time-out period; that is, he can rejoin the group when he is ready to behave.

"Docking" or "grounding" is also effective in changing persistent behaviors. You can dock the child from a TV show, from weeks of social activity, or from a specific activity. By "grounded" we mean that the child misses *all* activities in that period—his friend's birthday party if it falls in that time, the Thanksgiving parade, or whatever. To reinforce your own resolve and your child's understanding, you should make it clear that you mean business by saying to the child as the special day approaches, *I'm sorry you have to miss the* _____.

Another punishment is to set a non-negotiable time for doing what he was supposed to do. If the clothes on the floor are reaching the high-water mark, you can say, *You may not go to swim-club practice today; you must come home and clean your room. And, if you cannot get it under control and keep it under control, you will have to give up* _____ *for next session, because it seems you can't fit school and sports and orchestra and chores into your schedule.*

If you use this procedure, never pull the child out of the big game, or practice for the school play the week before it's going on, or anything that will seriously affect his status at school or with the other members on his team.

Having the child do compensatory activities for misbehaving, is another form of punishment. This is a little like a court assigning someone who has broken the law to some public-service duties for a period of time to make up for what he did. The child may be assigned to rake leaves, or to shovel snow, or to do an extra week of washing dishes, or to do any chore which the family needs to have done.

We've heard of parents who punish their kids by assigning them to do things that they want the children to learn to value. (For example, the child who misses a book report is told,

You have to listen to the symphony.) We don't recommend using as a punishment the things you'd like your child to develop a positive attitude toward. The child will naturally feel angry about the things you are using as punishment, and will probably develop a correspondingly negative attitude. Thus, don't assign extra practice to the child who didn't practice the piano. You might "ground" the child tomorrow afternoon and insist that he practice that day, but don't link the practicing with punishment.

If you need to punish your child, make the punishment appropriate for her age and appropriate to the goal you have in mind for changing her behavior. Also, it's important to remember that you and your child are human, and part of being human is making mistakes. Sometimes you're going to lose your temper and punish your kids for things that you'll later wish you hadn't, or in ways that you'll wish you hadn't. Likewise, your child will be sorry she broke the rules or misbehaved. That's part of being a parent and a kid. When you're wrong, apologize; then forgive yourself and let it go.

The punishment should always convey to your child that you want her to change a certain behavior but *not* to change her essential self. When you punish your child, you are punishing her for what she did, not for what she is.

Punishment *will* often cause an immediate change in behavior. Scolding Jane for hitting her sister will probably get her to stop while you are watching, but it is less likely to guarantee a permanent change than other forms of discipline. A procedure more likely to bring about permanent change is positive reinforcement. This means what your grandmother said more poetically: *You can catch more flies with honey than with vinegar.*

How does it work? Watch for opportunities to notice your child being good. Reward her for doing things you want her to continue to do, rather than punishing her for doing things you don't want her to do. Since children want your love and attention, they will most likely focus on the things you focus on. For this reason, you should focus on what your child is doing *right* rather than what she is doing wrong. Besides, a child who hears about her faults all the time will have much lower self-esteem than a child who hears a balanced presentation of her strengths and weaknesses.

Does this mean that you should ignore anything your child does wrong? Definitely not. But it does mean that, if you watch, you can frequently spot your child practicing behavior you would like her to repeat. By praising her for acting correctly, or better than last time, you increase the chances of her doing the right thing in the future. For example, Paul had problems doing his homework. His father decided to apply positive reinforcement principles to the situation. He kept quiet the next night, when Paul did *not* do his homework. But the following night, when Paul did do part of his homework, Paul's father made it a point to comment about several good things in the homework. He said he was very pleased that Paul had remembered to sit down and do his work without any reminding. He asked what Paul had done to get himself to remember the homework, and was geniunely delighted with Paul's response: *I set the oven timer to go off at 7:30 so I'd be sure to begin on time* (which is what Paul and his father had discussed). It takes a lot of patience to ignore behavior you don't like in favor of rewarding behavior you do like. But try experimenting to see if, in the long run, it takes less time than constantly nagging and fighting over long-standing discipline problems.

No matter what method of punishment you use, what's important is that the child realizes (through hearing you say it many, many times) that the punishment is because of the specific thing he did. It does *not* signal a withdrawal of your love for him, even though you may be angry. We've heard parents express this by telling their kids something like, *My job as a parent is to risk telling you when I think you're wrong even if you get angry with me. When I do that, it doesn't mean I don't love you; it means I don't want you to continue doing that thing.* Finally, once the punishment is done, it should be finished with forever. The incident should not be referred to again.

Punishment is a short-term, immediate reaction to specific broken rules. Discipline is the long-term development of an internal sense of responsibility for doing what one knows one should. Your child's long-term commitment to meeting goals comes, in part, from day-to-day activities which help him understand what he is supposed to do. For example, the calendars you build with him show what he has to prepare for; the chore charts show him what he has to do and when; family meetings show him how discussion enables family members to get what they need. When rules are broken you want to correct the situation immediately. You also need to take steps to prevent the same thing from happening again. For example, after you've punished your child for not keeping his room clean, you should sit down with him to discuss how he will keep the room clean in the future. Saying, *You've got to be more responsible,* is too broad a demand for your child to carry out. What is needed is a training plan he can follow.

There are two ways to evolve such a plan. One way is for the two of you to decide on specific steps for him to follow. If, after a while, that doesn't work, then *you* should decide what steps he should take, and impose them. Such training plans can be:

- Your child might get up ten minutes earlier to clean his room.

- You might change your requirements to meet your child's limitations. (In discussion, you may find, because of the child's schedule, he is able to clean only three days a week, so the room will be a little messier the other days.)

- Your child might trade off with one of his siblings, getting help with one task in exchange for doing another task that is easier for him. (If his sister, Mary, keeps her room neat but hates to clean up after dinner, they could trade: Mary will do both rooms if her brother will clean up after dinner.)

- You might reach an agreement with your child that says, *Your room is yours and you decide how you want to keep it. Whatever you decide is all right with me.* If you do this, set up any rules in the beginning. Don't expect your children to live by rules that are not made explicit and agreed upon. (One rule may be, *No food is to be left in your room because if it attracts ants, the whole household will be affected.*) If you decide on this option you've got to stick to it. If it upsets you to see an empty closet and two feet of clothing piled up on the floor, then don't go into his room.

- As a last resort, you may have to ground the child and insist that he miss something else in order to make time to clean his room. This will involve a discussion about the fact that there are only twenty-four hours in each day, and if he has piled too many things into his day, something has to go; when he gets his act together, he can begin to add more to his daily schedule.

Keeping his room clean is, of course, only an example of the many tasks that seem to generate continuous parent-child tension and conflict. We've handled this task in detail because it is such a common problem.

There's no clear-cut answer to the question, *Should parents remind their child about things he has agreed to do that day?* A reminder may be really helpful until a new chore becomes a habit. But too much helpful reminding may turn into nagging. Be sensitive to how you're coming across, and when in doubt, ask.

Our concept of discipline is similar to on-the-job training, where, rather than punishing the employee when he does the wrong thing, the supervisor builds a clear, step-by-step training plan for what the employee is to do, and then supervises him closely as he learns. The bad news is that you can't fire your kid when he does the wrong thing. The good news is the positive feeling when things go right.

There's no need to be particularly creative about punishment. The punishment should be clear, simple, and directly related to what the child has done. What's important is that the child learn that if he breaks a rule, something will happen to him. Children need to learn why rules are important: that breaking a rule causes everybody harm, and that being responsible means doing the things which benefit the family, community, society, and themselves—even when no one is watching. If you are feeling especially angry, however, it is advisable that you remove yourself from the situation until you have cooled off somewhat.

The issue of corporal punishment is a controversial and difficult one. The application of physical punishment is not a disciplinary method we recommend. Hitting the child changes the issue from one of helping her to master her own internal lack of control into one of a power struggle which teaches the child to do what the parent says because the parent is bigger, and bigger is "right." Parents should be able to say, *no,* or *do it now!,* and make it stick by helping the child develop her internal capacity to respond to her parents' demands. This learning is imperative if she is going to cope with the demands of school, work, and adult society.

THE ABUSED CHILD

For many reasons, the tensions of an intense relationship with a dependent child get to be too much for some parents to handle. We've all experienced to some degree the feeling that, *If that child asks me that one more time, I'm going to scream.* When this feeling gets out of control, it may be expressed in physical violence against the child. Most of us at one time or another have hit a child out of frustration and anger, but few of us do it repeatedly. The abused child is the child whose parent is so enraged by the pressures he or she feels, that he or she doesn't stop hitting. In fact, the expression of the anger can make the parent more and more angry, creating an escalating spiral of violence against the child. An incident which normally would merely upset a parent and provoke a needed reprimand may enrage this parent beyond control and result in severe arm twisting or beating or worse.

If you feel yourself losing control over your reactions to your children, there are agencies which can offer help. Many cities have child-abuse prevention centers, which you can locate by calling your city-government information center or the reference room at your local library. Also, the police can refer you to your closest agency, hot line, or self-help group.

Peer Pressure

Training children to form their own opinions, and to withstand peer pressure to do things they really don't want to do,
should begin very early. Don't wait till the child is a teenager
to teach him to stand up for what he believes. Why? Because
the ability to make decisions on one's own grows out of early
parent-child interaction. If the child is always told he's wrong
in discussions with his parents, then he'll carry that image of
being wrong into his relationships with his peers. If he feels
like a valuable person, he will not be driven to find acceptance among his friends by doing what they want—the mer-
its of the activity, rather than who proposes it, will determine
what he does.

What helps to develop this sense of self-worth which allows
the child to withstand peer pressure? Well, high on the list is
respectful communication between you and your child—particularly if he has received your approval for his ideas. Also, a
sense of self-worth is aided by your prohibiting yourself, others, and especially the child himself, from putting "failure"
labels on him (like dummy, clumsy, irresponsible, thought-
less). Practice in the home of making and sticking to decisions, even unpopular ones, gives him a sense of his right to
have opinions different from other people's.

Peer pressure is often seen by parents as "those people out
there making demands." Bring "those people" into the home,
so you know who your child's friends are, what kind of people
they are, what activities they participate in, what ideas they
have. Even if you are a very busy parent it's important to find
time to meet your child's friends. Inviting friends for dinner,

picking them up at activities, encouraging your children to have their friends over to watch the big game or to play at your house on the weekends are excellent ways to be aware of what is going on. If someone seems to be especially important to your child, and you have concerns about him, invite him on a family outing so you have time to see if your fears are well founded.

Your children may tell you about kids who do things you do not approve of, about kids who vandalize, smoke, drink, or use drugs. This leaves you with a decision to make: and the one that we favor is to butt out. Make the climate acceptable for your kids to come home and talk, so that you are their confidant. Listen! But you are *not* the school detective. Some of it may be mere gossip, some of it may be distortion, and some of it may be true. What is relevant is that your kids know what they think is right to do; that the kids feel comfortable coming home and talking about what they see, what they are feeling, and what they plan to do.

Teach kids to remove themselves from a situation in which they feel uncomfortable: a fight on the school playground; drugs or drinking at a party; "everyone" going someplace to play that isn't appropriate, or doing something that is against the law.

Teach your kids to say, *I don't know if I can come*, or *I don't know if I can do that—I'll let you know*. Children may not want to go to each and every party they're invited to. When a child is asked, he might not know how to handle it. Saying *I don't know if I can come that day—I'll let you know* buys him the time to think about it and talk to you, without sounding like a baby (*I'll have to ask my mother*).

Finally, try not to set up situations that will be hard for your child to handle. For example, if you are away from home often, there may be pressure on your child: *Let's go to your house; there's nobody home!* The child should know what the rules of the house are (No guests in the house when parents are away unless the parents have agreed to it in advance) so he'll feel comfortable saying to others, *No one goes to my house unless my parents are there. If you want to go to my house, let's arrange to do it when my mom and dad are there.*

Common Problems

Regardless of how happy the family is, there are bound to be some events that create hassles—for example, the event at school which requires items to be collected and delivered; the family dinner for which everyone has to be showered, dressed, and out by a certain time; the big homework assignment or work project. There are also some daily experiences that cause tensions. We've listed responses to some of the common child refrains that drive parents up the wall.

"*I want . . . newer, bigger, better . . .*" Toy manufacturers and doll companies make money only when people buy their products, so companies keep coming out with new and different products, though not necessarily better ones. Children are aware of new products from watching TV ads, and they ask for what they have seen. In that situation, talk to the child about how much time he has spent playing with the old item. When a child asks you for a newer toy he already has a similar version of, talk to him about it. Get him to think about the costs and benefits of the new toy. Ask questions like, *How much time have you played with your truck lately? When your friends come over, what have you been doing with them?* Often this will reveal his interest at the current time, and whether or not a similar toy is really the thing he will play with. Suppose the child says, *But the reason I'm not playing with my old truck is it doesn't have a new electronic dump the way the new one will.* Then the understanding has to be that there is always a choice to be made—if he has two of one thing, he'll be missing one of something else. This is a cost-benefit analysis; for every benefit, there is a cost. One of the things that separates children from adults is that children don't have to think about the costs—in money, energy, resources—or the benefits they receive. The older the child, the more he should be made aware of these trade-offs. Involve the child in the decision-making process. If the child helps decide what he wants, he has a commitment to what he's bought. And, the more he knows about the costs of his decision, the clearer his commitment will be.

"I'll do it later." Kids have a variety of excuses for not getting tasks done. We're sure you'll recognize them: *I'll do it later. I didn't have enough time. I thought I could finish it. I forgot.*

Your child can understand that when you pour too much milk in a glass, the milk spills over. You can use this as an analogy to packing too many activities into too little time. It's helpful to teach a young child about time management by making time concrete. Work up a short-range calendar—for the after-school period or a weekend, and then have the child help you write in the activities he is planning and the time in which he aims to do them.

The next step for teaching time management is to build a schedule when the child has a long-term project for school. All of us have memories of last-minute panic to get projects in on time. Help the child look at the steps that have to be done: go to the library (walk, bike, or ask someone to take her), do the research, draw the pictures, design the cover, write the report, assemble the report. Have the child write down how long each step takes, and then fit the steps into the schedule. This kind of training is important to help children learn to break complex jobs down into achievable steps to meet time-tables.

The ability to plan for goals is the hallmark of a successful person. All managers (be they managers of a household or of a corporation) know how to plan the steps necessary to reach their goals. In fact, as we get older, we need to be able to manage not just our own schedules but those of other people (children, employees, people on our committees, and so forth). These skills are not mastered all at once: they need to be learned. When you build a scheduling calendar with your children, it gives them a tool for mastering valuable planning skills. This allows children to see how their days can be stretched and used profitably, or just used up.

"He took the biggest slice." Lots of hassles can be avoided with some simple techniques for teaching fairness. "He took the biggest slice" problems can be eliminated by having one child cut and the other child get the first choice of what slice he wants.

The "She took the red balloon and I wanted that one" problem can be handled by flipping a coin for it, guessing a number from one to ten that the parent thinks of, or having one child choose this time, and the other child choose first the next time there is a conflict. (This puts you in the role of monitor of whose turn it is, but it does limit squabbles.)

"You got him a present and you didn't get me one." It's important to help your children realize that they will all get their needs met, but that because they are different people, they will get things at different times. Sometimes you may want to bring home a book that Rob's been looking for, and another time Jeff may need a new sweater. Don't get trapped into feeling that being fair means bringing the same thing to each of your kids each time you buy something for any one of them. If you are even-handed about distributing presents, your children will learn to handle their natural feel-

ings of jealousy. Help them learn to be pleased when a sibling gets something nice.

Siblings

You want to say right from the very beginning, *You and your brother (sister) are very special to each other because you are siblings.* That's an umbrella concept that says you hope brothers and sisters will remain close throughout their lives. You, the parent, need to build up the kind of affection that will override the intense short-term rivalries and disputes that frequently occur between siblings.

From the time a child goes off to his first birthday party, you can encourage him to bring home some candy or peanuts for his sister or brother. If a child goes on a class trip and he is allowed spending money for himself, give him a little extra to buy a present for each of his brothers or sisters.

Even though each child has his own friends and his own activities, siblings should go some places together—the zoo, for example, or a science museum. That way they are together not only for chores like raking the leaves but also to enjoy themselves and talk about fun things.

Make sure they remember each other's birthdays and special days. Help them to make gifts or contribute to their buying gifts for their siblings. Also encourage each child to be thoughtful in noticing the differences between himself and his siblings. For example, if he sees a book on tennis that his sister would like and points it out to you, commend him on his caring attitude.

Foster some things that they do together well—making a special dish at a family dinner; taking care of part of a family celebration. These shared happy events help build bonds which will outlast petty bickering.

Use the expertise of the brother or sister who has already gone to school, scouts, or sports; encourage an older sibling to talk about the new school—how to take the school bus, where to stand in line for lunch, where to go if you have to get an early dismissal. Allow each child to be helpful to the others. Encourage kids to ask, if they are going to the store or the library, *Do you need anything while I'm there?* Also, encourage them to be aware of and to attend each other's special activities: scout programs, sporting events, school plays, and so forth. Encourage the children to ask for and use their siblings' opinions on clothes, movies, books, and activities. Encourage them to share information, not only at the dinner table, but more personally with each other.

If you notice any intensification of rivalry and fighting between siblings, it may be a symptom of something else. A discussion is in order to find out if the hostility is being displaced from outside onto the "safer" target of the sibling. If a child is upset with a new teacher, he may fight more with his sister, because he knows better than to pick a fight with the teacher and he feels helpless and angry about the situation. Your discussion with the hostile child may uncover a real problem which needs attention.

Sibling rivalry can be reduced by assuring each child of your love for him, so that he doesn't feel the need to compete with his siblings for it, and doesn't feel the need to put a sibling down in order to appear better in your eyes. Focusing on each child's individual strengths can help reduce the conflicts.

Siblings will fight—that's a truism—but it's not necessarily bad. It teaches them how to stand up for their own interests, to handle competition and rivalry, being a winner sometimes and being a loser at other times. We want to emphasize that siblings are almost always very strongly attached to one another, and care very much for each other. What makes their relationship so intense when they are mad at each other is not just their being angry, but being angry with someone they care so much about. Siblings can probably be left to handle their own fights up to the point where bodily or property harm may occur. Then you should step in to establish some sort of cooling-off period.

THE NEW BABY

When a new baby joins the family, various feelings are stirred up in older siblings. A youngster who previously felt himself to be the center of his parents' universe may be shocked to have to share their attention with this intruder who not only takes a lot of his family's time and attention, but can't even do anything interesting like play ball. Of course, you will have to prepare the older child as much as possible. Talk about what the baby will be like, and involve the child in planning where the baby will sleep, where its clothes will be kept, what kinds of things he can do for the baby when it comes. This is the time to think about the times you will spend with the older child without the baby. Do some planning yourself to protect those times. And think about the things you can do to recognize the older child's status as someone who is growing up.

Children react differently to a new brother or sister. Some children may be openly angry; others may become babyish to regain the love they feel they're losing and try to share the baby's bottle or even begin bed-wetting again. On the other hand, a youngster may appear to have nothing but love for the baby and devote himself to the baby with care and concern. It is just as important to assure the very loving older sibling of his worth and your love by involving him in activities that don't include the baby. He needs to be reassured that he has roles and a value in the family other than as a "good brother" or "good sister."

Never discourage an older sibling from verbally expressing his anger at his parents and the new baby for the disruption and intrusion in his life that the infant brings. Let him know that if he says negative things to you, he in no ways risks losing your love. Assure him that it is okay for him to feel anger and to tell you about it. Allow him to lash out verbally, though not physically, to express his hurt feelings. In this way he can learn to gain control of his anger.

Moving

Parents need to recognize that moving is a separation and loss issue for children, requiring parental support and empathy. Separation from the people, places, and things to which the child is accustomed causes the underlying anxiety about a move. Reassure her that contact with the familiar will be maintained. *We will write letters and call old friends.* This linkage is important for her. She will reflect back on the old; tell her the old was fine and that the new will also be fine in time. *Emphasize reattachment;* assure the child that attachment to new people, places, and things will take a little time, but it *will* happen.

Don't defend the need for the move. It is a normal process and one for which you need not be defensive. Make clear that the move is a big step for the family as a whole. *We're in this together, and we will help one another with this move. Our family will be together, we will make new friends together and explore the new neighborhood.* Changing environments is a normal occurrence, and the anxiety is temporary. Remind the child of things that she was uncomfortable about when they were unfamiliar but that she likes now—people, school, sports, dancing, or whatever.

Every year, one in five families moves. Well-organized planning is a necessity to prepare for the move. Gather and preserve the records that have to go with your family—medical, dental, sports achievement certificates, and so forth. Make arrangements with someone at your child's school for the transfer of her records to the new school. Often schools will not give you the records to take yourself. Find out about the admissions policy of the school your child will be attending. If she is going to a private or parochial school, you may need a few months' lead time for admissions work to be completed.

Parents need to put themselves in their kid's shoes, imagine the child's concerns about the move. Only then can they help to alleviate the child's worries. Young children may not have a realistic grasp of what it means to move. They don't know exactly what they are leaving behind, and they certainly don't know what they will find ahead of them. Make yourself available for extra listening time, so whatever the child needs to say is heard. Help her share her concerns, so that those that are unrealistic can be dealt with.

Children in a new place are a little like foreigners entering a new land. The younger the child the more concrete you need to be when discussing the move. Describe the new house and the school. *It's near the science museum and around the corner from the tennis court.* If the children haven't seen the new school and house, parents should take pictures when they visit the new neighborhood prior to the move. Go to the library and get books about the new area to read as a family. Ask the Chamber of Commerce, tourist bureau, and your realtor in the new community for as much information as they have about the new area that will help you give your child a view of their new home.

Make it your business to find out what is available in the new community that will be of particular interest to your child. If possible, enroll your child in a favorite activity before the move. This will give her something exciting to think about. Without advance planning, you may arrive in your new location only to find that you have just missed the registration deadline for enrolling her in an art class or getting her on a sports team.

Order stationery for the child with her new address printed on it. Help her gather the addresses of all the people with whom she plans to keep in touch.

Make a moving calendar. Put everybody's important dates on it—last baseball game, end-of-term banquet, awards presentation. If possible, try to schedule the move so that the child will not miss any event she has long awaited.

Put on the calendar a day for her to make the important decisions about what to take and what to leave behind. Schedule packing time, and involve your child in the packing. She can make inventories, label boxes, and pack things like sheets and towels, while the adults pack breakable and heavy items. Allowing the child to be part of the packing and cleaning-out process reduces her sense of loss. In the moving process do not throw away objects that are meaningful to the child. Let her take anything she wants from the old house to bring to the new. Old items can be thrown out after you are established in your new home. Don't view the move as an opportunity to get rid of her old toys, stuffed animals, and so forth. Because they are familiar they may be more important to her now than they have been in the recent past.

Help your child answer the question which will prey heavily on her mind during the move: *Where will I fit in?* Basically your goal is to strengthen the family unit during this move, because the child really has no one else during this transition. Everything has to be replaced—friends, teachers, ways of doing things. The child needs to know that she is accepted and loved. Maintain familiar routine wherever possible.

Because the move probably involves separation from friends or family you care about, the feelings of sadness and loss as you leave them will be real for you as well as your child. But there are things you can do to make it somewhat easier. Start talking well in advance about what's going to happen on moving day. *We're going to pack the car, and the moving truck will come . . .* Ask your child to talk to you about how she thinks it is going to feel to say good-bye to her friends. When you arrive at your new home, allow the child to be part of the unpacking process. Let her arrange her own room, decide where things will go. It doesn't have to be perfect, and it gives her something to do and think about, which is important if she is feeling lonely.

Keep old traditions. If you always go to church on Sunday, even if you're not unpacked and can barely find two shoes that match, go to church. If it's somebody's birthday, get that person a cake and celebrate, no matter how busy you are.

Develop new traditions. If you've always lived in a warm climate, and you move to a place that's cold, throw a "first snow" party, or celebrate fall because *we've never had changing leaves before.* Or, if you're moving to a warmer climate, buy new bathing suits for the children.

It is essential that you spend adequate time helping your child make new friends and start attending the new school with ease. New home, new friends, new school, new neighborhood—these are the elements that add up to a difficult transition period for children. You can help by being accepting of your child's anxieties and being available with love and understanding.

Fears

Fears, like other strong feelings, are something a child can master only to the extent that he is able to put them into words and then can deal with them. If you ridicule a child's fears, or "explain" to him why they are unreasonable, you compound the child's problems by teaching him to feel guilty or foolish about having those apprehensions. Frightening or shaming a child by calling him a baby or throwing him into deep water as a way of making him swim tends to make fears deeper, rather than assisting the child in overcoming them.

When you take the child's feelings seriously, your child can talk to you about unbearable feelings, and will be able to get the help he needs. Often, once the child expresses difficult feelings, he can then take steps to resolve his own problems.

If your child expresses a fear of something (dogs, lightning, his parents' going away), take the time to explore his feelings in depth. Encourage your child to put his fears into words. Accept his feelings; don't disparage what he says. Give him all the information you have that is appropriate for his age. If you are secretive in a particular situation and there is unexplained tension in the household, the child may become fearful. Talk to others who may have information that will help your child. If the fear is not resolved easily, you might consider talking to the family doctor, other parents, or a mental health professional.

If the child is afraid of a specific object, like dogs, you may be able to lessen the fear through a series of steps which will have him approach a dog with you while he is feeling safe. First, show him how you enjoy petting the dog and how you have a good time playing with it. Then, very gradually, invite the child to come closer and closer to the dog, while you pet it at the same time. If there are other children the same age as your child, it helps to have them pet the dog and play with it too. Encourage the child to pet the dog himself, if he wishes. If he doesn't, keep letting him see you pet and play with a dog. Never force a child to pet an animal. Patience and time are important factors in overcoming a fear of animals.

Around the age of five or six a child begins to worry about what happens to his house and family when he is not home. This sometimes causes a fear of going to school. The child is afraid that something bad will happen to his loved ones or his home if he is not there. Take the time to explain to your child where you are when he is on the way to school, at school, during recess, at lunch, at after-school activities. Relating your schedule to his will help him create a visual picture of where you are. Show him a clock set to the time when you will see each other again. Be on time during any period when your child is experiencing fears about the welfare of his family. If you must be late, call to explain why.

We've taken one common childhood fear, fear of the dark, to illustrate ways of coping with a fear. *I'm afraid of the dark* (whether openly expressed or apparent by a child's reluctance to go to bed) can make bedtime a nightly hassle. Often the child does not understand what he is afraid of and as a result cannot tell you about his difficulty. Shadows encountered in a dark bedroom can be a source of terror for a child. Find any object whose shadows may appear scary and help the child see which light is casting the shadow. Many things look different at night. The tree which sways so peacefully outside the window all day, suddenly casts a scary shadow at night; the chair with clothes piled on it looks like a lurking monster. Look for these things during the day, and then associate them with nighttime shadows.

One way to help make shadows understandable and even fun for kids is to create your own shadow project, called "Silhouette." A silhouette is an outline of a person or thing viewed from the side, and filled in, usually in black. Ask someone to sit between a bright light (sunny window, candle, lamp) and a smooth wall on which you've hung a piece of light-colored paper. Focus the person's shadow on the paper by having him move closer to or farther away from the light. Talk to your child during this process about the shape of the shadow depending on how far the object is from the light source. When the person's shadow is the size your child wants it to be, have the child draw the silhouette on the paper. Then remove the paper from the wall, put a piece of black paper behind the tracing, and cut out the silhouette on both pieces of paper. It is very effective to mount the dark cut-out on light paper. Do a silhouette of every member of the family.

Anything unexpected can be frightening. Children often are upset because shadows suddenly appear in their rooms at night. They may be startled by the lights going on in a neighbor's house, a sudden light in the street, a traffic light casting shadows, or a neon sign on a store window. You can help your child lose any fear of these shadows by preparing him for their appearance. Stay with him while it starts to get dark, and watch for these shadows to appear so you can explain what is happening. The next night, let him explain the process to you. Anything that can be predicted or explained is easier to handle than something mysterious.

Allowing your child a night light in the bedroom can sometimes help ease a fear of the dark. Likewise, leaving the door to his room open, with a hall light on, can help reduce fear. A flashlight allows the child to feel in control of the dark, without having to get out of bed to turn on a light. By flashing his light around the room, the child can reassure himself and then can turn over and fall asleep. Company, in the form of a familiar soothing record, can also help your child relax and fall asleep. Be sure to use a record player that turns off automatically.

Sometimes children develop a fear that something is in the room with them. It is important to take the time to assure the child that you take his fear seriously. Search the room with the child, if that's what he would like, to help him see for himself that nothing is there. Examine closets, drawers, under the bed. Ask the child, *Where else should we look?* Do not say, *There is no such thing as a monster, ghost,* whatever. Belittling a child's fears will only convey to him the idea that he cannot really discuss them with you. It does nothing to help him learn to deal with his own fears. By searching with him, he sees for himself that there is nothing in the room. Search as often and as completely as necessary when your child wants you to.

Drugs, Alcohol, and Cigarettes

A common, but surely anxiety-provoking aspect of being a parent is teaching children how to deal with the wide range of chemical stimulants and depressants that are so much a part of today's society. These substances range from aspirin to cigarettes to alcohol to marijuana to tranquilizers. They offer the potential for abuse and they are readily available to your child. It is totally unrealistic to expect to isolate any child from our society's drug culture.

Because of seeming acceptability, children think of these substances as part of everyday life. Even those children who do not smoke or drink know others who do. The medicine cabinet has been promoted to the twentieth century's answer to all problems. Taking a pill, smoking dope, or taking a drink have become solutions to everything, whether one is feeling up, down, sad, nervous, or afraid.

Children need to understand that life is sometimes boring, sometimes lonely, sometimes distressing, sometimes unhappy. They also must learn that taking a drug to get through a difficult situation doesn't allow them to gain the strength they'll need for dealing with life's unpleasantnesses.

Parents have three tasks in teaching their children about the use of various substances:

- Education—telling your child about the substances she will be exposed to and what their effects are

- Modeling—demonstrating appropriate behavior to your child to set a good example

- Setting limits—making clear what your rules for substance use are

Education. Learn as much as you can about these substances so you can be clear and straight with your child. Magazines and newspapers are excellent sources for the latest information. Keeping abreast of what's new is important since certain fad drugs seem to become a major problem almost overnight, like "angel dust" (PCP).

Drug, alcohol, and cigarette use should not be discussed in moralistic terms with your child, nor should their use be presented as a privilege of adulthood. The dangers associated with the use of these substances are real and should be presented that way.

Do not exaggerate. Overwrought claims of danger will only undermine your credibility. The real consequences of substance abuse are a far better deterrent than old wives' tales. The dangers can be spelled out in a nondramatic fashion.

Encourage drug and alcohol education programs in your child's school. There is often a stigma attached to these programs by people who believe they indicate there is already a problem. Think about these programs as preventive medicine, something like taking your child for an annual check-up at the physician or encouraging her to eat properly.

Educate yourself so that you are knowledgeable about the street names and catch phrases associated with the drug scene. In this way you will be alerted to your child's possible use if she begins adopting drug related jargon.

Modeling. You cannot live your child's life for her. Ultimately, the crucial decisions will be up to her. But what you can do is establish a clear sense of what you consider a responsible role to be for her and provide her with the basis for making informed, reasonable decisions.

Look inside yourself to sort out your own feelings and to determine your own values. How do you honestly feel about smoking and the use of alcohol and other drugs? What do you consider abuse? Sort out these feelings critically and then square them against your social behavior. Talk these feelings over with your spouse. Only after you clearly have defined your own principles will you be prepared to offer guidance to your child. Your value system will be the first one she will try out, but it will not be received in a vacuum. As children grow, they come in contact with many different life styles.

You serve as a role model for your child. Remember that you probably administered her first drugs to her, whether it was a teaspoon of cough syrup or an aspirin. A child can be taught at an early age to respect medicine, to use it only in carefully monitored situations and only when it is absolutely necessary. Children should not get their own medicine or be allowed to dose themselves. Poison control centers report that the two most common child overdoses are of aspirin and vitamins. When children are given medicine, they should be told exactly what its purpose is and why the special circumstances call for its usage.

Just as parents give their children their first exposure to medications, so they also provide the first example of adult use of substances like alcohol and cigarettes. Your teenage child may reach for a cigarette as a symbol of adulthood. So, if you are a smoker and do not want your child to smoke, the most powerful lesson you could give would be to stop yourself. Similarly, if you drink and do not want your child to use alcohol, make sure that you only drink moderately.

If you do smoke or drink or take some form of drugs, then discuss with your child your reasons for doing so, how and when you started, and how you feel about it. If you feel you have made bad choices which you now regret, be open about this.

Setting limits. Don't be afraid to say no. This is an area that is non-negotiable. Maintain your firmness. Listen to what your child has to say, but be prepared to refute arguments. Tell her that most drugs are illegal, addictive, and harmful to the body and mind.

Set clear rules. Don't be afraid to repeat yourself—just make sure your child understands what is acceptable and what isn't. Cut off discussions about what other children are doing by making it clear that your family has its own rules and regulations by which the child must abide.

Remind your child that she can always leave a situation where she doesn't feel comfortable. Be sure she has a way out of a situation if she wants to leave. Give her money for transportation or let her know where she can call you.

Don't hesitate to forbid your child to use drugs of any kind. This is not an infringement of her rights; it is a protection of her health and is your responsibility. This is possible, however, only if your child understands the ground rules or the limitations and the reasons behind them. Be strict when it's called for.

OVERCOMING THE ATTRACTION OF SUBSTANCE ABUSE

- Help your child develop respect for her body. Explain that these substances break down her body's good health and have a negative impact on her mind.

- Set a good example by showing the same respect for your body. Participate with your child in activities that help reinforce a health-oriented life style.

- Be aware of the prevalence of pushers in your child's school. They may be fellow students or other children or adults who hang around the schoolyard. Pushers invade all schools—public and private. Teach your child how to say no to anyone who offers her something to try that will make her feel good. She should say *No, I'm not interested* and then get away from the person offering the substance. Make sure your child does not carry around a lot of money, making her a target for a pusher.

- It is important that your child be occupied after school. She should not be coming home to an empty house with nothing to do and with liquor and medicine cabinets easily accessible.

- Be aware of why children take drugs. Many say they do because the drugs make them feel good. Make sure you build things into your child's life that make her feel good without turning to drugs. There is a time for doing chores and schoolwork, but there is also a time for relaxation and fun. If you point out to your child how she can and does have a good time through her own efforts and does not need artificial means to help her feel good, she will develop a sense of mastery and pride useful in rejecting the enticements of drugs.

WHAT TO IF YOU
FIND YOUR CHILD
EXPERIMENTING WITH DRUGS

- Don't panic or run for a mental health professional or the police.

- Listen to your child. Talk with her to determine if her use was a one time experiment or if she really has a problem she was trying to run away from.

A child who sneaks a beer or a drink of liquor from the family bar or who puffs a cigarette or a joint in the attic once or twice is not a juvenile delinquent. She may just be growing up and be curious about the world around her. Such experiments call for very firm action and a laying down of the family law, but they are not reasons to get hysterical. Of course, within any family there is the possibility that a child might develop a real problem, and part of your responsibility as a parent is to be sensitive, to recognize unusual behavior when use has gone beyond infrequent experimentation, and to try to solve the problem. Then, if you are unable to solve the problem, seek professional advice and support.

Divorce

It's a rare elementary-school-aged child who has no aware-ness of divorce. Your child is certain to have had some expo-sure to this fact of twentieth-century life if he watches televi-sion, listens to conversations between adults, reads maga-zines, newspapers, and so forth. Almost all children will know friends, classmates, cousins, or neighbors whose par-ents are divorced. Because divorce is a part of life and some-thing that has probably touched all of us in some way, you as parents need to be ready to discuss this topic with your chil-dren.

When your child has questions about the dissolution of a marital relationship, try to provide some simple, factual answers to his questions about why this is happening. If there are children in the family where the adults are divorc-ing, be sure to include them, and what happens to them, in any explanation.

DIVORCE IN SOMEONE ELSE'S HOME

Your child comes home from school and says *Tom told me that his parents are getting a divorce. Will he still go to my school and be my friend?* Advise your child that this will probably be a difficult period for his friend but that he is still the same kid he was before his parents split up. Certainly don't try to hide the fact that there is a divorce, but also don't give your child personal information that the child is too young to handle. You can tell your child *Tom's parents can't be happy together anymore. They both love Tom and will always be his parents, but they won't live in the same house any longer. They are getting divorced because of the problems between them, not because Tom did anything wrong.*

You may know that your child's friend's mother is in love with a man other than her husband, or that there is a problem with alcoholism within the family, but it is not necessary for you to share this information with your child. When discussing any serious subjects, the level of information you provide will depend on your child's age and emotional maturity.

Don't talk to your child about impending divorces when you are merely speculating about a possibility or are repeating rumors. When you are talking to your child about anyone's divorce, what you want to convey to him is that divorce is between adults, and is not because of the children.

Your child may show signs of concern about the state of your marriage. He may be very aware of all fighting between married people—his parents, his friends' parents, neighbors, relatives. He may focus on the marital problems not only of the people he knows but also of people he sees on TV. He may frequently request that the members of his family participate in activities together. He may always be on his best behavior and not act in a relaxed, normal fashion. Just because you know that the marital tensions between you and your spouse are not serious, don't assume that your child understands that you are not headed for a divorce. It is a good idea to explain to the child that a certain amount of tension, and an occasional argument, is normal behavior, and that it is often a way of getting problems solved.

If your child asks if you and your spouse will ever get a divorce, don't promise *Never!* Don't pretend, in an effort to protect your child, that divorce is an impossibility in your family. You want to build your child's trust in you, and you don't develop trust by allowing him to retain misconceptions about the real world. Do tell your child that you and your spouse are happy together and enjoy him and your family life very much. People only get divorced when they're not happy with each other.

Your child deseves truthfulness. Never ignore his questions or pretend that he doesn't have serious concerns. Be prepared to help your child understand divorce and to help him get answers to his questions about it. Read about divorce, talk about it with other adults, and listen to others who can give you constructive advice.

DIVORCE IN YOUR HOME

There is never a right time to tell your children about an impending divorce. And it's never easy. However, when talking about your divorce, there are some guidelines which can help you lessen the chances for serious repercussions.

Never allow your children to be the last to know. Be careful about discussing your troubles with family and friends. Don't speculate about the potential for a divorce with family and friends before you tell your kids something like *Your mother and I are having some hard times right now, but we are working to straighten things out.* They might hear about it from someone else, and have no way to make sense of it. Never discuss the possibility of divorce with your child unless you are certain. However, once you decide, immediately prepare yourself to tell your children about it.

Agree in advance with your spouse on answers to the questions that children will probably ask right away. *Where will I sleep? When will I see Daddy (Mommy)? Will we be together on my birthday? Who's going to come see me in the school play? Will you divorce me? Why can't we all stay together?*

You can say: *I think you have noticed that we are arguing a lot and don't agree on things. We have different ideas, and we are not happy together. We think we can be happier living apart, so we are going to make some changes. Mommy and you will continue to live in our house; Daddy is going to move to an apartment about ten minutes away from here. We both love you very much, and will both still be your parents. We want to take care of you.*

As the children ask you questions, you can expand. *We have tried to work things out. We have gone to a special doctor who helps married couples settle their differences, but the marriage cannot be fixed, and we are not happy together.*

Even though both parents are probably in a muddle at this time, it is important that you both give your attention to your children when you talk to them about your impending separation. Both parents should agree in advance to talk to the children at a quiet time when the phone is not going to be answered, the TV is turned off, and the door is shut against friends walking in.

Be sensitive to the child's schedule. Don't tell him the day before an exam or a major school event. If possible, wait for a Friday evening, so you have the weekend to spend with him, when he can talk to you after a night's sleep and after he has had time to think about his real questions.

If the separating parents are too angry with each other to be able to see the children together, each parent needs to tell the other that he is going to talk to the children, what he is going to say, and when. This prepares the other parent for the questions that will probably follow.

Don't be mysterious and secretive about the divorce. Tell your children what they want to know, but don't give your child personal information that he's too young to handle. This will differ according to the age of the children. Help them to ask questions, and answer their questions. You may be surprised that the things you want to tell them don't interest them as much as things you never thought of, such as *Can I still go to camp?*

Almost universally, children believe that the divorce is something they caused. You want to convey to them that the divorce is only between adults. Parents do not divorce because of children, they divorce because they cannot get along. This concern may show up in the form of questions such as *Did I do something wrong? Do you love me? Do you know that I didn't really mean to be bad? Are you going to keep me? Do I cost too much money? Will you stay if I don't fight with my sister?*

Be alert for questions that don't get asked. Your child may need help expressing what he is feeling. You can encourage him to open up by asking him what his concerns are regarding the impending divorce. *You've been thinking about what I told you; what are your feelings? Are you worried about what things will be like with Daddy (or Mommy) away? Are there things you want to know?*

It's important to help the child talk about his feelings and clearly to separate the difference between *Mommy and Daddy don't love each other anymore* and *Mommy and Daddy don't love me anymore.* Reinforce this point until you are sure that the children understand that *Even though we can't get along, you are the best thing about our marriage. You will always be our child, and we will always love you. We both still want to see you and be with you. Mommy will always be your mother and Daddy will always be your father.*

The time to tell your children that there will be a separation and that one spouse will be leaving the house (or everybody will be moving) is dependent on the age of the child. The younger the child, the closer to the actual separation your talk should be. Not only do you have to tell children clearly about the divorce, but you also have to be ready to tell them who is leaving the house. *Daddy (Mommy) will be leaving on Wednesday. When you come home from school, he will not be here. He will be packing his things Monday, Tuesday, and Wednesday, and moving a little bit each day. He is going to have dinner with you on Thursday night.*

Promise only what you can fulfill. Tell your children as much as you can about what will happen now—*You'll live in this house with Mommy, and you'll see Daddy on Tuesdays and Fridays*—and a little about what will happen in the future—*You'll go to the same camp next summer. You'll go on the same vacation, only you'll go with Daddy alone to the beach.* Tell them about the things they like that will stay the same. *You'll still see Grandma and Grandpop.*

Tell the truth. Don't say *Everything's great,* say *Some things are hard now, but we're working to get them straightened out* or *Some things are a little confused right now, but we're talking together to get things clear.*

Review with your kids what to say if someone asks questions. Tell your kids *You tell them what we've told you. My Mommy and Daddy aren't getting along and are going to separate—that means live in different places. They were unhappy and tried to work things out. They both still love me.*

Sometimes it takes a while for the children's reactions to surface. They may appear unmoved the first time you tell them about the divorce, but have many questions later. Reactions will vary from child to child. Some will be indignant, some moralistic, some angry, some frightened. Most feel guilty. They may need to take your side or your spouse's side. Some children reject one parent or the other for a time; some get depressed.

Children have great need to keep in contact with both parents. *Visitation is the right of the child, not the parents.* For continued good mental health, visitations with the non-custodial parent are vital. It is equally important to keep in mind that children do not divorce from grandparents, uncles, aunts, cousins, and other family members, and that contact with both families should be maintained.

AFTER THE SEPARATION OR DIVORCE

Parents may feel that the children have been through so much that they're entitled to a little "extra" indulgence: not having to clean up their rooms, extra sweets, staying up later than they are supposed to, or whatever. Don't confuse setting limits and sticking to your household rules with depriving the child. When other things are in flux, it is most important that children know what they are supposed to do. Continue to make it clear to your children that rules, and knowing that you can all count on each other to do what you are supposed to do, help make it possible for people to live happily together. The extras that you should give them are your time, your care, your support, and your attention.

Also, after the divorce, it's very important that the parents act like a team with respect to the children. Even if there is great hostility between the parents, it's important that the child not sense that the two parents are in conflict about him.

Work out disagreements with the spouse directly, not through the child. Don't say *Tell your father that I said you can stay up past 9:00* or *You tell your mother that I'll pick you up at 6:15 sharp, and she'd better have you ready this time.*

Children need the sense of clear parent/child roles so that they do not learn to take sides or get what they want by manipulating one person against the other. If the child wants to go see a horror movie while visiting one parent, and that parent says *No, you are too young and I think it is not appropriate for you,* the other parent needs to support that, and not say *Well, that's your mother's (father's) craziness; you're certainly old enough, and I'll take you on Saturday.* If you have a different opinion concerning the child, talk with your former spouse privately and make the decision together. Then decide how you will tell the child. It is important that the child continue to feel that both parents are looking after him. You can afford to support the other parent's decision at least for the few days that it will take you to get in contact and to make a joint decision for the future.

TIPS AND HINTS

Keep your word. If you say you are going to visit or call, do it. It's vital to keep your credibility intact during this period, when the child is already suffering from loss of trust in the things that he took for granted.

When your child goes to his other parent's home overnight or for the weekend, help him pack if he is very young, or help him learn to pack if he's older. It is very upsetting for the child to arrive at the home of his other parent and be missing his blanket, homework, underwear, or whatever. It may help both parents, as well as the child, to tape a reminder list inside the lid of his suitcase, so that they can check to be sure that needed items are going back and forth with him. The checklist should include the items appropriate for each child: blanket, bear, sleepwear, underwear, jeans and shirts, shoes, homework, special clothing, sports equipment, library and school books.

Communicate any special needs to the custodial parent. If the child needs a party dress, good shoes, shirt and tie, or sports equipment for the weekend, the custodial parent should be sure that these items get packed.

The non-custodial parent should keep a set of underwear, extra clothes, and toothbrush, in case these commonly needed items are forgotten. He should also keep some books, games and toys that the child looks forward to using. These help make the new apartment or house feel more like home.

Plan in advance for holidays, special occasions, and the children's birthdays, so your children have a clear expectation of what will be happening and where they will be. Try to avoid "spend the morning here and the afternoon there" routines. It doesn't seem to work well. Rather, spend Christmas here this year, and "there" next year, or Christmas Eve at one place and Christmas Day at the other.

Don't be rigid. Give and take on visiting schedules. If you don't, the real losers will be the children. Help your children to remember to keep in touch with their other parent by calling often. The custodial parent, no matter what the feelings are toward the spouse, should continue to encourage the children's relationship with their other parent.

If your spouse has moved to a different house due to separation or divorce, make a small sign for your children that says either DADDY or MOMMY and right under it your spouse's home and work phone numbers. Tape this to the refrigerator, or anyplace else the children know to look for it. Do not make a child's calling the other parent contingent on your giving him the phone number.

Remember the other parent's birthday, Father's Day or Mother's Day, and holidays by helping your child get or make a present or card. Good relations between child and both parents are important for the child's development.

Make it a policy to report information pertaining to your child's health—including trips to the doctor, allergist, dentist—the same day or evening that you get the information. Keep the other parent aware of school progress, functions, and activities.

It is especially important after a separation or divorce that you keep in touch with your child's school. When so many other things are changing, school is your child's anchor, and he needs to know that you find it important and valuable, too. If a problem arises, such as poor grades or misbehavior, you and the child's other parent should get together as a team. You want to communicate that you both care about school. *How can we help you? I'll quiz you on your multiplication tables while you're here, and Mommy will help you at home.*

Although most children can profitably and comfortably take on some additional chores, be careful not to overwhelm your child with things he has to do *now that we're alone and have to be partners in running the household.* Your child will be having his own hard times during the divorce, which may make him less capable of dealing with even the ordinary things for a time.

Be aware of a custodial parent's tendency to turn to a child to fill the void of the missing spouse. Young children cannot be a substitute for a spouse in providing emotional comfort. It is important to develop and sustain adult support systems for yourself after the divorce.

Make arrangements to go out. Leave the children with a trusted friend, hire a baby-sitter, let them stay at their grandparents', but do go out, even if you go alone to a movie. In this way, your children will not expect that you will spend all of your time either alone or with them.

When you start dating again, one way to help reduce children's confusion about "what's happening" and to lessen the chances of the *Are you going to be my Daddy (Mommy)?* question, is to introduce your dates by their last names. *This is Mr. (Ms.) Johnson*, instead of *This is Max (Mary)*. Teach your children to call them Mr. or Ms. You can explain that if someone becomes very important, then you'll decide something else to call him (maybe his first name, maybe "Uncle Max"). The formality will help your child know that dates are not all potential parent replacements.

Try to have your children be part of whatever model of family life you approve of. Take your kids to visit with people who have a good married relationship. If nobody invites you, invite them to your house.

If you have custody of the children, try to have them see and become friends with people of the same sex as your spouse. Your children need role models—cousins, neighbors, aunts, uncles, friends.

There are certain personal things that are important. Learn how to buy personal items for whatever sex you're dealing with, such as a razor, a jock strap or a bra, if these are your responsibility. Ask friends or relatives who have children of the same age for help.

Encourage other members of your family and friends to spend time with your kids. An invitation to dinner, to watch TV, or to go to a movie and talk—anything that extends the range of the children's contacts and gives you some time off is helpful. Nobody can love somebody, or even like somebody, all the time. It's perfectly normal and natural to want to get away from your children sometimes, and for them to want some time alone, too. A favorite aunt or friends who have children the same age can be a good back-up *if* they really enjoy visiting with your child and *if* the child genuinely likes to go there, too.

Sex

This section provides suggestions and guidelines for talking with your children about sex. It has a point of view—that sex is a wonderful and natural part of life. We want children to grow up knowledgeable and responsible about sex, and able to take great pleasure in it. We believe that the more sex education children get, the better prepared they will be to have a healthy, caring, responsible sex life as adults.

Sex is a topic that often makes parents feel uncomfortable, perhaps even frightened. Thus, they tend to avoid talking about it with their children. As a result, kids get most of their sex education from older siblings and peers, when they really want to get it from their parents. Recent studies show that fewer than 15% of children get their sex education from their parents, while 75% get it from their peers.

Clearly, the kids we are writing about are too young for "sex." So why give kids information about sex at such an early age? First of all, TV and peer pressure are making children aware of sex at younger and younger stages of their lives. Teenage pregnancies among girls of fourteen, thirteen, and even younger, are on the rise. More and more children are exposed to pressures to experiment or do what the other kids are doing so they do not feel left out. In addition, pre-adolescent sexual events "happen" to children (wet dreams, menstruation, body changes). Without prior knowledge of the naturalness of these events, children can react with anxiety and fears which could have been replaced by positive feelings at these eagerly anticipated milestones in each child's development.

Often sex education is limited to talk about the parts of the body and their roles and functions. It is unrealistic to assume that your child will not want to learn about what's involved in making love, where babies come from, what the grown-up male and female bodies look like. If there are things you don't want your children to do, it is better to give them the information about the topics and tell them your feelings and answer any questions they may have, than to assume that their ignorance is permanent as well as blissful.

It is important that you do not give your child the misconception that adults engage in sexual intercourse only when they wish to conceive a child.

Choose a quiet time and place, when and where you will not be interrupted when you are talking to your child about sex. Make sure there's room to spread books (if you are using books), and try not to be rushed. These discussions set the stage for activities, feelings, and events that are major parts of your child's life. Warmth, caring, and interest should be important elements of these talks. Remember, there's never a dumb question—do not belittle your child when he doesn't understand. Try not to become impatient if you have to say something two or three different ways until it is clear. Try to set an atmosphere for these conversations that will reflect the importance and beauty of the subject.

Your child will benefit from understanding that sex is one way that two people show their love for one another. About the same time that you explain this to your child, you should also begin to tell him about the responsibilities involved in

making love. The child should understand the consequences—pregnancy and caring for and making the partner
feel good.

Talk to your children about the things you believe in. Children need to know the limits of what you think is healthy and
acceptable. If you feel you cannot talk about sex with your
children, they will get their information from the "street."
There they may get an impression of sex that you don't agree
with, as well as misleading information.

Books can be very useful as a springboard for future discussion. Although there are many books on the market introducing and explaining sex to children, and books for adults
and kids to read together, not all bookstores have them. If you
can't find them easily, keep looking, or try a local library.
We've suggested some books for the five- to twelve-year-old
that will still be useful as your children mature. Use only
those sections of the books that are relevant to your child's
age, maturity, and physical development. Make sure you
thoroughly read any book you give to your child. We suggest
that if you plan to supplement your child's sex education with
reading, you give him more than one book, so that he gets
more than one perspective on each topic. Discuss with your
child what he has read. In this way you can put the new information in the perspective of your family's own values and
religious beliefs.

Some of the books we've found helpful are:

Carrera, Michael. *Sex, The Facts, the Acts and Your
Feelings.* New York: Crown, 1981. (This is not for chil-
dren. It is an exceptional adult reference book.)
Comfort, Alex, and Comfort, Jane. *The Facts of Love—
Living, Loving and Growing Up.* New York: Crown,
1979.

Gardiner-Loulan, Jo Ann; Lopez, Bonnie; and Quacken-
bush, Marcia. *Period.* San Francisco: Volcano Press,
1981.

Johnson, Eric W. *Love and Sex in Plain Language. 3rd
rev. ed.* New York: Bantam, 1977.

Mayle, Peter. *Congratulations, You're Not Pregnant: An
Illustrated Guide to Birth Control.* New York: Macmil-
lan, 1981.

_____. *What's Happening to Me?* Secaucus, N.J.: Lyle
Stuart, 1975.

_____. *Where Did I Come From?* Secaucus, N.J.: Lyle
Stuart, 1973.

Pomeroy, Wardell B. *Boys and Sex.* New York: Dell,
1981.

_____. *Girls and Sex.* New York: Dell, 1981.

Sheffield, Margaret. *Where Do Babies Come From?* New
York: Knopf, 1981.

Don't be upset if your child isn't interested in the things
you want him to read. Children report a fair amount of disin-
terest in the mechanics of reproduction. So, don't be concerned if your child only turns to certain sections of the books
you give him, rather than reading them in order. Don't force
your child to read more than he wants to, and encourage him
to ask you questions about any part of the book.

You can also find opportunities to talk with your children
about sex without placing undue emphasis on the topic by
discussing magazine articles or newspaper stories that you
have just read: articles about curfews, youthful marriages,
even rape, all present opportunities to talk about sex in general without relating it specifically to your behavior or your
child's behavior. These discussions will allow you to share
your values and attitudes toward responsible sexual behavior

without lecturing. They will also allow you to offer factual information about sex without the mutually embarrassing *Now you're old enough to learn the facts of life* talk by the father and mother. Questions about sex education aren't something that happens once—they're an ongoing part of a parent's responsibility.

Some parents believe that talking about sex will stimulate kids to do things they wouldn't have done without the discussion. This is a myth. Children are naturally curious, particularly about their own and others' bodies. They will seek answers whether you talk to them or not. Children express their sexual curiosity from birth on, by seeking to explore their own bodies, and to experience the pleasure the body can give. Information will satisfy some of your child's curiosity and will help to diminish the need he feels to find out about sex from irresponsible sources.

Values about relationships and sex, as well as other areas of life, are formed as the young child is growing, and they come from his everyday experiences and observations. Therefore, teaching your child to be responsible about sex should not start when the child is a teenager—by then he has formulated his sexual role and most of his beliefs. Whether you have a son or a daughter, from the earliest age you should be helping the child learn that sex is both a pleasure and a responsibility. Both boys and girls should learn to feel responsible for their actions, and for the consequences of those actions.

You'll want to help your child learn that good sex is associated with good relationships in general: coercion and force are wrong. You can introduce the term "rape" to the older child as an extreme form of sexual force. Seeing an article in the paper about a rape is a natural way for you to share your beliefs about such an act.

When a child starts to go to boy-girl parties, it is the parents' responsibility to find out who is going to be at home. Allow your child neither to go to a party where parents will not be at home, nor to give a party when you won't be home. Make it routine to talk to your children about their parties, so they expect to find out in advance who will be chaperoning. When your kids are older (past the age where you always pick them up at parties), you can still ask *When will you be home?* and negotiate a mutually agreeable time.

It's hard to start asking the fifteen- or sixteen-year-old child *Where are you going?* and *Who's going to be there?* But if you begin asking those questions when your child is still little, your child will grow up expecting to give that information to you. Likewise, you should volunteer this kind of information when you go out.

Girl-boy parties sometimes begin in elementary school. And though they put many different names on it, "Spin the Bottle," "Post Office," and "Turn Out the Lights" are still party activities. You should teach your child to know he can say *No, I don't want to play that game* if he really doesn't want to play. This is a good place to reinforce his skills in resisting peer pressure. You can say *Sometimes it is hard not to do what your friends want you to do. But, when you believe in something, you have to stick to it, even though it is uncomfortable.* On the other hand, if the activity is appropriate for his age, you'll want to explore why he doesn't want to play this game. *Kissing games are a part of growing up,* or *Is there a special reason why you don't want to play "Spin the Bottle" with your friends?*

TALKING ABOUT SEX

Your child may begin to ask questions about sex before the age of five. Try not to make the answers to his questions about sex different from answers to the other questions children constantly ask. An attitude of embarrassment, impatience, or fear may make your child feel there is something wrong with his curiosity on this subject, and he may not ask again. A relaxed, comfortable, straightforward attitude toward sex will have a positive influence on your child's attitudes toward sex and toward his body.

What happens if you don't feel comfortable talking about sex with your child? The best thing is to get a book in language appropriate to the child's age and reading level, one that you've already read. You can say something like *I've looked carefully to find this very special book for you. I'd like you to read it and we can talk about it whenever you want to.* Or, you can read it together with the child. We recommend the use of a book rather than sending the child to a doctor, a coach, or someone outside the family. This keeps this important topic a part of family life. This is vital, because you want the child to be able to talk to you about any topic at all, and not feel that there are some things which you don't really want him to bring to you to discuss.

ABOUT TRUST

As the child has grown, he has learned to trust your opinions, reactions, and information. The questions he will ask you about sex will range from the simplistic, requiring only one- or two-word answers, to the more specific questions of the twelve-year-old that require accurate, detailed responses. Whatever the child's age, and no matter how complex the question, there is no substitute for the truth. Search for ways to say what you want to say simply, yet truthfully, so as never to put your credibility with him in jeopardy. Trust is built on experience, and you want your children to have the kinds of experiences that enable them to depend on your telling the truth. Children tend to be literal-minded, and well-meaning folklore about storks or analogies about seeds and plants may only confuse them.

USING THE RIGHT WORDS

It's important to use the correct vocabulary concerning sex right from the beginning of your child's education. This practice should start from the time you say to your child *Do you want to go to the bathroom?* rather than saying *Do you want to make a wee-wee?* The words *penis, vagina, breasts* and many other parts of the body can be taught early and naturally when you are bathing your child.

TEACHING CHILDREN THE DIFFERENCE BETWEEN PRIVATE AND PUBLIC CONVERSATIONS

Children are known for their lack of tact. This is at once their charm and a source of parents' discontent. Parents rightfully associate sex with privacy, and the young child does not. So you can easily find your five-year-old asking *Why is that lady so fat?* at the top of his amazed lungs while he's standing with you in the supermarket line behind a pregnant woman. Embarrassing situations like this can be handled best by keeping calm. (For example, catch the eye of the pregnant woman and smile if she has overheard.) You can lean over to the child and tell him, quietly, *That lady is pregnant; there is a baby growing in a special place inside of her. We'll talk more about it a little later.*

As soon as you can be alone with the child, explain that there are public and private conversations. *We don't talk out loud about the way someone looks—how fat, how tall, how old someone is. Whisper it to me.* Then show the child: *This is how you whisper.* As the child gets older, you can teach him to wait until you are alone to discuss private or sensitive matters.

CURIOSITY

At around the age of five, children begin to be very curious about their bodies. It is not unusual for them to want to see their own genitals and those of their friends, of both sexes. Children thoroughly examining each other does not have the same meaning to them as it does to the alarmed adult who sees them. To the adult, it has a decidedly sexual connotation, but for the young child it is merely an act of innocent exploration—of getting to know about the body. Reactions of horror or distress if you find your child "playing doctor" with children of either sex are inappropriate, because such reactions suggest that the child is wrong to want to know about his body.

Instead of outrage, use the next convenient time, when your child is alone with you, to tell him *Many children don't think that this is a good game.* Explain that people shouldn't take their clothes off in public. Say *I will talk with you about anything you want to know, so that you can find out more about boys' bodies and girls' bodies.*

NUDITY

On the question of nudity, parents should do what feels comfortable and is consistent with their own attitudes and feelings. Trying to change the way you feel could lead to self-consciousness and nervousness, and does not set a good example. There are both positives and negatives to a parent's being nude in front of the children. If they see you with your clothes off, it helps them understand what they will be like when they grow up. It may make them more comfortable when they have to get undressed at camp, at the doctor, in the gym, or at someone else's house.

On the other hand, some psychologists feel that the disproportionate size of the parents' sex organs may be frightening to the child. Since the parents are probably the only adults he sees naked, he may not realize that all adult sexual organs are larger than his own. Instead, he may conclude that *I am little, weak, and insignificant.*

If you don't make it a regular practice to walk around nude in front of your kids, they may at some point "surprise" you when you are undressed. Try not to react in an embarrassed fashion: don't clasp your hands over your genitals or order the child harshly to leave the room. Instead, try to walk normally toward a covering and put it on, so that you don't convey the impression that there is something shameful about the human body. If your child does see you naked, he's likely to ask questions. A common one is *Why do you have hair there?* Explain that growing hair on the body is a normal part of growing up, and when he grows up, he will have hair under his arms and on his legs, as well as in the pubic area.

CHILDREN OBSERVING
PARENTS' LOVE-MAKING

If your child wanders into your bedroom during intercourse, try not to act as if you were doing something wrong, although that's the way most people seem to feel. Tell the child that this is your time to be alone with your spouse, and you would like him to leave the room. Later you can explain, in a simple way, that love-making is a way of communicating the feelings of closeness and tenderness that each spouse feels for the other. By reinforcing to the child that his mother and father love each other very much, that love-making is pleasurable, you can help the child be assured that *Mommy wasn't being hurt* and *Daddy wasn't being mean*, and that both were enjoying the activity.

Some children who overhear the noises of love-making, or see their parents making love, associate the love-making with violence. It is very important that the child be made aware of the difference between sex and violence. You can explain that great pleasure often is associated with noisy activity, and you can point out examples from the child's own excitement when something pleases him.

MASTURBATION

Masturbation is normal for all children, both boys and girls. Even infants enjoy rubbing their genitals. As they get older, children find additional ways to masturbate to increase pleasure and release tension. Letting your child know, by your attitude, that masturbation is natural and that everybody does it and enjoys it, is likely to have wide-ranging positive effects on his feelings about himself and his body. Children will naturally feel good about masturbating unless they are exposed to the old-fashioned myths: that it leads to insanity, will make you blind, causes illness, and so forth. These myths could make a child feel worried and guilty unless they are countered with the facts that masturbation is not harmful and is an excellent preparation for more adult sexual activities.

Masturbation, like other sexual activity, should be done in private. If you see your child touching his genitals or masturbating in public, don't make a big fuss, but go to him unobtrusively and take him aside where you can talk to him privately. You might say something like *Although it feels good to touch yourself, that is something that people don't do in public. There is nothing wrong with it, but other people may not enjoy watching you.* You might go on to point out that when he is with other people, he ought to be paying attention to them, and to what is going on around him.

DISCUSSIONS ABOUT SEX

It is best that discussions about sex happen over a long period of time, beginning when the child expresses interest in where babies come from, what various parts of the parents' bodies are called, and why there are differences between himself and adults, and between men and women. The child's education can keep pace with his developing curiosity, and this enables you to avoid overburdening him with information he has not requested and may not be ready to understand.

Try to explain the parts of the body in natural, day-to-day conversation as part of bathing or dressing. Your child's earliest questions about parts of the body will probably demand nothing more from you than naming the part. You should know the name of the body part and its function so that you can answer accurately. The anatomical differences between men and women can sometimes be a source of anxiety for children. Reassure the child by indicating that these differences are not only normal, but special.

The young child can be told that grown-up people make babies. *A woman and a man who care very much for each other can decide they want to share their life with a child, and then they come together to make a baby that will grow inside a special place in the mother's body.* Watch for reactions, and make time for any questions your explanation may provoke. When you see a pregnant woman, you can quietly mention it to the child and point out the woman to him unobtrusively.

Depending on your child's maturity, the next time he asks about babies and sex may be the time to get a little more specific, and explain that *having a baby is a big decision made by two people. A lot of discussion and planning go into the decision. A baby is made by the father and mother coming together and making love (having sexual intercourse).*

If it is appropriate to the child's level of maturity and he seems to want to know more about the mechanics, you can give him a simple explanation of intercourse, including the functions of the male and female sexual organs. You should be sure that the child wants to know this much detail before offering it, and then make it simple and easily understood. It is also important to let the child know that intercourse is a pleasurable activity in which adults may engage for its own sake, and that while it is necessary activity for having a baby, having a baby is not the only purpose for having intercourse.

It may also be useful to accompany this explanation with study of the development of the baby's body in the womb. There are many excellent, illustrated books which examine the growth and development of the fetus and are intended for children. Encyclopedias may also be of some value and many have useful illustrations.

In other, later, conversations introduce your child to the preparations his body is starting to make for his maturity. Tell children of both sexes about such things as wet dreams and menstruation, and in equal detail. You can discuss some or all of the following topics in one or more conversations, depending on your child's age, interest and development.

You can begin by saying something like: *From the time you were a baby, your body has been growing and changing. It gets ready for different things at different times: for example, when you were born, you couldn't crawl, then you could crawl but not walk. Your body has continued to grow and develop, and there are many big changes that your body will start to make in the next couple of years. These changes don't happen to everybody at the same time, and it doesn't matter when they happen.*

The following is a hypothetical conversation with a boy, telling him about changes in his body and the changes in a girl's body.

You will soon get hair on your pubic area—around your penis. You will also begin to get hair on your legs and under your arms. Your glands will begin to develop and you'll begin to need to use a deodorant. Your penis, hands, and feet will grow, your shoulders and chest will get larger, your voice will change and get lower.

Help your child notice anything about himself, or his friends, that has already begun to change.

Later, you'll begin to get hair on your face and we'll buy you a razor because it will be time for you to begin shaving. Other things will also happen. Sometimes your penis will get stiff and hard—that's called an erection. It happened when you were a baby, but it will probably happen more often now. It may happen for no reason, or when you think about being with a girl, or when you wake up in the morning or touch yourself. The reason it happens is because extra blood moves to the penis. Almost anything can trigger an erection; this is natural and normal and should be explained to your child.

All of these are outside ways of showing that you are growing up. Your body is also changing in ways that you can't see. It is starting to manufacture sperm so that,

*years from now, when you are ready, your body will be
able to help make a baby. If the sperm that you are starting to make do not have a way of escaping your body,
your body takes care of eliminating them, normally and
naturally, by an involuntary spurt or stream while you
are sleeping. This is called a wet dream.*

Tell him that it is nothing to be embarrassed about. If he
asks what his mother will think, reassure him that it is nothing unusual, any more than a girl's menstruating is unusual
or a source of embarrassment. You should also remind him
that his mother already knows about such things and, far
from being upset, will simply acknowledge them as evidence
that her son is growing up. It is a milestone which marks the
beginning of his adolescence, and should be treated by both
parents and children as significant but ordinary.

Only a small percentage of fathers talk to their sons about
sexual development. In the preceding example we have
assumed the parent speaking to be the father because,
although either parent can discuss sexual topics with sons
and daughters, the male talking to his son and the female to
her daughter have the added advantage of being able to share
their first-hand experiences with the children, and can relate
more easily to the specific anxieties likely to beset children at
such moments.

In a later part of the conversation, or perhaps on another
occasion, the changes happening to the opposite sex at about
this time should also be explored. The boy, for example,
should be informed that *Just the way this is happening to
you, and you are getting more interested in girls, they are
getting more interested in you, too. And there are changes
happening in their bodies, as well, some of them quite
similar to those which you are experiencing. Like you,
they are getting taller and stronger, and they are growing
hair in the same places that you are. Their voices will
change, but won't get as deep as yours.*

But some different things will happen to them. Their breasts will start to grow, the nipples on their breasts will start to stand out, their hips will get a little wider so they can carry a baby during pregnancy, and they will probably, over the next couple of years, start to get their periods.

Just as you are having wet dreams, which show that your body is getting ready to be able to have children, a girl is showing the same thing by menstruating. Once a month, her body makes a new lining for that special place called the womb (which is near her stomach) so that it can be ready to hold a baby. She produces the eggs that will meet the sperm from the man's body if she decides to have a baby. If the eggs are not fertilized by the sperm, which means that the new lining of the womb won't be needed to hold a baby that month, then the body gets rid of it (just like your body gets rid of the extra sperm). Because one of the things in the lining of the womb is blood, the liquid that leaves the body each month through the vagina is red, and looks like blood. Sometimes girls are surprised by their first periods as boys are surprised by wet dreams, but after a while everybody grows to understand that this is a normal, natural part of what happens as people grow up.

In discussing menstruation with a girl, it is a good idea to go into a bit more detail, since it concerns her much more intimately than it does a boy, and she is likely to be more embarrassed by menstruation which can affect her for longer periods of time and have a greater impact on her in her public life. You should warn a daughter that menstruation can be uncomfortable and even messy, but reassure her that it gets easier as she gets used to it. Emphasize that it is a natural process that is part of the miraculous functioning of the human body and an essential process in the sequence of sexual maturation and childbearing, which, while uncomfortable, is nevertheless a significant milestone in her life cycle.

Talking to a daughter about growing up creates a special bond and requires extra care because there is so much to discuss. Tell your daughter about menstruation at one time, and about how boys change and develop at another time. Very often, parents tell girls what to do when they get their periods without discussing what happens and what it means. We hope your conversations will include all three. In addition to the details about the menstrual cycle itself, there are a number of related topics which will require some discussion.

There are clear signs that will help a young girl realize that her body is changing. Tell her to watch for pubic hair growing near her vagina, as well as hair under her arms and on her legs. When that happens she will probably need a deodorant and a razor. Her glands will create more perspiration, so personal hygiene will become even more important. Explain the need for washing, drying, and general cleanliness, and give her tips about talcum powder, and so forth. This might be the time to let her choose a perfume or cologne that she would like to use.

Be alert for signs that her breasts are developing, and, when she needs to begin wearing a bra, take her on a special shopping trip to celebrate her growing up—lunch out is a nice way to talk and to share time. She will probably be concerned that she has no breasts or that her breasts are too large. Help other members of the family understand her sensitivity so that they do not tease or embarrass her. Explain to her that her nipples will also begin to stand out, her hips will widen, and her waist will narrow a bit. All of this is in preparation for her body to be able to create, carry, and nurse a child—if she chooses.

Use one of the books listed, or an encyclopedia, to trace another change that will occur inside. Explain that *your ovaries will begin their work of carrying the eggs that enable a woman to help create a baby when one is joined by a sperm from the man. One of these eggs matures each month and breaks loose from an ovary. It then gets pushed down the fallopian tube. At the same time, the uterus or womb begins to build up a protective lining of tissue and blood in case a baby is formed. If a sperm fertilizes the egg, then a baby begins to grow. If there is no fertilization, then there is no need for the lining and the egg, and they leave the body through the vagina. When they come out of the body, the fluid which contains them looks reddish because of the blood. This is called menstruating or having a period.*

Very often, a girl's first period begins without warning. If she has not been told about it before, and what to do, she can be very frightened. So it is especially important to discuss this with her. Explain the beauty and wonder of a woman's body that grows so beautifully and can create human life. Help her understand how very special her own body is—and how to respect herself and her body by taking proper care of it.

Teach her what to do when her period comes. Let her experiment to see which kind of pad or tampon suits her best, explain the variety of aids available, and show her how to use them. Warn her that they'll all feel funny at first, but that in time, as she finds the one that she likes best, she will feel natural and comfortable.

Explain that the entire cycle takes about a month, but that it is different for each woman. Every young girl has concerns about menstruation. You should recognize that they are very important to her and deal with them thoroughly and thoughtfully. Some typical concerns and advice on how to deal with each one are detailed below:

- *Everyone's started and I haven't* or *No one's started*

and I have. Explain that there is no best, or right, time to start. There is just the appropriate time for her body.

- *What can I do when I have my period?* Everything you feel like doing—anything you planned to do—your period needn't stop you.

- *Why don't I feel good?* (and other complaints about discomfort). Explain that most times she will feel little or no difference—once in a while she may feel a bit uncomfortable, but it usually won't last long. Tell her that when she does feel uncomfortable she should feel free to ask your advice, and that if you can't help, you will get advice from a doctor.

- *It smells funny.* Explain that there may be times when there is extra sweat-gland activity, but that if she washes a bit more often and changes pads or tampons more frequently, there won't be any odor. Warn her that sometimes she'll think she smells something, but no one else will.

- *Will everyone know I have it?* Ask her to look in the mirror and see if she can tell.

- *What if it just happens unexpectedly?* Once your daughter gets her period, encourage her to carry a pad or tampon, safety pins, and change for dispensing machines. If she's stuck, teach her how to fold paper towels, toilet paper or some other emergency substitute and how to pin it to her underpants until she can get what she needs.

- *How do I know when it will happen?* Tell her that it's different for each woman but that it will happen about once a month. She should expect to be irregular at the beginning and may skip a month, or even several months, until she becomes regular.

- *How long will it last?* Between two and eight days.

- *Am I losing too much blood?* No, only a few ounces. This is seldom a problem.

Because, in the first year or two of menstruation, girls can experience considerable embarrassment, it can be very helpful if the parents take responsibility for securing sanitary pads. The child should assume the responsibility of informing her parents of her needs. As she gets more comfortable with the process, she can gradually assume the full responsibility.

Responsibility. Another conversation you should have with your children is on responsibility, care, and birth control. It is preferable to build into your kids the concept of how to act appropriately rather than just setting curfews. Whatever can happen at midnight can happen at noon, and the issue is helping your children want to behave responsibly rather than simply adhering to the "letter of the law," or being home "because my father said I have to be home by nine o'clock." Encouraging your kids to use their own good judgment and not listen to or give in to peer pressure should be an ongoing process.

Birth control. The fundamental goal of birth control is preventing a live sperm from reaching a live egg. There are many different methods available, to suit a variety of personal preferences and needs. When birth control is an appropriate concern, you should be certain that your children have an understanding of the basic process of menstruation and ovulation. A frank discussion of the number and types of birth control devices available to men and women may be in order. The depth of this discussion, and when it should take place, should be determined by the depth of your child's understanding. You should also be certain that the possible side effects and physical risks involved in any form of birth control under consideration are fully explored and well understood by the child.

CONCLUSION

Whenever discussing sexual concerns with your children, be as relaxed, open, and forthright as possible. Gently but firmly help them to understand that sexual intercourse is an activity with great responsibility attached to it, for both the man and the woman. If your children learn at an early age that all humans are sexual beings and that sex is a normal, natural, and healthy part of being human—that in fact it is one of the glories of being human—you will have helped to provide them with a firm foundation for their sexual development and to avoid many of the pitfalls which confront the unprepared child.

Death

Death is a topic that frightens most people. It is especially overwhelming for a child who has never been exposed to death and is suddenly confronted with the death of a pet, his friend's grandfather, or a member of his own family. The child has almost no perspective with which to understand that death is part of the natural process of living; thus, he may believe he caused the death because he was "bad," or had angry thoughts about the person who died. In addition, children often feel that death is temporary and that somehow the dead pet or person will come back to life.

Because of the trauma that death causes, parents need to provide a structure that enables the child to understand death and to cope with the pain it brings in a manner that allows him to mourn and, in time, overcome his grief and resume his normal life. Your own fears of death will complicate the issue for your child. If talking about death is difficult for you, and if your attitude is that death is something you don't want to think about, you will need help in discussing the subject with your child. Often a trusted friend or relative or religious leader whom the child knows and feels comfortable with can advise you on what to say, or could speak to your child with you. There are also many books about helping your child to cope with death which could be of assistance to you as you prepare yourself to speak with your child.

When telling your child about a death, pick a place to talk where you won't be interrupted. Make your explanation simple. Use words the child will understand. Tell the truth and follow the child's lead. You can say something like *I have something very sad to tell you. Uncle Henry died today. He died because he was very sick (in an accident, very old).* Then stop and wait for a reaction.

Be as honest as possible. If you don't know the answer to a question, admit it and try to find out the answer later. Don't lie or say anything you might have to change later when your child is older and wiser. Explain that there are questions about death that no one has the answers to. Avoid myths and half-truths. Use the words "dead," "death," and "dying." Be careful to avoid using euphemisms that give a false impression, like "going to sleep" (your child will surely ask when the person is going to wake up), "going away" (when is he coming back?), "passing away" (children think of "passing' as something you do on a test in school). It is crucial that your credibility with your child remain intact so he can trust that what you say is true.

Some children will react to the news of a loss with a need for lots of physical contact. The child may regress and want to climb onto your lap; the child may want to be hugged and held. Other children may want to withdraw for some period of time. Be supportive of whatever your child seems to need. Give him lots of nonverbal messages which say you know he is sad, that you love him, and that you are there for him.

Do not protect your child from your sad feelings. If you cry when you tell your child about a death, it shows you have feelings and that you are free to express them. This leaves the child free to have his feelings. Children sense when an adult holds something back. This is worrisome for them since it implies there is something wrong with expressing (or even feeling) those (sad) emotions. The child participating in a family experience where everyone is expressing sad feelings about the loss helps him see that the death of a person is an extraordinary experience, and that people are valued and missed when they die. It helps him increase his value of life and his knowledge that people are "special" because they have these feelings. *I know you will miss him; so will I. It hurts when someone you love dies. It's not wrong to cry and feel sad. I understand.*

How much you talk to your child about death will depend on the child's age. It is vital that you tell the child the truth, no matter how young he is; however, the younger he is, the simpler the explanation needs to be. Fears of death are typical around age five, and even without directly experiencing the death of someone close to him, the child may have questions about dying.

Young children are often unaware that death is irreversible and permanent. They may believe that doctors, or magic, or time will bring the dead person back to life. You should be conscious of this attitude and watch for any behavior that indicates the child is thinking along the lines of *if I do the right thing* or *if I'm very good* or *if I promise to kiss him good night*, this will bring the person back to life. Make sure your explanation is simple and to the point and stresses the finality of what has happened.

The young child may seem to take death very matter-of-factly. A few hours or even minutes after hearing about someone's death, the child may want to play with his friends or go to a movie or turn on the TV. This short span of sadness is a natural reaction for a child. Children commonly cope with severe grief by denying that anything is wrong. The child's seeming indifference toward the death does not mean he does not care. It usually signifies the opposite by communicating that the child is not ready to give up his fantasy and wishes to be with the loved one. He is able to handle this difficult time by putting it out of his mind for a while. In this way, he prevents himself from being overwhelmed by his grief and loss. With parental support, his sadness will emerge over a period of time. Parents should watch for signs that show the child is ready to talk about his feelings of loss. He should be encouraged to do this. Reminiscing with the child and recalling happy times and good feelings associated with the person are of tremendous help, as is admitting to one's own sense of loss. Giving the child a personal item that had belonged to the deceased—cufflinks, a book, a photograph, a ring—can provide a remembrance the child will treasure for many years.

A child who has experienced the death of someone he knew may worry that his mother or father will now die and leave him alone. The child may want to talk to you about these fears. Children who have these concerns often ask such questions as *Are you going to live for a long time?* Help him to address his fears by asking him if he is worried about something happening to you.

Reassurance is vitally important. Convey to the child that you expect to be around for a long time to take care of him until he's all grown up. If the child continues to be fearful, tell him about the options there are. (*If something were to happen to me, then Daddy [or Mommy] would take care of you, and if something were to happen to both of us, then [guardian] would be with you and take care of you and make sure you had a good home.*)

Between the ages of seven and nine, your child may typically become interested in the details and arrangements surrounding a death: the casket, the cemetery, the burial, the funeral service, and what happens after death. His interest in these details may even seem excessive, but this is his way of coming to terms with the loss. Parents must try to be patient and to answer the hundreds of questions the child may want to ask.

Be prepared to deal with such queries as: *What will happen to his body? (There are people specially trained to take care of someone who has died. His body will be taken to a place and cared for until the funeral.) What is a funeral? (A funeral is a time when people who care about the person who died come together to honor him and to say good-bye.)*

Many children are terrified about the thought of being buried alive. Be alert for signs of this fear, and be ready to explain that people are never buried alive—that they are carefully examined by a doctor to make sure that there has been no mistake and that they are really dead.

By the age of nine or ten, a child is capable of understanding what death is. He can comprehend the finality and that other people feel sadness and loss too. He may even understand the biological facts (no pulse or heartbeat, no breathing, etc.).

You can offer the child who is five or older the choice of going to the funeral or not, and older children the option of going to the cemetery after the services. Feelings about funerals and cemeteries vary widely among people. Some want to remember the person as he was in happier times, and some feel better about the reality of the symbol of the burial marking the passage from life to death.

Including children in discussions about death and in the

family's plans for the services reassures the child that he is not going to be left alone with his sadness. Don't be mysterious about death and its ceremonies. If you are secretive, your child's fears and anxieties may increase.

Often adults assume they are "saving" the child from additional sadness by not taking him to the funeral. In some cases, this prevents the child from being part of a community of fellowship to honor the person who has died (which lessens his chances to be comforted by other family members). Allowing the child to observe other people grieving can help him overcome his own feelings of loss. Since different children react differently, you will have to observe your child. Clearly it is an individual family decision as to which child will be allowed to go to the funeral and/or cemetery.

If the child and parents have decided together that he will attend the funeral, some time should be spent in explaining the events that will take place (including the greeting and comforting of the bereaved family by other family members and friends, whether or not the casket will be open, what the cemetery looks like and what will happen there, who will be speaking, how long the services will last, and that some people may cry).

The child should not be left alone during the services, so arrangements should be made toward this end to take into account the possibility that immediate family members may be too grief-stricken to be able to pay adequate attention to him.

It should be decided prior to the funeral where the child will be taken afterward if he does not go to the cemetery. A good solution is to take the child home so he can help get ready for the family's return from the graveside. He should be allowed to participate in some meaningful way (setting the table, meeting the guests, taking the coats). Useful tasks allow him to feel a part of the process.

After the funeral is over and the "official" period of mourning is ended, watch for signs of continuing grief. Your child may need your help to overcome some unresolved anxiety or fear. Be alert to such questions as *What will happen to me if something happens to you?*, or fear about his own death. Continue to give your child opportunities to recall the person who died and reinforce the fact that the child had nothing to do with the person's dying. Encourage his talking about the deceased and communicate your own feelings of loss and sadness as being normal.

Your child may need to be told that sometimes people feel hurt and angry because the dead person has left them.

It is particularly traumatizing for a child to be confronted with the death of another child. Everyone expects older people to die before younger ones, and it is extremely painful for both adults and children when a youngster dies. The same techniques apply here in helping your child cope as you would use at the death of an older person; however, you will have to be particularly alert to be supportive of his fears that he, too, might die. Reassure him that you always take good care of him (take him to the doctor, make sure he is properly dressed, see that he eats correctly, etc.). Spend as much time as necessary with your child. Often the physical presence and contact is most reassuring.

The loss of the family pet may be a child's first experience with death. How he deals with this situation may affect his feelings about all subsequent losses. Grieving over the loss of a pet is perfectly natural. You can best help your child by letting him talk about his loss, about how much he misses his pet, and about the fun he had with it.

If the pet dies suddenly, tell the child directly and without unnecessary detail. Use words the child can understand. (*I have something very sad to tell you. Fudge is dead. She was hit by a car this morning.*) Help him express his feelings. Let him know you feel sad, too. Don't try to distract your child from exploring his grief. As with a human death, his feelings of loss and sadness are real. Let your child tell you if it is too painful for him to talk about.

Never treat a child's pet as being worthless. Even a fish or a guinea pig may have strong emotions attached to it and the situation requires some sensitivity to how the child feels. Never tell a child his pet "disappeared." The child will grieve for an interminable length of time because he's waiting for the pet to reappear, and worrying about it while it's gone. Acceptance of a death is what allows the child gradually to let go of the feelings of sadness and move on to thinking about other things and other feelings. Offer your child the opportunity to have a "funeral" for his pet. Let him decide if he wants to have a burial, or if he would like you to take care of it for him. This, too, is part of the mourning process.

If it is ever necessary for a family pet to be put to death by a veterinarian, don't use a euphemism like "put to sleep." You risk confusing an already difficult issue for your child if you are not honest. Don't rush out to replace a dead pet. This minimizes the importance of the dead animal and can convey the idea to a child that someone or something you love can be easily replaced. Let your child go through the mourning process. When her grieving is behind her, she will be ready to reattach to another pet. Don't ever try to fool your child by replacing a dead pet with another just like it without her knowledge. Trying to protect her by not acknowledging a death and pretending it didn't happen is not constructive.

It is not uncommon for elementary-school-aged children to become aware of death and dying without having experienced a personal loss. Many children today are involved in the issue of nuclear war. Don't be surprised if your child expresses a fear of dying from this cause. Older children may take comfort in actively working for disarmament by signing petitions or writing letters to elected officials or joining with other children who are organizing to stop this threat. The younger child who is not able to participate in such activities may still share these concerns. In this instance, the only thing that may comfort him is to assure him that you will do everything in your power to keep him safe.

THINGS NOT TO DO

- Don't try to distract your child from talking about his sad feelings.
  Child: *Grandpop won't take me to the park anymore.*
  Parent: *Don't think about that. Let's go bake some cookies.*
  In this situation, the child will realize that you don't want him to talk about his feelings, and may begin to think there is something wrong with feeling the way he does about his loss. Try using approach behavior.
  Parent: *You really had fun with Grandpop when you would go to the park. What did you two used to do there?*

- Try not to change your behavior with a bereaved child. These children often end up feeling that there is something strange about them because everybody acts embarrassed or restrained with them. Not only are they coping with the very real loss but they are left feeling alienated, almost as if people don't know how to deal with them because they are different. A child grieving for the loss of a loved one may feel isolated and deserted.

- Don't take a child away from his family when there has been a death. Often the child is sent to a relative's house. This prevents him from experiencing how the rest of the family is feeling. He needs his loved ones around him to talk about his grief, his fears, and his needs. The feeling of solidarity that can evolve in a family going through a crisis is sustaining to a young child.

- Don't delay telling the child about the death of someone close to him. If you tell the neighbors before you tell the child, he may overhear the conversation which could be devastating for him.

- Don't expect your child to be a source of comfort to you when you are mourning. It is appropriate for your child to see your tears and suffering, but do not expect him to help you through your grieving process. Expecting comfort from a child may deter him from turning to you when he needs empathy and support. If you indicate you depend on him to be your "little man" or a friend to you, he will not get the comfort he needs from you at this time.

In times of the loss of a loved one, trying your best is the best you can do. Don't dwell on what you didn't do perfectly, or what someone tells you you should have done differently. Whatever you do with care and honesty is all that you can expect from yourself.

Failure

"Nothing succeeds like success" is one of our favorite mottos, because it's true. A child with confidence can do fantastic things compared with a child who has the same level of skills and lacks the confidence to try.

Thus, giving your child a sense of perspective when things

don't go right for him is a very important part of being a parent. What happens when your child doesn't make the team, doesn't get a part in the school play, is rejected by a classmate, or fails an exam? What is likely to happen to your child at such a time is the same thing that's likely to happen to you—a thinking distortion: *I'll never be good at sports. Nobody likes me. I can't really act. Why did I ever try?* These are really "lies"—non-truths about himself because they are so exaggerated as to be untrue—but your child doesn't see that. Encourage your child to talk about what this event means to him. If your child didn't make the team, he may think, *I'm never going to make the team,* so get him to talk about his past sports successes and failures. When you feel he's ready, start talking about how he plans to prepare to try again in the future.

The biggest problem about failing is not the failure itself. We all have to cope with disappointments—it is part of growth. The biggest problem is helping your child refrain from feeling like a failure. Never trying, and therefore never risking a failure, is much more harmful to a person's growth than trying for six challenging activities, and succeeding in only three of them. Help your child see how many good things he's doing, and that, if he's really acting to his fullest capacity, he's going to succeed at some but not at all—otherwise he's not challenging himself enough.

The same is true for making mistakes and saying things that may seem foolish to others. One important lesson that isn't ordinarily taught in schools is that we learn by making mistakes. We learn by saying what we think and feel, and getting feedback.

What should you say when your child comes home after experiencing a major disappointment? If you sense that things didn't go well, you can either wait till the child brings it up, or ask a noncommital, *How'd it go today? That must have been very disappointing. What a shame, I know you worked very hard.* If he handles his disappointment by being angry, accept it. This is not the time for a lecture on sportsmanship. A supportive statement like, *You must feel really angry about not making the team*, maybe all your child needs to hear to ease his concern. He may also be afraid that others will think badly of him because of his "failure." Follow your child's lead about what he wants to talk about, until you sense that the worst of his upset is over. Then you can bring the conversation into perspective by helping him talk about his past successes and future plans. Once he is feeling better, you can work on teaching him that real growth requires that we try for things which are a little out of our reach, so he will succeed at some and fail at some.

To cope with failure the child needs to learn that there are resources in the world which he can, and should, draw on when things aren't going well—friends to talk with; teachers to get information from; books to show how others have coped with the same situation; professional people to give technical help. You can help by asking your child questions like, *Who can be helpful here? What else can we do now? What do you think you need to do next?* Help him dispel his notions of inadequacy by realistically answering what he needs and helping him to go after it.

ACCIDENTS

The milk spills!
The vase breaks!
The gloves are lost!

And you yell and make an enormous fuss. These are situations that happen to all of us. Often, after such an experience the parent says, *Why did I holler? Why did I act like that? It's not what I really meant, but I'm not sure exactly what to do.*

If you have a plan for what you're going to do when accidents happen, you won't be at a loss. You'll be able to think clearly, to sort out what's important, to realize when you have control, when you have no control, and when you can teach control.

No one means to break, spill, lose, or drop—an accident is an unexpected happening or unintentional event. And yet we *all* spill things and drop things. When a child spills something he will probably feel bad. This is a no-control situation. The adult's first question should always be, *Are you all right?* This shows what's most important to you: the child.

After an accident, you need to help children with their embarrassed or guilty feelings. Avoidance behavior such as *You're clumsy, Why aren't you more careful?* is not helpful. Action to help remedy the harm or loss is helpful. Let the child help. Mopping up the milk after all the pieces of glass have been removed, setting the table again, getting clean napkins are ways in which the child can participate, feel helpful and better about the situation.

Although spilling something is not an action which the child can usually control, this is different from the case of, for example, kids rough-housing and breaking the vase that sits outside on your front step. In this situation, there is an opportunity for teaching control, although your first question should still be *Are you all right?* Allow kids to help by cleaning up, and by looking at what should happen in the future. Show them how to look for things to move when they are going to play ''rough.'' Teach them that this is an accident-prone situation in which they *can* have control. And, you can explain, in future *if you break, you pay.*

An important goal is to prevent children from becoming self-defensive about mistakes and accidents. They should be able to admit fault and say *I'm sorry*, but not feel abnormally upset about accidents over which they have no control.

When Mother Goes to Work

More than half of all American children younger than eighteen have mothers who work away from home. When the mother leaves for work for the first time, it is a big change for her, but it is an equally big change for her children. Ordinarily, the mother makes intensive preparations for the change—everything from buying new clothes to deciding how to handle the household chores and the kids' car pool.

But that is only half the preparation that is needed. The other half involves getting the family ready for the change. Your first step in preparing your family is to get yourself ready, which means not only knowing what you're going to be doing, how you're going to get there, what time you have to arrive, but also gathering the information that your kids will ask about: *Who's going to take me to school? Who's going to be here when I come home? How will I get to scouts? What are we going to eat for dinner? Will you still come to see me in the play?*

One major choice will affect many other decisions: Will there be someone to handle the adults' early-morning and after-school responsibilities or will the children be taught to do these things themselves? Once this decision has been made, the steps are more clear-cut. If someone will be in your house, getting the children off to school and welcoming them after school, then the changes in daily family life will be fewer. Still, even though you may leave long notes for the caretaker about the family's routine, there will be some changes. When the hot chocolate is made differently, it is a change for a child that takes getting used to. If someone else is in the house, there must be a clearly posted day-to-day routine written out. This includes what time the school bus comes, how much milk or lunch money to give, and the activities of each person in the family for every schoolday (dance class, swimming team, paper route, religious school, etc.).

All planning should be done before your child is told anything about your going to work, so that when you talk with him, you are prepared, and don't have a lot of "I don't knows" to add to his confusion.

If you are not going to have someone be with your kids when they get home, the same planning has to occur, but what you tell your kids will be different. The same listing of what has to be done is necessary, but who will be doing the various necessary tasks will differ, as the family picks up the chores that the working mother can no longer do.

Tell the kids the truth about why you're going back to work: money, new opportunities, new experiences. Stress the positive! While they are at school, which is their work, you will be doing some new work of your own. Mention other children they know whose mothers successfully combine working and parenting.

We recommend the following steps for both working parents: Give your children a clear understanding of where you work, how you get there, whom you work with, what you do all day, what your work space is like. Make it as real as you can: *I go to a big building in town. I take an elevator to the fifteenth floor. I hang up my coat on coat hooks in a big room that just holds coats and hats. My desk is in a big office with lots of other desks. . . .* Tell them where you go to lunch, whom you eat with, and if a bell rings when it is time to go home, like in school. Share with them any details you feel they can relate to which will assist them in getting a visual idea of your workday.

We also recommend taking your child to your place of work as soon as possible. Drive him by the outside of the building several times, and take him inside as soon as it is appropriate. It's a good idea to time your ride while he is in the car, so he understands that, if you are needed, it takes only *x* minutes to get home. When you take him into the building, have him meet as many people with whom you work as is convenient. Show him where you have your meetings, where you check merchandise, all the places where you actually do your work, so that when you later talk about what you did that day, he can visualize where you did it and with whom.

One of the biggest changes is that you will not only have less time to do household chores, but you may also feel tired from working at a new job. It is wise not to expect the house to be as sparkling, the garden to be as carefully tended, if these are jobs the mother did without any family help. It is easy to fall into the trap of using the weekends to play "catch up" with all of the chores that didn't get done. This may cause the children to associate your new job with drudgery and reduced quality of life. Therefore, special efforts should be made to plan some fun things for weekends that the children can look forward to with you. These need not take a lot of time, but they should be definite "events" that you can talk about with them: get pizza, go to a movie together, go bowling, drive to see the fall leaves or the decorations at the mall.

When talking to your kids about changes, it is important to stress what will be the same: *We'll still all be having dinner together every night. We'll still go to Grandma's on Sundays. We'll still be going to the circus next Friday night. You'll still be going to scouts and taking piano lessons.* Then say, *What will be different is that Mrs. Green will be here after school,* or *You will be coming into the house alone after we have practiced* (or, *as you have done when I had volunteers' meeting on Thursdays.*) You can also set realistic expectations by saying, *We may have to postpone some things till we see how it goes, but the things that are important to you will stay the same.*

Expect the first week or so to be tough, and that some of

your plans will not work out as you thought they would. Help your child to realize this too, and tell him you will be talking about how things are going every day, and will change the plans as you all learn to do things better. Remind him how it was when he first went to his new school, because he can use his own experiences with change to better understand what is happening. Also, we recommend telling the child that *it's new for me, too,* so he sees that adults also find some changes hard, as well as exciting.

It's also wise, when and if appropriate, to invite some of the people you work with to your house to meet your children. Seeing these people relaxed and having a good time will help extend your child's life space, so he won't feel you are disappearing into a void for which he has no feelings or connections.

Frequently, teachers will start the school year by asking children for their parents' names, addresses, and phone numbers. They will ask, *What does your father do? What does your mother do?* Your children will find that mothers who work are clearly not in the minority. What is important to the children's security then is simply planning so that all goes well.

What the working parent needs to do is stretch time, steal time, and create time. Following are some tips which may be helpful to the working mother whose time is particularly scarce:

- Have a batch of birthday presents stored away and ready to be given for boys and girls—to make birthday-party invitations easier to accept. Keep gift wrap, ribbon, and tape on hand with the presents. If all else fails, the Sunday comics make a wonderful wrap for a child's gift.

- When you're running an errand, use the time also to do

something that is pure pleasure with your child. Not all the time, but often enough that the child learns that going out with you is not just a routine of carrying packages and going dull places.

- Make every trip count. Consider what you can drop off or pick up (including a child) along the way when you run errands.

- Find a special storage place at home (that only you know about!) to save yourself emergency trips to the variety store. In it keep loose-leaf paper, colored paper, notebooks, magic markers of all colors, and the ever-necessary report covers.

- You can stretch time by always carrying something to read or work on when you're delayed—while waiting to pick up the kids at activities, in doctors' offices, on public transportation.

- Use your resources: a grandmother who is available to pick up your kids at the library; an aunt who would love to spend time with your kids; a special friend who will keep them company at dinner. You have to learn to ask. Frequently people don't ask because they don't "want to impose," but other family members might be very happy to pitch in. Be equally gracious when your neighbors or friends are in a pinch.

- One of the things that we've found most helpful is substituting phone calls and notes for face-to-face talks, when you just cannot be at home. Try to call home every day after school, to talk to each child for a moment, to see how the day went, to reinforce plans for after-school activities and chores, to say a personal word of caring, and to try to give a warm feeling to the rest of each child's afternoon.

- Look for ways to cut corners and save time. When you suddenly find out that you have to take a child to the library and do an extra car pool, don't make the big dinner you had planned; instead, serve eggs or grilled cheese sandwiches. Showing up at the table in good humor counts a lot.

If your job requires you to travel away from home, it's important to tell your children what will be happening, where you are going, when you will leave, and when you'll return, so they don't feel that you are off on a vacation without them for no good reason. Explain why you are going and tell them why you cannot take them with you. Mark the calendar so they can tell when you will be back. You can make a separate calendar with days you'll be gone for them to check off.

The mail and phone are your only methods of contact while you are away. It's important to know what to write. Don't write anything which will make your kids fearful, because the child doesn't have you there to talk it through with. It's nice to phone early in the morning and wish everyone a good day as well as at night. Write frequent short notes. It's more fun for the child to get a lot of postcards than one five-page letter. Don't be stodgy and formal; include a fun cartoon or an article of interest from the paper of the city you are in, especially something in that city's paper about your own city's sports team or local events.

This is a good time to leave little presents that can be opened on different days. Be sure to leave information about where you are going to be: the hotel number, meeting days, how to reach you, and what to do when they cannot reach you. If you have a tape recorder, you might tape some of their favorite stories or a fun message for them to play while you are away.

Networking

Networking means using your resources and contacts to make good things happen. In business, the famous "Old Boys' Network" consists of people who use connections to find job openings and get promotions. This concept has been extended these days to mean talking with everyone you can about the activities you want to be (or are) involved in, so that "connections" can be made. Unless you talk about it, you might never find out that your cousin has a friend who teaches the very thing your child is interested in learning.

Networking is an important concept to teach your children. Extended-family members—aunts, uncles, cousins—can form a warm and supportive network for them to call on when they are seeking expert information in a wide variety of areas. Cousin Charles may know about woodworking, and Cousin Sandy may have just completed a course in automobile repair. The extended family may also prove a good source of people for your children "just to talk to" when they need a sympathetic ear.

Using extended resources is a way to help your child branch out from depending just on parents and teachers for information and assistance. You will have to teach him how to network. *Who can help with that problem, assignment, task? Whom do you know who has skills in the area? Who would be a good listener? Cousin Mark studied history in college—maybe he'll have some good ideas for your history project.*

Also another idea which falls under this topic of networking is learning to talk in positive terms about what you are doing. Many people do not reach the level of success they otherwise might because they bury their light under the proverbial bushel. Successful people tend to talk in a positive vein about what they are doing. This lets their bosses (or teacher) and peers get involved in and excited about their projects and interests. It's harder to feel warm toward a child who just stands there mute than toward a child who tells you about his team's winning the football game or about joining the swim club, or who shows you his wonderful puppet that he made in art class, or who asks you if you know where he can get a chef's hat to wear in the school play.

Teaching your children to talk about their interests, hobbies, or school projects does two things:

1. It networks—lets people hear about them, so connections to needed resources can be made.

2. Gets other people involved with your children, creating positive feelings all around.

Caring for People and Showing It

The ability to care for people develops slowly as the child moves from the totally self-centered, self-loving infant to the fully mature adult who values significant others in his life. The ability to relate lovingly to others comes from a sense of being loved, and being secure as a child. If one is sure that the parents' love, as well as food and shelter, is available, then one has the energy to stop focusing on filling one's own needs and can be concerned with the needs of others.

Caring for people and showing it is one of the marks of a maturing child. For most people, showing affection for someone is easy. For some, it is hard. Giving a hug, a kiss, a big smile, a good word are all ways you show people you care, and recognize that they are important to you. There are other ways to show you care—a note that reads, *I'm proud of you*; a message written in soap on the bathroom mirror reading, *You make me happy*; a letter in the mail congratulating a child on something special she's done; notes stuck in boots, pockets, and lunch bags—these are all special ways of saying, *I care for you.*

A "happy happy present"—a present given for no special reason at all—can be a joy for both giver and receiver. Parents can give these to children and to each other, and through these children learn to express caring for parents and for siblings too. There's just one rule about these happy happy presents: make sure that they are things the child really wants, not something you were going to get her anyway. For example, new underwear or a new rake is not a happy happy present. A present does not have to be for being the best. For example, it can be for showing team spirit, making a good catch, helping another player, or acting especially nice.

Certificates that can be left in your child's room, stuck in a schoolbag, put under a pillow, or stood up at the dinner table are fun conversation starters, and clearly show you care. A certificate can be an unusual, surprise of giving your child something he's been wanting.

To: _____

THIS CERTIFICATE IS GOOD FOR . . .

A VISIT TO THE ZOO

Some ideas for certificates that kids, as well as parents, can give are:

- A five-minute back rub
- One clean-up after dinner
- Tickets to the ball game
- A new book
- Three "make-your-beds"
- Two breakfasts in bed

Caring and learning to show love are a wonderful part of the maturing child's growth. Caring and showing it is setting a place for your child even if she thinks she can't be home for dinner, so if she comes in there's a place waiting for her. Having alone time with your child is another way to show you care, as is talking about or helping with a special project, or going out and helping the child with "her" chore—raking the leaves, or whatever.

Take special notice of the times your child gives you a happy happy gift—a flower, some of her original artwork, an invitation to attend an event with her—because these are the beginnings of her awareness that she cares for you and wants to share with you, too. Don't miss them.

A meaningful happy happy gift that costs very little and gives a lifetime of pleasure is a scrapbook in which you record the treasures that your children have brought home to you since they were little: the cards they sent you, their drawings, their scribblings, their school compositions, even scraps of paper on which you jotted down memorable things they said.

> The airplane is blinking its
> lights and riding carefully
> so it doesn't hurt a star.
>
> Mommy, were there roads
> when you were little?

There's a prevalent fantasy that everybody lives together as a family happily ever after. The reality is that family life is not always wonderful and not always terrible. *It is what we create* as we cope with the thousands of tasks and treats that daily life entails. There are lots of things that we as adults "must do," many things we "should do," and lots of things we "want to do." We hope this book has given you ideas for creating an environment that will allow you and your children to plan for more of the "want to do's" in an atmosphere of love, sharing, understanding, curiosity, and enthusiasm.

Index